The LOST DIVISIONS

THE INEFFECTIVE SOLDIER

Lessons for Management and the Nation

THE LOST DIVISIONS

BREAKDOWN AND RECOVERY

PATTERNS OF PERFORMANCE

The LOST DIVISIONS

by Eli Ginzberg

James K. Anderson, Sol W. Ginsburg, M.D.,

John L. Herma

With a Foreword by

Howard McC. Snyder, Major General, MC, USA

GREENWOOD PRESS, PUBLISHERS
WESTPORT, CONNECTICUT

Library of Congress Cataloging in Publication Data

Ginzberg, Eli, 1911-
The ineffective soldier.

Reprint of the ed. published by Columbia University Press, New York.
"Investigation ... undertaken by the staff of the Conservation of Human Resources Project."
Includes bibliographies and indexes.
CONTENTS: [1] The lost dividions.--[2] Breakdown and recovery.--[3] Patterns of performance.
1. United States. Army--Recruiting, enlistment, etc. --World War, 1939-1945. 2. United States. Army--Personnel management. 3. Psychiatry, Military--Cases, clinical reports, statistics. 4. Soldiers--United States. 5. Manpower--United States. I. Columbia University. Conservation of Human Resources Project. II. Title.
[UB323.G5 1975] 355.2'2 75-29042
ISBN 0-8371-7812-6

Originally published in 1959 by Columbia University Press, New York

Reprinted with the permission of Columbia University Press

Reprinted in 1975 by Greenwood Press, a division of Williamhouse-Regency Inc.

Library of Congress Catalog Card Number 75-29042

ISBN 0-8371-7812-6 (Set)
ISBN 0-8371-8467-3 (Vol. I-The Lost Divisions)

Printed in the United States of America

P

To

Dwight David Eisenhower

CONSERVATION OF HUMAN RESOURCES

The Conservation of Human Resources Project was established at Columbia University by General Eisenhower in 1950. It is a cooperative research undertaking involving the University, the business community, foundations, trade unions, and the Federal Government. Since 1955 the Project has been under the administrative supervision of Dr. John A. Krout, Vice President of the University.

SPONSORING ORGANIZATIONS

American Can Company
Bigelow-Sanford Carpet Company
Cities Service Company
Cluett, Peabody and Company
Columbia Broadcasting System
Consolidated Edison Company of New York
Continental Can Company
E. I. du Pont de Nemours and Company
General Dynamics Corporation
General Electric Company
General Foods Corporation
Radio Corporation of America
Standard Oil Company (New Jersey)
The Coca Cola Company
The New York Community Trust

In addition to the foregoing, the Ford Foundation has also contributed toward the financing of the Conservation of Human Resources.

STAFF

DIRECTOR
Eli Ginzberg, PH.D., *Economics*

ADVISOR
Howard McC. Snyder, *Major General, MC, USA*

CONSULTANT
Sol W. Ginsburg, M.D., *Psychiatry*

RESEARCH ASSOCIATES
James K. Anderson, A.B., *Manpower and Personnel*
Douglas W. Bray, PH.D., *Social Psychology* (1951–55)
Henry David, PH.D., *Labor History* *
John L. Herma, PH.D., *Psychology*
John B. Miner, PH.D., *Industrial Psychology* (1956–57)
Robert W. Smuts, M.A., *Economic History*

RESEARCH ASSISTANT
William A. Jordan, M.S., *Statistics* (1957–58)

ADMINISTRATION
Bryna Ball **

SECRETARIAL AND STATISTICAL
Edith Garshman, *Secretary* (1952–57)
Judith Nadelmann, *Statistical Assistant* (1955–57)
Gloria Tofano, *Secretary* (1952–57)
Jeanne Tomblen, *Secretary to the Director*

* Executive Director, ** Associate Director, National Manpower Council

ACKNOWLEDGMENTS

THE LARGE BODY of statistical information that underlies the present volume could never have been developed and evaluated without the wholehearted cooperation of various government agencies. While we know many of the individuals who helped us, we never learned the names of many others who worked so conscientiously and competently to meet our myriad requests for information.

We wish to acknowledge specifically the assistance of the Armed Forces and the Selective Service System. At all levels, from the senior officers on the General Staff to file clerks, we received unstinting cooperation. Official reports were tracked down and made available to us, and we were given access to file copies of statistical worksheets and backup material. When these proved inadequate for our research needs, special tabulations were prepared.

The Navy's Bureau of Personnel and Bureau of Medicine and Surgery provided data about Naval personnel and the Marine Corps; additional personnel information for the Marines was provided by the Headquarters of the Marine Corps. The Selective Service System made available unpublished as well as published data on the men rejected for military service during World War II and provided valuable assistance in the interpretation of these data.

This volume deals primarily with the Army, which in World War II included the Air Corps, and it is to the Department of the Army, particularly to the Adjutant General's Office and the Surgeon General's Office, that we wish to acknowledge our special indebtedness. In the Adjutant General's Office the Statistical and Accounting Branch and its Machine Records Unit provided the basic information on soldiers who had been separated, and prepared the special tabulations of the 5 percent sample of the separation cards. The Medical Statistics Division of the Surgeon General's Office provided information on men discharged for medical disabilities and assisted us in the interpretation of these data.

The manuscript was read in its entirety and many valuable suggestions were made on it by the Honorable Hugh M. Milton, II, Under-Secretary of the Army; Lieutenant General Lewis B. Hershey, Director, Selective Service System; Eugene L. Hamilton, Chief, Medical Statistics Division, Office of the Surgeon General, and Bernard D. Karpinos of the same Division; and Douglas W. Bray, Personnel Research Supervisor, American Telephone and Telegraph Company.

Although the data in this volume were derived almost exclusively from official sources and the above mentioned agencies and individuals helped us interpret them, final responsibility for their accuracy rests with the authors.

During the course of the research, part-time statistical assistance was provided by the following students of the Graduate School of Business, Columbia University. From 1951 to 1955 these included: Leo Tansky, William Wright, Edward Epstein, Stewart Knapp, and Thornton Lockwood. Judith Nadelmann aided in the final statistical analyses, and William A. Jordan prepared the tables for publication.

Douglas W. Bray, for five years a research associate on the staff of the Conservation Project, assisted materially in the design of the research and the initial evaluation of the materials. Ruth Szold Ginzberg through her careful editing of the manuscript improved its readability. Jeanne Tomblen, Secretary to the Director, typed the successive drafts of the manuscript.

CONTENTS

TABLES

For explanation of abbreviated titles used in sources of tables, see page 205

FIGURES

MAPS

FOREWORD

THE CIRCUMSTANCES which permit me to introduce this first of three volumes growing out of a major investigation into personality and performance undertaken by the staff of the Conservation of Human Resources Project can be briefly described. It was my good fortune to have participated in the establishment of the Conservation Project, to have joined actively in the research work in the early years, and to have enjoyed a continuous relationship with the Project since its inception. Because of my long and intimate acquaintance with the Project, I welcome the opportunity to provide for the reader, even though briefly, background information about the origin of the Conservation Project, its research objectives and working methods, and the place that *The Lost Divisions* and the companion volumes, *Breakdown and Recovery* and *Patterns of Performance*, have in the overall research program.

In the 1956 Progress Report of the Conservation of Human Resources, I outlined in detail the steps that led to the establishment of the Project, and so I will limit myself here to the highlights. During the North African Campaign, and even more in the European Theater at the time of the Battle of the Bulge, General Eisenhower encountered marked shortages in manpower. At the same time he knew that large numbers of young Americans were being rejected for military service or were being prematurely discharged because they were judged to be deficient in the mental and emotional qualities that make good soldiers. After his return to the United States and when he was serving as Chief of Staff, General Eisenhower explored the possibilities of making use of the rich personnel records of World War II as a basis for a comprehensive investigation into this nation's human resources. His hope was that research might develop answers that would prove of value not only to the future planning of the Armed Services but also to the nation as a whole.

Shortly after he became president of Columbia University, he took the initial steps that eventually led to the establishment late in 1949 of the Conservation of Human Resources Project. General Eisenhower placed the Project under the direction of Professor Eli Ginzberg, who had worked on frontier problems in human resources before the war and whose war experience had alerted him to the potentialities of using military data for research purposes. Some of the questions that General Eisenhower hoped could be illuminated by research were whether the men who proved to be ineffective during World War II came primarily from rural or urban backgrounds, whether their schooling had been adequate, whether they gave evidence of prior physical or emotional disabilities, and whether they had been able to readjust after their return to civilian life.

From the start the Conservation Project adopted a broad approach focused on *work*, in civilian as well as in military life. Two of its publications—*The Uneducated* (1953) and *The Negro Potential* (1956)—have investigated themes closely related to the present effort. The other published studies have contributed to illuminating important aspects of talent and superior performance and the changing role of work in American life. The staff of the Conservation Project has also assisted materially in the preparation of the major reports of the National Manpower Council on student deferment and national manpower policy, scientific and professional manpower, skilled manpower, and womanpower. Each of these reports has had a significant impact on public policy.

Important as these earlier studies of the Conservation Project have been in advancing our understanding of how our society utilizes its human resources, it is my belief that the three related volumes on personality and performance, of which the present is the first, will prove even more significant. I would like to present my reasons for this conclusion.

The Conservation staff, which is a truly interdisciplinary team, recognized the importance of establishing at the outset a firm statistical foundation before proceeding with the analysis of the central problem of performance. Moreover, early in its investigation the staff was fortunate in eliciting the support of many senior psychiatrists who had served in important positions with the Armed Forces in World War II. It encouraged them to reappraise the manpower policies and procedures in effect during the course of the war, and this survey was later published in a monograph (*Psychiatry and Military Manpower Policy: A Reappraisal of the Experience in World War II*). In all of its work the Conservation staff is as responsive to the ideas of others as it is critical of its own formulations. And at all times it remains alert to the need of seeking answers that can be useful to the Armed Forces, industry, and the community at large in developing policies aimed at the more effective utilization of the nation's human resources.

This volume on *The Lost Divisions* represents a new approach and an essential one if we are to move out of the realm of opinion and speculation into the arena of fact and proof. It sets out in definitive fashion what really happened during World War II in the screening and utilization of the several million young men who had mental and emotional handicaps. I am satisfied that the Conservation staff analyzed and utilized very effectively the great store of military records to which it was granted access and upon which its studies were based. This volume introduces the reader to this broad study of personality and performance. To appreciate its full significance, he will want to read the two related volumes, for the three together reveal the comprehensive manner in which the Conservation staff have developed their studies of *The Ineffective Soldier*, from which they have drawn important lessons for management and the nation.

It is my conviction that the staff of the Conservation of Human Resources Project rose to the challenge that General Eisenhower set it and that this nation will be the stronger as it puts their findings to constructive use.

HOWARD McC. SNYDER
Major General, MC, USA
Personal Physician
to the President

The White House
Washington, D.C.
January 1959

The LOST DIVISIONS

Introduction: THE STUDY OF PERFORMANCE

STUDENTS of human behavior have long bemoaned the fact that, unlike their confreres in the physical and biological sciences, they are unable to test the validity of their hypotheses. In fact, they are frequently unable even to garner the basic facts and figures necessary to formulate reasonable hypotheses. The relatively slow advance in our understanding of the intricacies of human behavior has quite correctly been ascribed to this difficulty of studying it. For this reason social scientists must be particularly alert to exploit significant bodies of social data which do become available.

World War II presented just such a unique opportunity. More than 20 million men were examined as to their physical, mental, and emotional suitability for military service. This screening operation which extended over five years resulted in the largest personnel inventory in the history of this country, possibly in the world. During the course of the war more than 14 million men were called to active duty and served as enlisted men in the Armed Forces of the United States. From the day that a man was sworn in until the day he was discharged, a record was kept of the most important developments in his military life. These notations resulted in an important increment to the initial screening record. And the accumulation of information continued after these men returned to civilian life. Since most discharged servicemen were entitled to various benefits from the Veterans Administration and since the scope and scale of their benefits depended not only on their military experiences but on their current circumstances, considerable additional information about many veterans was accumulated and evaluated.

The combined records represent a unique repository of information about a large sector of the American population. In addition, the records reflect operational decisions reached by the Selective Service System, the Armed Forces, and the Veterans Administration: whether an eligible man was available for military service, whether he was acceptable under military standards, whether his performance justified discharging him, and whether he needed and was entitled to special assistance to speed his readjustment to civilian life. And, of course, the records also include information about the many other aspects of a man's military career such as his assignments, promotions, disciplinary action and medical care.

The foregoing suggests that the records of World War II represent a laboratory experiment in individual and group behavior. Millions of men were subjected to special performance tests—tests of their suitability for military service and tests of their performance as soldiers. The records of World War II contain therefore a wealth of data about the judgments reached by key organizations on the ability of these men to perform effectively in time of war. Since the records also include at least a rough indication of how these men performed in civilian life prior to entering military service, and again on how they performed after discharge, they provide a broad base for studying performance.

Military service provides the fulcrum for our study of performance, not only with regard to the individual citizen-soldier, but also in assessing the impact of organizational policy on the utilization of manpower. A recent cartoon showed a recruiting sergeant explaining to a potential enlistee that among the other advantages of military service is the fact that men need not spend time traveling to and from work. The sergeant did not go further and elaborate that the serviceman, unlike the civilian, is under twenty-four-hour surveillance by his employer. The World War II soldier was, of course, under stricter supervision than his present-day counterpart. How he cut his hair, how he made his bed, what he ate, when he went to bed—all this and much more was predetermined. The all-pervasive influence of the Army on the life and actions of the soldier actually created a laboratory situation that makes possible the study of group behavior.

But is not the military environment by its very nature so abnormal that any conclusions that emerge will have little or no relevance for the appraisal of performance in civilian organizations? Before venturing an answer, let us state how the term "performance" is used in this study. We have defined "performance" as the ability of the individual to meet the minimum demands of the organization and the community to which he belongs. In our society a man must find an employer who considers it profitable to hire him, and he has the further obligation to take care of his wife and children and to stay out of conflict with the law. These are the minimum performance standards required of a citizen in the ordinary course of events.

In times of national emergency or war a citizen has additional responsibilities. If he is selected for military service, he is obliged to meet the demands of the military organization. From one point of view this is a very special order of demand, for it may require a man to kill and to assume the risk of being killed. Nothing in civilian life compares with such a demand. Yet in a democracy the obligation of every citizen to respond in an emergency to the call to arms is as real as his obligation to earn his livelihood, maintain his family, and abide by the laws of his community.

It is these obligations of a citizen—whether his country is at peace or at war—that justify concern with conclusions growing out of an investigation into the ability of men to perform effectively in the Army. In both instances—in peace as in war—our concept of performance is limited to the minimum. No question is raised about whether a man's job is commensurate with his abilities; we are concerned only with whether he is self-supporting. Likewise a man is credited with effective performance in military service if he is able to remain on active duty until the termination of hostilities. This concept makes no distinction between an outstanding combat soldier and one who performs only simple routine duties. We have therefore used the premature discharge of a soldier for mental, emotional, or behavioral reasons as prima facie evidence of ineffective performance. And since prevailing policy held that no soldier was to be separated during hostilities until he had been carefully assessed, considerable additional information is usually available about those who were prematurely discharged.

As we have stated, to kill and to run the risk of being killed is an obligation that has no parallel in civilian life. Yet a democracy that is challenged by war can survive only if it is victorious on the field of battle. Hence, during a war soldiering must be considered to be a proper demand on all who are eligible to serve. The measure of a man must be his ability to meet the test. It is not the only measure, but it must remain a crucial one.

Even though our concept of performance is severely restricted to bare standards of acceptable behavior, it is still too complex a phenomenon to be pursued by only one line of analysis. It invites inspection and study from multiple vantage points. We are therefore presenting the conclusions arising from the detailed investigations that we have carried on for almost eight years in three separate though related volumes, each independent, yet each contributing to an understanding of performance from a special vantage point.

This volume, *The Lost Divisions*, traces the impact of military manpower policies on the efficiency with which the Armed Services utilized the human resources available to them. In each area of manpower policy—selection, training, utilization, separation—the mass data have been systematically organized and reviewed in light of the changing goals and policies regarding the utilization of manpower resources developed by the Armed Forces during the course of the war. The focus of this volume is not primarily on the large numbers of young men who, when screened for service, were found deficient and rejected. It is rather the impact of military manpower policies on the performance of those who were selected that is our concern.

Psychologists and psychiatrists, largely because of their concern with therapy, seek explanations of adult behavior within the life experience of the individual, particularly his experiences in early childhood. But most personnel officers know that the work situation in which a man finds himself—his relations to his supervisor and his fellow workers, the demands of the job, the conditions in the shop, his pay, and a host of similar factors—will materially influence the level of his performance. Organizational policy has a crucial influence on the ability of men to perform effectively.

Certainly, the ability of individuals sets outer limits on their performance, but the fact remains that there is wide scope for an organization to use well or poorly the manpower resources available to it. The burden of this volume is to establish, on as sound a statistical basis as possible, the results of changing manpower policies on the utilization of military manpower during World War II. The entire analysis is built around the basic operational concept of performance—namely, whether a man was judged capable of serving in the Armed Forces and whether, if selected, he was able to meet prevailing standards or had to be separated prior to the cessation of hostilities.

The second volume, *Breakdown and Recovery*, as the title suggests, is also focused on performance, but particularly on the various types of soldiers who failed to perform effectively. In this book we attempt to deepen our understanding of performance by a more detailed evaluation of the experiences of individual soldiers who were separated prematurely. We search for the strategic factors responsible for their breakdown. The records of the Veterans Administration, as well as replies to questionnaires which we developed, provided detailed information about the postwar adjustment of many of these ineffective soldiers. The materials made it possible to go beyond a study of breakdown and to include an analysis of the factors that enabled many of these men to rehabilitate themselves to a point where they were able to perform effectively in civilian life.

The third volume, *Patterns of Performance*, represents our most comprehensive approach to the study of performance. Personality factors. situational stresses and strains, and organizational policies and procedures are considered in their dynamic interplay. The conclusions in that volume are based on statistically valid samples that have been carefully controlled. In each volume, but particularly in *Patterns of Performance*, attention is focused on considerations of public policy.

Just as there is a clear and definite connection between a man's prior performance in civilian life and his performance as a soldier —for it is the same man who performs in both environments—so the lessons learned about the utilization of manpower in the Army have relevance for the management of large civilian organizations, business and nonprofit alike. Although the specific mission of the Army to defeat the enemy in combat has no parallel in civilian life, a very large number of soldiers, even during a major war, do not directly engage the enemy. In many respects the Army is confronted with problems of organization, supply, and personnel that have direct counterparts in large civilian organizations. Just as the Armed Forces have long sought to profit from civilian experience, so their experience should prove of help to civilian organizations.

But the relevance and pertinency of these studies, grounded as they are in the records of World War II, are not limited to the contribution that they can make to civilian life. As long as force remains a major factor in the relations of nations to each other, it behooves a country that values its freedom to improve to the maximum possible degree the efficiency of its Armed Services. A reassessment of the manpower logistics of World War II should contribute to this important end.

WORLD WAR II— A LABORATORY CASE

Millions of young Americans underwent a performance test during World War II in an army that, aside from its name, bore little resemblance to the institution in existence when Hitler's legions marched into Poland in September, 1939. The unique qualities of that transformation must be inventoried and briefly reviewed in order to assess the military manpower experience of World War II. This section will set out in brief compass the scale and quality of the changes within the Army against a background of the major changes in the civilian community.

When the war began, the total officer and enlisted personnel of the U.S. Army, which then included the Air Corps, was less than 200,000. Kaiser Wilhelm had referred to the British Army in 1914 as a "contemptible little army." Hitler, in developing his timetable for world dominion, considered the American Army of the 1930s in the same light and did not give it a second thought. Victory would be his long before the Americans could train, equip, and deploy any large number of troops. Reflecting on the state of the war less than a month before Pearl Harbor, Hitler stated that he had been right to attack Russia, for even if the United States "worked like crazy for four years, it could not replace what the Russians had already lost."

Legend has it that there was a colonel on the General Staff of the peacetime Army who knew how well every officer played bridge. But it was fact, not supposition, that during the 1930s the Regular Army was in such straitened circumstances that only a few troops could be sent on maneuvers at any one time. Even the Surgeon General, in reassigning medical personnel from one post to another, had to give more weight to transportation costs than to considerations of professional competence and need. No wonder that Hitler felt that he had nothing to fear from the American Army.

The president of one of America's largest and most successful manufacturing corporations recently estimated that it might be possible for his company to expand indefinitely at an annual rate of 15 percent. Applying this rate to the Army as of 1939, the total strength in 1944 would have amounted to slightly above 400,000; in point of fact it was over 8 million! At an annual rate of growth of 15 percent, it would have taken the Army until 1966 to reach this peak figure. Actually, the expansion of the Army was at a rate of 109 percent or more than 7 times greater than that which the corporation president put forward as the most optimistic estimate of his organization's capability. Chapter One will review this spectacular expansion which, more than anything else, was the source of most of the manpower difficulties with which the Army had to cope throughout the war.

One important reason that organizations encounter difficulties in growing very rapidly is their inability to obtain adequate numbers of qualified supervisory personnel. For the efficiency with which an organization utilizes its resources, human and material, and the effectiveness with which it performs its mission depend more on the quality of its supervisory force than on any other single factor. But the development of competent supervisory personnel at all levels of management is greatly influenced by time and experience.

These may be foreshortened by various devices, such as the establishment of special schools and training exercises that simulate reality. And the Army resorted to both: it established Officer Candidate Schools and specialists' schools and it resorted to realistic training exercises in which live ammunition was used. However, despite these and other efforts the Army was unable to solve its leadership problem during the course of the war. There is no way to calculate at this date, nor could we have calculated even during the war, the losses in efficiency arising out of a shortage of qualified noncommissioned and commissioned officers. But that they were very high is beyond question. It is interesting to note that many war industries that expanded very rapidly also experienced great difficulties as a result of an inadequate number of qualified supervisory personnel.

Hitler's comment about the length of time that the United States would require to mobilize its resources effectively points up the crucial role of time in war. When the enemy is on the march, he must be checked before he entrenches himself in forward positions if he is eventually to be defeated. The most difficult problem that the Army faced during World War II was to train and deploy its manpower as expeditiously as possible. For each day's delay gave the enemy an opportunity to strengthen his position and made the eventual task of defeating him that much more difficult. Many policies that the Army adopted with respect to the selection, training, and utilization of its manpower, which are considered in Chapters Two and Three can be appreciated only against the background of the overriding importance of time.

Here, too, the civilian economy provides a useful parallel. Those sectors of American industry on which the success of the Allied cause so largely depended—airplane, shipbuilding, munitions, to mention only these—adopted policies and practices that they would never have entertained had they not been under instructions from the government to trade money for time. To illustrate: these industries were willing to transport potential workers hundreds, and sometimes thousands, of miles, find them living quarters, pay them at the full rate while they were learning, put them to work before they were adequately trained, and tolerate many deficiencies—all in the hope that these exorbitant costs would be justified by some increase in output, some advance in the date when the essential items would become available for use by our troops.

Under pressure from events the War Department in turn placed tremendous pressure upon the Army Ground Forces to assemble divisions in the shortest possible time so that they might be deployed either in North Africa or in the South Pacific to stop the headlong advances of the Germans and the Japanese. No one in Washington could be long concerned, especially early in the war, with the cost of getting the job done—cost in this instance measured in terms of the number of men required to bring a division to its authorized strength. If necessary, 40,000 would be assigned to get 20,000 effectives.

The economizing of time at the cost of the wasteful use of manpower resources was not limited to the training period. As we shall see in Chapters Four and Five, the Army did not hesitate to adopt liberal discharge policies during the first years of the war. The Army was not only willing, but eager, to return soldiers to civilian life if they proved difficult to train and absorb. At one period during 1942 the Army culled from its ranks as many men as the Selective Service System was able to furnish. The materials on premature separations illuminate one of the most interesting and little understood aspects of military manpower policy in World War II. Chapter Six presents in summary fashion what we have learned about the performance records of soldiers who were prematurely discharged by the Army.

The Army released men when it estimated that they would not repay the investment required to train them, or at certain periods of the war when its manpower requirements lessened, or because an individual was discovered to have an emotional or physical disability. In civilian life, employers also discharge men during a probationary period, they also let the inefficient go when business slackens, and they also are forced to discharge or retire some for cause.

However the Army was confronted with a problem that has no civilian counterpart. In civilian life men seek jobs and try to do well when they are hired. During a war soldiers are very much aware that sooner or later they may be seriously wounded or killed. Hence the pull to escape is always present although most men are able to withstand it. However, if the Army itself establishes easy discharge policies, many with low motivation to succeed as soldiers will try to be discharged.

The identification of the different types of soldiers who failed to perform satisfactorily is only a first step in a systematic study of performance. We must then attempt to differentiate the ineffective performers from the many whose war service was satisfactory. The evaluation of the background characteristics of ineffective soldiers, which is the concern of Chapter Seven, is specifically directed to this central problem. Are there significant factors in the lives of these soldiers prior to their entrance into military service, such as their family background, education, health, work experience, and social adjustment, that would help to explain why they failed to perform effectively while others were able to meet prevailing standards?

Both industry and the Armed Forces have devoted considerable resources since the end of World War II to seeking the answer to the question of whether a man's background can provide a reliable index of his future level of performance. The fact that the present investigation deals with such very large numbers makes its findings on this point highly relevant. Although the military and civilian information which is available does not include many items that would have been helpful in assessing the determinants of performance, they do permit answers to such questions as whether a man's age, race, residence, education, marital status, were significantly related to his ability to perform effectively in the Army.

Chapter Eight considers still another facet of performance, the extent to which men broke down after they had been exposed to situations characterized by a high order of stress. Chapters Nine, Ten, and Eleven present a detailed analysis of the results of the educational and psychiatric screening of the millions of men who were called for military service and relates the findings about those rejected to the characteristics of those who later broke down in the service for the same reasons. This comparison provides the first comprehensive test of the efficiency of the screening mechanism. This mechanism was predicated on the simple assumption that if men with actual or latent defects could be identified at the time of induction and rejected for service, the performance level of those accepted could be significantly raised. Although the records of those rejected and prematurely separated have limitations from a research point of view, they do enable us to reach many important conclusions about the logic and efficiency of the selection process in World War II. Despite the widespread use of selection procedures in industry, no opportunity has arisen for undertaking a comparable large-scale test.

The concluding chapter seeks to place the preceding analyses in broader perspective. Although this study has been focused on the performance of men in a military organization, most of the findings can be used directly, or with modification, to illuminate key manpower and personnel problems in large civilian organizations. As the analysis proceeds, many of these extensions are suggested, and in Chapter Twelve they are systematically developed and illustrated. Here it is that our comprehensive investigation of the military manpower experience of World War II, of which this volume forms a part, is able to contribute to advancing the understanding of manpower in large organizations, military and nonmilitary alike.

Since no organization ever operates independently of the environment of which it is a part, we want to set out at this time the more pervasive influences in the American scene that conditioned and limited the functioning of the Army during World War II.

When the war erupted, the United States was still in the backwash of the most devastating depression in its history. For ten years this country had been victimized by large and continuous unemployment; not even the venturesome policies of the New Deal had succeeded in bringing the economy back to a level where all fit men had jobs. As late as 1939 1 out of every 6 persons in the labor force was still unemployed. Small wonder, therefore, that in the years prior to the outbreak of World War II those charged with mobilization planning gave scant consideration to a possible manpower shortage. They simply did not envisage a situation where manpower could be the limiting factor in any future war effort. Business planning had been characterized by a similar neglect: management paid little attention to developing either executive personnel or skilled manpower. It was not until the United States had been in the war for some time that a change in approach was finally forced on those in authority by the increasing evidence that manpower was indeed the limiting factor to our war effort.

The military planners knew very little about the characteristics of the nation's human resources. Many policies, some sound and many unsound, were developed. It was indeed unfortunate that the

Armed Services had to learn by trial and error once the war was under way. Yet this was the inevitable consequence of lack of knowledge and prior planning.

For instance, it was only after several years of experience with Selective Service that the Army came to appreciate the variability in the American population and the need for caution in applying national norms. It had to make special allowance in assessing the potential usability of men from some parts of the South, who because they had been brought up in relatively isolated rural areas, had had only a limited amount of schooling, and had little knowledge of modern technology, and had only a limited exposure to group life.

Many a man was unnecessarily lost to the Army because the screening officers were unfamiliar with the cultural mores of different regions. For instance, a medical officer from New York or Chicago frequently had little or no experience with the behavior patterns of rural Americans. Errors of judgment occurred when inexperienced officers confronted with the excessive taciturnity of a Tennessee mountaineer or the feigned "dumbness" of an Alabama Negro concluded that they were dealing with mentally deficient persons.

The Army was particularly handicapped by the fact that its experience with modern war was limited to the less than twenty months that we participated in World War I. In that war our Allies initially carried us, while in World War II, especially in the later years, we carried our Allies. Some of the experiences of World War I were so deeply engrained that they led to serious defects in policy, such as the conviction about the limited value of Negro manpower. Other valuable experience was lost and had to be discovered anew at a high cost. An outstanding example of this was the failure of the General Staff and of the Surgeon General of the Army to make effective use of Volume X of the History of the Medical Department of World War I,[1] which summarized the experience with soldiers who suffered from emotional disturbances and which detailed the best ways of avoiding such manpower losses. The British sought out copies of this volume but we neglected it.

Even if we had made maximum use of our experience in World War I, the problems that we faced in World War II were so different in degree as to constitute almost a difference in kind. Instead of sending an expeditionary force to France, the United States was engaged in a global war with the active fronts stretching from its own coastal waters to Western Europe, North Africa, the South Pacific, and China. Not only were we without experience in fighting such a war but there was no experience in history to serve as a guide.

One consequence of having to engage the enemy on so many fronts so far from home was that the Army was forced to decentralize authority. This made it very difficult to secure uniform interpretation and action on the fast changing personnel directives issued by headquarters in Washington. Another consequence was that many troops, forced to wait or fight in out-of-the-way places, and unable to see how their efforts were contributing to victory, developed low morale. Their discontent and despair were frequently augmented by officers who shared their fear that they were the forgotten men of World War II.

We must recall that the United States had to fight a global war with men who had been brought up in a culture that, if not dogmatically pacifist, surely had little concern with international problems. When President Roosevelt sent up his trial balloon in 1937 about "stopping the aggressors," it was deflated so quickly that many did not know that the President had even launched it. Yet it was the younger men of this generation who had to endure the very heavy burdens that war brings to all fighting men. The surprising fact is not that the Army had to deal with many soldiers whose motivation to fight was low, but that it did not have to cope with even larger numbers of poorly motivated soldiers.

Another factor illuminates the setting in which the Army had to operate. American culture is conspicuously child-centered and the dominant trend in the 1920s and 1930s in the upbringing of the young was sympathetic understanding rather than rigid discipline. Largely as a result of the influence of modern psychiatry and psychology, the focus of efforts to deal with bad behavior had shifted increasingly from religious and legal restraints and punishments to a search for causes and their control. What the Army could or could not do in handling that segment of the nation's manpower that came under its direct control is illustrated by the fact that one of America's most skillful field commanders just missed being relieved of his post because in a moment of excitement he slapped a soldier. The Army was forced to shape its policies in terms of what the country would accept.

This, then, is the framework within which the Army operated. It entered the war with little concern about the manpower supply. For many months the Army directed all of its efforts to building divisions and getting them ready to fight, ignoring the manpower costs involved. At some point the need to conserve manpower resources became apparent. This required the Army to reappraise its policies and procedures. Limited in what it could do, not only by the nature of the war itself but by the attitudes and feelings of the American public, the Army improvised. Sometimes it was successful, other times not. From the beginning to the end of the war, the Army attempted to improve its management of the millions of men in its ranks. This book sets out some of the more important aspects of this unparalleled undertaking in manpower logistics. It is our conviction that no experience of such magnitude can fail to yield valuable and constructive lessons for those who seek to learn and profit from them.

Chapter Two: SELECTION FOR SERVICE

COMPETENT observers have provided the following picture of how manpower was mobilized in Nationalist China in the latter part of World War II. A squad of soldiers would suddenly block off a populated street. They would grab all likely looking male civilians and tie them to a very long rope. When fifty or so had been snared and tied, the soldiers would march the "recruits" off to a nearby collection station. There a few, obviously unfit for service, would be released and a few others might be able to wangle their freedom. The rest, under guard, would be marched to the fighting front. The further away the front, the larger the number that would desert or die en route.

American officers assigned to the Chinese army estimated a yield of no more than 15 new soldiers for every 100 thus recruited. The only way they were able to reduce the desertion rate towards the end of the war was to fly new recruits to a front a thousand or more miles from their homes. A high-ranking medical officer in the Chinese army explained that the senior staff, aware of the nation's fantastically large manpower reserves, insisted on this method of mass selection. They saw no reason for a selective approach. Even the provision of medical services for soldiers who took ill or were injured was considered a luxury. For all who died, the army could always get replacements.

At an early stage in our own industrial history employers pursued much the same unselective hiring approach. When they needed new workers, they accepted all who appeared at the hiring gate except those obviously disqualified. They knew that they could easily fire any man who was unable to do his job and just as easily replace him.

males. Navy data are for Navy personnel only and exclude Coast Guard personnel serving with the Navy. The total male and female Coast Guard personnel on active duty ranged from 13,756 on June 30, 1940 to 171,192 on June 30, 1945. It should be remembered that the Coast Guard is under the jurisdiction of the Treasury Department in peacetime and the Navy Department in wartime.

As this table indicates, in 1945 the Army accounted for 68 percent of the total Armed Forces' strength, and a consideration of its problems will illuminate most of the military manpower issues that arose during World War II. Of course, if the manpower problems of the Navy and Marine Corps were studied intensively, such an analysis would yield additional insight into manpower utilization.

Table 2. GROWTH OF ARMED FORCES MALE PERSONNEL STRENGTH DURING WORLD WAR II, BY SERVICE *

DATE	NUMBER OF MEN				ARMY PERCENT OF TOTAL
	Army [a]	*Navy* [b] †	*Marine Corps* [b]	*Total*	
30 June 1940	267,000	161,000	28,000	456,000	59
31 Dec. 1941	1,679,000	382,000	75,000	2,136,000	79
31 Dec. 1942	5,366,000	1,252,000	238,000	6,856,000	78
31 Dec. 1943	7,387,000	2,329,000	395,000	10,111,000	73
31 Dec. 1944	7,918,000	3,111,000	455,000	11,484,000	69
30 June 1945	8,113,000	3,288,000	456,000	11,857,000	68

* Officer and enlisted male personnel. † Data exclude Coast Guard personnel.
[a] *Strength of Army*, STM-30, p. 51.
[b] NAVPERS-15115, table 1, pp. 4–5; except 30 June 1945, *Stat. Ab. U.S. 1957*, table 289, p. 240.

Table 2 indicates that the Army's expansion was not only much greater but also much speedier than the Navy's. Since most of the analyses undertaken hereafter are based upon total enlisted male personnel rather than total male personnel, Table 3 has been prepared.

The differential rate of growth of the services is evidenced in Table 4 by index numbers which show that the expansion of

Table 3. GROWTH OF ARMED FORCES ENLISTED MALE PERSONNEL STRENGTH DURING WORLD WAR II, BY SERVICE

DATE	NUMBER OF MEN				ARMY PERCENT OF TOTAL
	Army [a]	*Navy* [b] *	*Marine Corps* [c]	*Total*	
30 June 1940	249,000	147,000	27,000	423,000	59
31 Oct. 1940	477,000	179,000	38,000	694,000	69
31 Dec. 1940	573,000	197,000	45,000	815,000	70
31 Dec. 1941	1,562,000	344,000	71,000	1,977,000	79
31 Dec. 1942	4,989,000	1,135,000	225,000	6,349,000	80
31 Dec. 1943	6,739,000	2,116,000	367,000	9,222,000	73
31 Dec. 1944	7,128,000	2,820,000	420,000	10,368,000	69
30 June 1945	7,284,000	2,976,000	420,000	10,680,000	68
31 Dec. 1945	3,533,000	2,476,000	281,000	6,290,000	56

* Data exclude Coast Guard personnel.
[a] *Strength of Army*, STM-30, p. 51; except 31 Oct. 1940, AG, MRBr., XTQ-13.
[b] NAVPERS-15115, table 1, pp. 4–5; 30 June 1945, *Stat. Ab. U.S. 1957*, table 289, p. 240; 31 Dec. 1945, Navy Records, unpub. tables 172 and 179.
[c] NAVPERS-15115, table 1, pp. 4–5; except 30 June 1945, *Stat. Ab. U.S. 1957*, table 289, p. 240; and 31 Dec. 1945, Marine Corps, unpub. summaries.

Table 4. RELATIVE GROWTH OF ARMED FORCES MALE PERSONNEL STRENGTH DURING WORLD WAR II, BY SERVICE [a]

Index: 30 June 1940 = 100

DATE	*Army*	*Navy* *	*Marine Corps*	*Total*
30 June 1940	100	100	100	100
31 Dec. 1941	630	240	270	470
31 Dec. 1942	2,010	780	850	1,500
31 Dec. 1943	2,770	1,450	1,410	2,220
31 Dec. 1944	2,970	1,930	1,630	2,520
20 June 1945	3,040	2,040	1,640	2,600

* Data exclude Coast Guard personnel. [a] Calculated from Table 2.

the Army between 1940 and the end of 1943 was twice that of the Navy—28-fold as compared to 14-fold.

Table 2 shows that the Army expanded by almost 1½ million between 1940 and Pearl Harbor while the Navy and Marine Corps together added only about 270,000. A year later the Army had already reached two-thirds of its peak strength while the Navy was at 38 percent of its peak and the Marine Corps at 52 percent.

At the end of 1943, the Army was at 92 percent of its wartime peak but the Navy had only reached 71 percent. The rate at which an organization expands provides a greater challenge to management than the level of expansion that it finally reaches. Without question the Army had the more difficult problem, primarily because of the speed with which it had to expand.

The strength figures reveal only net changes and therefore actually understate what transpired. Each of the services, but particularly the Army, found it necessary up to the end of 1943 to take in many more men than it would otherwise have required to replace those whom it had found wanting. Accession figures therefore provide a more valid picture of the magnitude of the expansion. Table 5 presents the accessions of enlisted personnel to the Armed Forces during World War II.

Table 5. ACCESSIONS OF ENLISTED MALE PERSONNEL TO THE ARMED FORCES, BY SERVICE, 1 JULY 1940—31 DECEMBER 1945

PERIOD	NUMBER OF ACCESSIONS				ARMY PERCENT OF TOTAL
	Army [a]	*Navy* [b]	*Marine Corps* [c]	*Total*	
July–Dec. 1940	376,000	50,000	21,000	447,000	84
Jan.–June 1941	850,000	58,000	10,000	918,000	93
July–Dec. 1941	490,000	89,000	26,000	605,000	81
Jan.–June 1942	1,371,000	254,000	71,000	1,696,000	81
July–Dec. 1942	2,444,000	619,000	100,000	3,163,000	77
Jan.–June 1943	1,850,000	413,000	73,000	2,336,000	79
July–Dec. 1943	809,000	583,000	93,000	1,485,000	54
Jan.–June 1944	680,000	617,000	76,000	1,373,000	50
July–Dec. 1944	434,000	266,000	18,000	718,000	60
Jan.–June 1945	568,000	292,000	27,000	887,000	64
July–Dec. 1945	369,000 *	189,000	31,000	589,000	63
Total	10,241,000	3,430,000	546,000	14,217,000	72

* Excludes 323,000 men who reenlisted in the Regular Army, Aug.–Dec. 1945.

[a] *Strength of Army*, STM-30, pp. 84–85, 102–3.

[b] NAVPERS-15115, table 1, pp. 4–5; July 1940—June 1941 estimated from tables 3–4, pp. 8–11; July 1941–Dec. 1944, table 36, p. 50; Jan.–Dec. 1945, Navy Records, unpub. summaries.

[c] Marine Corps, unpub. summaries.

As Table 5 shows, the Army, Navy, and Marine Corps enlisted, inducted, and called to active duty a total of more than 14 million enlisted men from the beginning of mobilization through the end of the war. During the period 1941–45 the Army alone returned to civilian life more than 2½ million men. This figure does not include men demobilized in 1945 on "point scores," and of course does not include soldiers killed or missing in action. Only a relatively small number of these men (under 100,000) were so severely wounded in action that they could no longer serve effectively. The majority, about 1½ million, were men whose performance was so questionable that the Army believed it could gain by releasing them and if possible replacing them with better men.

Unlike the private employer whose additions to his work force are sometimes severely limited by the labor market, the Army, through the Selective Service System, had recourse to the entire national manpower pool within the age limits set by law—eighteen through forty-four. The Army therefore was tempted to seek replacements for men whom it found wanting. This was particularly true during the early period of the war when it seemed impossible that such a large pool could possibly run dry. Only in time did the Army realize that its own demands, when added to the demands of war industry, might exhaust the suitable supply, the more quickly because of the large numbers that were being rejected or deferred.

Although, as we have seen, many of the Army's difficulties were a direct outgrowth of its rapid expansion, our basic military planning actually contemplated just such a development. Ever since colonial days, our country has manifested a negativism towards, even a fear of, large standing forces. In peacetime the nation would tolerate only a small professional Army and Navy. In emergency, citizens were expected to answer the call to the colors. Until the Civil War, it had been hoped that volunteers would come forward in sufficient numbers to meet their country's need; but in that war, as later in World War I, it was necessary to have recourse to the draft. A small professional Army in peacetime, reliance on the draft in case of major emergency—these were two of the three legs of our military manpower planning. The third was a strong reserve to be built up in time of peace so that if an emergency occurred the Army would have trained units ready and would also have the commissioned and noncommissioned officers required to train the draftees.

We noted earlier that the Congress was niggardly during the 1920s and 1930s in allotting funds even for the small regular forces that it had authorized. It was even more niggardly in its appropriations for the reserves. Not until 1935 could the graduate of the Reserve Officer Training Corps enter voluntarily on active duty and even then a ceiling of 1,000 a year was established. Moreover, only 50 per year were permitted to secure a regular commission. Thus, very few reservists had an opportunity to gain the practical experience they would require if they were to carry important responsibilities in an emergency. Likewise, the status of most National Guard units was inadequate. Like the Reserve Corps, they were starved for funds; moreover, many of these units were crippled by politics and favoritism.

One fortunate development that helped the Army during these lean years was the opportunity to operate the Civilian Conservation Corps that was established by Act of Congress in March, 1933, and which within a very few weeks had reached its authorized strength of 300,000. The Army was given the responsibility to receive the recruits, equip them, house and feed them, send them to appropriate camps around the country, and organize them into effective work groups. This was valuable experience, especially for an Army that had long been short of funds for training.

Throughout most of the '30s Hitler's bellicosity did not impress itself on the American public. As we have seen, the President was unable to gain support for a more active policy aimed at checking him. It was not until Hitler marched into Poland that we began to respond, and then only slowly. The passage of the Selective

Training and Service Act in September, 1940, reflected a significant alteration in mood. For the first time in its history the nation authorized compulsory military training in time of peace. But a year later in August, 1941, when the Congress had to decide whether to release recruits who had been called up to serve twelve months or whether it would declare "the national interest . . . imperiled" and prolong their service, the vote in the House of Representatives in favor of extending the period of service was 203 ayes, 202 nays. And in the weeks immediately following, the Army did begin to release to civilian life selectees who had served one year and who were over twenty-eight years old. Because of cumbersome administration some men who were eligible for discharge were still in the service when Pearl Harbor was attacked.

The period prior to Pearl Harbor enabled the Army to begin to mobilize, although the lack of public support for a strong defense position proved a serious handicap. Nevertheless the Army grew by more than a million during this period and, as the official history on *The Procurement and Training of Ground Combat Troops* points out: "The further training of National Guard and Reserve officers, and the elimination of the more obviously unsuitable, were two of the advantages gained by prewar mobilization." But the history reports that the early training had not provided first-class combat troops by February, 1942. One of the major reasons offered was that "Officers from the civilian components, instead of being immediately ready to assist in the task of converting a mass of civilians into soldiers, had themselves required a long period of further training." [2]

The weakness of the reserve components represented one of the most serious hurdles that the Army had to surmount. It meant that civilians without prior knowledge of or interest in things military had to fill not only the enlisted ranks but also had to comprise a large part of the commissioned and noncommissioned officer personnel. Table 6 sets out the various sources from which the Army drew its officers.

At the onset of mobilization the Army had just under 14,000 regular officers on its rolls. During the next five and a half years it added 4,200 Regular Army officers; total officer accessions were 877,200. Thus, 63 officers were mobilized from civilian life for every professional Army officer on active duty in mid-1940. Some of the officers from civilian life had had some degree of military experience, largely from their reserve training, approximately 150,000, or 17 percent of the total. Most of the others, about 3 out of every 4 accessions, were commissioned directly from civilian life or were sent after a relatively short period of service as enlisted men to officer training and aviation schools from which they were commissioned.

Table 6. ACCESSIONS OF MALE OFFICERS TO THE ARMY, BY COMPONENT AND SOURCE OF APPOINTMENT, 1 JULY 1940—31 DECEMBER 1945

COMPONENT AND SOURCE OF APPOINTMENT	ACCESSIONS	
	Number [a]	*Percent of Total*
Regular Army	4,200	0.5
National Guard	20,500	2.3
Reserves and Army of the U.S.		
Officer Candidate Schools	289,700	33.0
Aviation cadet training	250,800	28.6
Civil life and others	112,600	12.8
Reserve Officer Training Corps (ROTC)	87,200	9.9
Direct commissions to enlisted men	47,900	5.5
Warrant and flight officer status	22,400	2.6
Former World War I officers	17,500	2.0
Officers Reserve Corps (ORC)	16,600	1.9
Citizens Military Training Camps (CMTC)	5,800	0.7
National Guard	2,000	0.2
Total: All components	877,200	100.0

[a] *Strength of Army*, STM-30, pp. 68–71.

Although the Regular Army officers, assisted by National Guard and Reserve officers, carried most of the responsibility for the initial expansion up to December, 1941, after we entered the war, primary reliance, particularly in the lower grades, had to be placed on the recently transformed civilians as depicted in Figure 1.

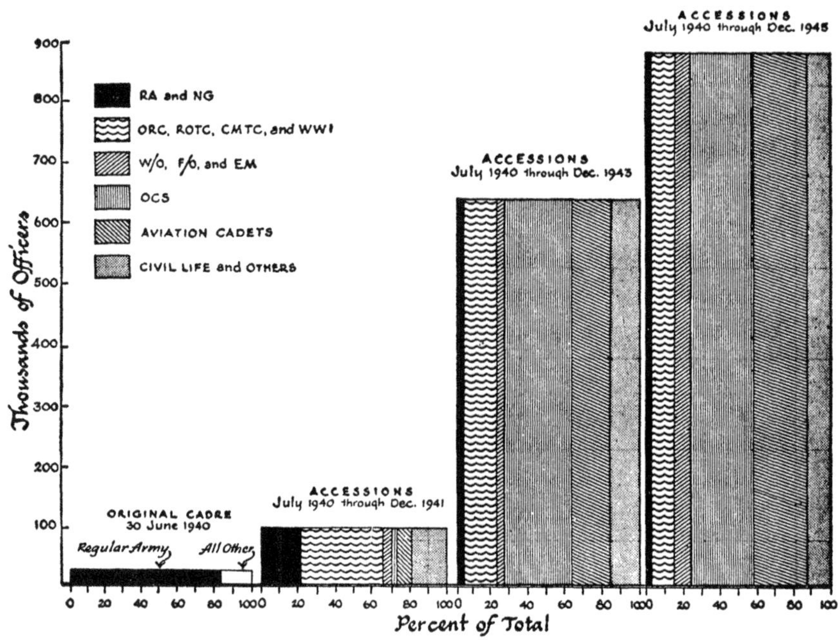

Figure 1. SOURCES OF APPOINTMENT OF MALE ARMY OFFICERS, JUNE 1940 CADRE AND SUBSEQUENT ACCESSIONS, WORLD WAR II

Source: *Strength of Army,* STM-30, pp. 68–71.

The extent to which the Army had to train civilian soldiers with civilian officers is even more vividly portrayed in Figure 2, which compares the accessions of officer and enlisted personnel and shows how closely the one paralleled the other throughout the war, even during the major expansion of 1942.

In the early part of the war a "ninety-day wonder" might receive his lieutenant bars one day and be in command of a unit the next. Men learned by doing. In the process they undoubtedly made a large number of mistakes, some minor, others serious. But they could not possibly provide, at least initially, the quality of leadership that many recruits sorely needed. If he was lucky, the young

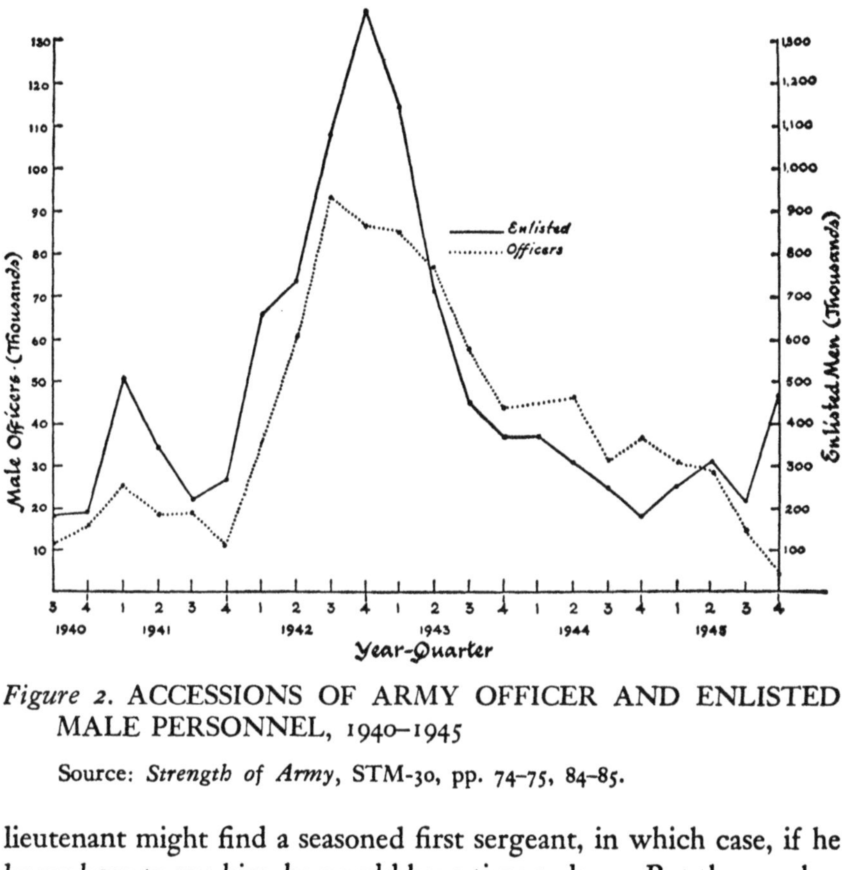

Figure 2. ACCESSIONS OF ARMY OFFICER AND ENLISTED MALE PERSONNEL, 1940–1945

Source: *Strength of Army*, STM-30, pp. 74–75, 84–85.

lieutenant might find a seasoned first sergeant, in which case, if he knew how to use him, he would have time to learn. But the number of experienced first sergeants was far below the number of new lieutenants. Shortly after we started to mobilize, the more able enlisted men in the Regular Army were promoted to officer status and their positions were filled, in turn, by those from the initial call-ups of 1940 and 1941. But by and large this was not a strong group. Many were drafted in 1940 and 1941 because there was no basis for their being deferred—they were no longer in school, they had no dependents, and many had no jobs. Others thought it best to get their military service over with as quickly as possible. Yet these early recruits formed the base of "experienced" military personnel from which noncommissioned and commissioned officers had to be drawn for the wartime expansion.

The Army, even more than industry, traditionally places heavy weight on seniority as a basis for promotion. Men are regularly advanced as long as they make no errors. In the precipitous expansion of 1942–43 the Army could not take time to assess carefully whether a man had positive qualities of leadership. While the expansion was sufficiently rapid to afford most good men a chance to move ahead regardless of their length of service, many were promoted largely because they had accumulated sufficient months in grade.

An interesting analogy in civilian life was found at many colleges and universities when enrollments soared in the immediate postwar years. Many mediocre men were added to the teaching staff, and a considerable number were eventually promoted and given tenure for no other reason than that they had performed adequately and their records were unblemished. Actually, many lacked the qualities required for academic distinction. In many large corporations men of limited ability also can be found fairly high in the organization because they were available when expansion occurred.

Almost all manpower difficulties that arose during the war can be traced back to acts of omission or commission during the initial build-up of 1940–41. The assumption that the manpower pool was bottomless and that it was not only feasible but sensible for the Army to discharge men whenever it determined that they, individually or as a group, were found lacking stems from this early period. It was not until the latter part of 1943 that the Army was rudely awakened to the fact that this basic assumption about the inexhaustible nature of the manpower pool was an error and that many of its manpower policies would have to be modified.

Closely related to the foregoing and deriving from the same

basic assumption was the Army's approach to screening standards. The Army wanted men without any blemish—physical, mental, or emotional. For this reason during most of 1941 and 1942 it rejected among others men who were illiterate and those who were suffering from venereal disease. Unfortunately, the number of each, as well as the numbers rejected for other deficiencies, mounted rapidly and soon reached a very high figure. Tremendous backlogs of rejectees with one or another handicap accumulated at each local Selective Service Board throughout the country. When the tightness in the manpower pool began to manifest itself the Army had to readjust its standards and begin to accept men with defects that had previously been disqualifying. Despite its use of quotas, the Army was inundated by individuals with particular handicaps at the very time it was under the greatest pressure to train men quickly. This inflow of handicapped personnel presented a much more severe management problem than would have occurred had the backlog not been built up in the first place.

As we have seen, the Army mobilized in the conviction that the nation's manpower would be ample to meet all of its quantitative requirements no matter how great they might turn out to be; it also gave only scant consideration to any prospective qualitative difficulties. In this, as in many other respects, its experience in World War I and in peacetime weighed heavily. It thought in terms of basic soldiers and it was committed to the doctrine of interchangeability. With a little training a selectee should be convertible into any type of soldier and if the situation changed and requirements were altered, he should be reconvertible. There was much logic to the Army's stress on convertibility and interchangeability, for only thus could millions of civilians be transformed into an effective military force. The Army's firm commitment to this doctrine helps to explain its disinclination to accept men whose handicaps reduced the range within which they could be trained and assigned.

But the war revealed, although it took considerable time for the facts to make themselves clear, that the proportion of specialists required was much greater than the Army had anticipated and that the training of some specialists was a long and difficult process. Further, the war brought into sharp focus the qualitative limitations in the nation's manpower. A high percentage of recruits did not have the needed intellectual and other qualities to enable them to acquire skills quickly. Failing to anticipate such a high requirement for specialists, the Army paid insufficient attention to developing policies aimed at identifying and utilizing men with high ability and readily convertible civilian skills.

Finally, as we had occasion to note earlier, the Army, confronted with a very high requirement for junior officers, focused on quantity production. Successful as it was in this area, it encountered other difficulties, some of which it could not solve. The extent to which poor phasing in the call-up operated to the disadvantage of the Army is illustrated by the fact that by 1943, when its requirements for junior officers had largely been met, the Army drafted many older men with demonstrated leadership qualities. These able and experienced men had few opportunities to qualify as officers although they possessed the maturity and experience that was conspicuously lacking among so many junior officers. The principal requirement for officer personnel later in the war was for combat assignments where young men had the edge.

Some of the manpower problems that have just been pointed up the Army was able to cope with, not to the extent of preventing them from arising, but at least to alleviate them once the evidence became clear that something was awry. But others were beyond remedy. The policies in force early in the war determined the outcome.

The major difficulties with respect to military manpower policies in World War II must be traced back to the tripod on which all planning had been based—a small professional corps, a strong reserve system, reliance on the draft. Among the duties of the small professional Army was the preparation of mobilization plans, including military manpower programs. Manpower planning was inadequate. The military experts, like most civilian experts, misread the experience of the country during the 1930s and failed to appreciate fully the large requirements for competent leadership and technical specialists in the advent of a full-scale mobilization.

Next, the reserve structure which was scheduled to play a crucial role in any large-scale emergency was much weaker than the mobilization planners had recommended. It made a significant contribution, but not until many valuable months had been lost in culling out the misfits and bringing units and men to a reasonable level of proficiency.

Finally, the selective service process, which from many points of view operated with outstanding success during the war, was much less selective than would have been desirable. In particular, more care in planning the call-up of men with varying abilities and handicaps could have alleviated many of the manpower problems that the Army encountered.

Considering the serious weaknesses that existed in each of these major respects the performance of the Army, in building up an outstanding military organization within a reasonably short period of time, is that much more commendable. The Army was able to give the lie to Hitler's forecast and in so doing saved this country and the Western world. The following chapters will review in detail how the Army adjusted its plans and policies as it gained greater insight into the manpower problems that it faced during the successive stages of the war. Much of the recital will deal with error and waste. But since the outcome is known—a resounding and overwhelming victory five years after the onset of mobilization—the shortcomings along the way, while they should not be minimized, must be kept in perspective. Moreover, the value of such a review is not to apportion credit or blame but to extract the important lessons that can contribute to the improvement in policy in the future.

Chapter Two: SELECTION FOR SERVICE

COMPETENT observers have provided the following picture of how manpower was mobilized in Nationalist China in the latter part of World War II. A squad of soldiers would suddenly block off a populated street. They would grab all likely looking male civilians and tie them to a very long rope. When fifty or so had been snared and tied, the soldiers would march the "recruits" off to a nearby collection station. There a few, obviously unfit for service, would be released and a few others might be able to wangle their freedom. The rest, under guard, would be marched to the fighting front. The further away the front, the larger the number that would desert or die en route.

American officers assigned to the Chinese army estimated a yield of no more than 15 new soldiers for every 100 thus recruited. The only way they were able to reduce the desertion rate towards the end of the war was to fly new recruits to a front a thousand or more miles from their homes. A high-ranking medical officer in the Chinese army explained that the senior staff, aware of the nation's fantastically large manpower reserves, insisted on this method of mass selection. They saw no reason for a selective approach. Even the provision of medical services for soldiers who took ill or were injured was considered a luxury. For all who died, the army could always get replacements.

At an early stage in our own industrial history employers pursued much the same unselective hiring approach. When they needed new workers, they accepted all who appeared at the hiring gate except those obviously disqualified. They knew that they could easily fire any man who was unable to do his job and just as easily replace him.

It was not until after World War I that American industry developed elaborate screening devices. These efforts were in large measure inspired by the psychological testing employed by the Army during the war. The adoption and strengthening of workmen's compensation laws also stimulated industry to be more selective, for thereafter employers had to pay increased insurance premiums if their accident rates were high. Still another factor that encouraged employers to intensify their selection procedures was their growing recognition of the costs of training new workers. As industry made increasing use of expensive equipment that required skilled workers, management became sensitive to the need to improve its personnel selection procedures.

Another consideration that played a part in determining the approach of the U.S. Army to the selection of manpower in World War II was the aftermath of World War I when many thousands of young Americans drew disability payments from the Federal Government because of injuries or diseases incurred as a result of their service. In the mobilization of 1940 the Armed Forces sought to reduce the number of potential pensioners by rejecting men who it thought might have to be discharged later for disability. But this interest was really secondary to their desire to select only those men who gave promise of being able to meet the severe demands of war. Furthermore, the Armed Services appreciated that time was their most valuable and most limited resource and that they must use it economically in order to defeat the enemy. Some men could be trained more quickly than others. There was a clear military advantage to selecting those most likely to succeed, and succeed quickly, as soldiers.

To this end, the Armed Forces set up screening standards aimed at eliminating all those young men who, because of a physical or mental defect, appeared to be bad risks. And the screening had a further aim. World War I had alerted the Army to the serious manpower losses which could result when soldiers were unable to withstand the emotional stress of war.[3] In the summer of 1918 General Pershing, who had been plagued by heavy losses resulting from "shell shock," cabled the War Department to be sure that all troops sent to France thenceforth should be carefully screened in order to eliminate those likely to turn into psychiatric casualties. Therefore at the outset of mobilization in World War II the Army made provision to screen all men before their induction to assess whether they were emotionally fit for service.

There is no direct counterpart in civilian employment to this type of psychiatric screening. Although every employer seeks to avoid hiring a person who is obviously mentally unbalanced, he does not generally attempt further testing. Nor is there much reason that he should. Most people can handle a job for which they have been trained even if they do suffer from some degree of emotional unbalance. But in the Army a man is under constant surveillance; he is always subject to the commands of others; he is trained to kill; and the threat of injury or death is never far removed—this job has no counterpart in civilian life. This environment exerts a major strain on a man's emotional resources.

Just as the intelligence testing used by the Army in World War I was taken over by many sectors of industry during the 1930s, so many corporations have uncritically introduced into their employment procedures psychiatric screening adapted from the experience of the Armed Services in World War II. A considerable number of firms will not hire a man for even a minor managerial position without subjecting him to a personality test. And some enterprising organizations will not hire or promote a senior man until they have given him an elaborate personality evaluation, usually administered by a skilled psychologist or psychiatrist.

The Army procedure in World War II provided for still one additional screen. Some men were rejected for military service on moral grounds. Those who had been in serious trouble with the law comprised the largest part of this group. The Army decided that a man with a history of poor social behavior was not likely to reform simply because he put on a uniform. The odds were that not only would such a man prove ineffective but he might infect others with whom he came into close contact. Civilian industry has long followed similar practices. Probation officers have great difficulty in persuading employers to give a former convict a job. The employers are usually unwilling to take a chance.

The Armed Services applied the foregoing four screens—physical, mental, emotional, and administrative—to all those in the population whom the law of the land declared liable and the Selective Service System declared available for military service. Congress extended the age limits on several occasions and finally determined that men between the ages of eighteen and forty-four were subject to call. The law exempted some groups of individuals, such as ministers; deferred others, such as certain public officeholders; and protected conscientious objectors from combatant service. It gave to the President, who exercised his power through the Selective Service System, the authority to defer other groups in the national interest. The law provided guidelines to the Selective Service System concerning the order in which men were to be called up. The major task of Selective Service was to provide the numbers that Congress had authorized for the Armed Services in a manner that would cause the least disturbance to the war economy and to the social structure. Its primary responsibility therefore was to determine which men should receive deferments because they were essential workers in war industry or agriculture or because they had important obligations towards dependents which no one else could discharge.

The operations of the Selective Service System were anything but static. Its determinations, within the law, were influenced by the fluctuating demands of the Armed Services on the one hand and the realities of the manpower pool on the other. For instance, although early in the war men up to the age of forty-five were drafted, it was not long before the Army, which under the law had the right to determine the standards of acceptability, realized that it was difficult to convert men above thirty-seven into effective soldiers. Within a year after Pearl Harbor the Army had stopped inducting these older men and had actually moved to discharge those it had already taken in. Shortly before D-Day in Europe, in the early spring of 1944, a further adjustment in the age of acceptable men was made. At this time, the Army had just about reached its peak authorized strength. Henceforth, its requirements for new manpower would be limited to replacing the losses it would incur in combat. Young men definitely made the best replacements. Therefore, the Army instructed the Selective Service System to limit its future call-ups to men below the age of twenty-six. These changes in age standards were paralleled by frequent changes in the criteria for deferments for fathers, farmers, and essential workers. There were also frequent changes in the physical and mental standards. These changes in standards necessitated the re-examination of many men who had been initially rejected for service.

At this late date it is impossible to determine exactly how many men were screened for military service during World War II. In fact, such a determination was never possible because the Selective Service System maintained statistics only on its own registrants. However, about 14 million men of all ages were taken into the Armed Services by enlistment or induction either directly or through a reserve component between the beginning of mobilization in 1940 and the end of the war. During the same period more than 6 million men were examined at least once and rejected, and never served in the Armed Forces. The total number examined for enlisted military service therefore exceeded 20 million.

The best available figures about the vast manpower screening relate to the group of men who were between eighteen and thirty-seven years of age inclusive on August 1, 1945. It must be recalled that men above thirty-seven years of age were no longer accepted for induction after December, 1942. Table 7 summarizes, as of August, 1945, the results of screening this age group during World War II.

As Table 7 indicates, approximately 18 million of the estimated total of 20 million examined were found in the age group eighteen through thirty-seven. The other 2 million included those not yet eighteen who were examined and accepted frequently directly by the Services, and those over thirty-seven, many of whom were examined and some of whom served, for at least part of the war. On the basis of comparable census data, males within the eighteen to thirty-seven age group totaled about 22.4 million. Thus, predominantly all males in this age group, except for about 4.4 million, were examined for military service during the course of the emergency. Those not examined were men over twenty-six years of age deferred on occupational grounds or because of dependents. It must be recalled that the passage of the Tydings Amendment to the Selective Service Act in November, 1942, encouraged the

Table 7. RESULTS OF PHYSICAL EXAMINATIONS GIVEN THROUGH 1 AUGUST 1945 TO MEN AGED 18 THROUGH 37 AS OF THAT DATE [a]

Examination and Results	*Number of Men*	*Percent*
Examined	18,000,000	100
Rejected	5,250,000	29
Found acceptable	12,750,000	71

[a] SSS, Monograph 15, Vol. 1, table 23, p. 154. Estimated number examined adjusted by the addition of an estimate of nonregistrant enlistees 19–37 years of age as of 1 August 1945 who were examined and accepted and were still in service on that date.

deferment of those engaged in farming, especially if they were above twenty-six years of age. Of the nearly 3½ million men deferred at the end of the war in nonagricultural occupations, more than 3 million were between thirty and thirty-seven years of age.

The 5¼ million men who Table 7 shows were rejected for service were unable to meet the physical, emotional, mental, or moral requirements. Thus, 3 out of every 10 men examined were found wanting. Approximately 2 out of every 3 of these men were rejected because of physical disability while 1 out of every 3 was judged to be unsuitable for military service because of an emotional, mental, or moral defect. The numbers rejected for these several causes are shown in Table 8.

It is easy to appreciate why the Armed Services, pressed for time, sought to avoid inducting men with physical disabilities. As was pointed out earlier, the Armed Services feared the creation of a large pensioner group that would have claims against the government for the rest of their lives because of an aggravation of a physical or emotional disability as a result of military service. But the nub of the issue lay elsewhere. The Armed Services eventually had to accept some men with poor eyesight, poor hearing, perforated eardrums, flat feet, those who were underweight and those who were overweight, men with skeletal defects, and those who

Table 8. WORLD WAR II REJECTEES AGED 18 THROUGH 37 ON 1 AUGUST 1945, BY MAJOR REASON FOR REJECTION

Reason for Rejection	*Number Rejected*	*Percent of Total Examined* [b]	*Percent of Total Rejected*
Physical defect	3,447,000	19.3	66.2
Emotional disorder	970,000	5.4	18.5
Mental or educational deficiency	716,000	4.0	13.6
Nonmedical, administrative	87,000	0.5	1.7
Total	5,250,000 [a]	29.2	100.0

[a] Totals and gross data from SSS Monograph 15, Vol. 1, tables 23 and 27, pp. 154 and 157. Distribution of various classes based on pub. and unpub. SSS data.
[b] See Table 7 for total number examined.

had recovered from tuberculosis, infantile paralysis, and other serious diseases. But the proper assignment of these men created serious problems. They could not be sent as replacements to an understrength unit. They had to be specially assigned. Under pressure of time and with a personnel system with limited experience the Armed Forces understandably sought to avoid accepting large numbers who required special treatment. And, as we shall see later, they discharged many thousands of "limited service" men soon after their induction because they could not be readily fitted into a rapidly expanding organization which was in constant flux.

The same logic led the Armed Services to set up minimum educational requirements for induction. Since no civilian was ready for a combat assignment at the time of his induction, all had to be trained before they could perform as soldiers. The need for men with ability to learn—to learn quickly and to learn with the aid of written materials—explains why the services were reluctant to accept men who were illiterate or who had only limited intellectual capacity. The Armed Services knew that many men with little or no formal schooling could be converted into effective soldiers if sufficient time and effort were devoted to instructing them. But again, time was the limiting factor. In an earlier volume, we reviewed in detail the experiences of the Armed Services with illiterate and poorly educated men during World War II.[4]

By far the most striking innovation in the screening practices of World War II related to the procedures for assessing the emotional capabilities of men called up for service. Every community had experience with a few seriously unbalanced individuals who were unable to make even a minimum adjustment to civilian life. Unable to hold a job or discharge their family responsibilities, many were hospitalized. They were wards either of their relatives, the local community, or the state. In peacetime the Armed Forces sought to keep such men out of the service and when they slipped in, to get rid of them quickly. Thus, the truly emotionally disturbed, the psychotics, presented no new or special problem.

The innovation in psychiatric screening related rather to an assessment of the very much larger numbers who had been able to make an adjustment in civilian life, frequently a very good adjustment as reflected in the fact that they were college graduates, earned good salaries, and were the responsible heads of families. Many such men, as well as many others whose civilian adjustment was less good but still adequate, were rejected for military service on the ground that they did not possess the emotional resilience that would enable them to absorb the hardships and strains of a soldier's life. The Armed Forces sought a screening procedure that could identify at the point of induction all who were likely to fail. They wanted to save precious time by not training men who sooner or later would fail, unable to take the punishment of modern war.

It is doubtful that the Armed Services would ever have committed themselves to such a radical screening procedure unless the leaders of the psychiatric profession had encouraged them in the belief that it was possible to separate the strong from the weak, the reliable from the unreliable, on the basis of a quick psychiatric evaluation. In this connection it is important to recall the environment in which the examinations were carried out during the most important months of the war. In one metropolitan center 3,000 men were processed between the hours of 7 a.m., and 4 p.m. It was, necessarily, an assembly line operation. If a man's educational background was adequate, he was passed on immediately to the doctors who examined him from head to toe, quickly but thoroughly. One physician examined his eyes and ears; another his chest and lungs; another his abdomen; another his genital organs; another his legs and feet. Routinely a blood specimen was taken, as was an X-ray of his chest.

At the end of the line the selectee was confronted with a psychiatrist who had about three minutes per selectee. As one respondent to our earlier inquiry remarked, "These were the hectic days during which my examinational procedure consisted of four rapid-fire questions, 'How do you feel?' 'Have you ever been sick?' 'Are you nervous?' 'How do you think you will get along in the Army?' One day I saw 512 men." [5]

In many stations the psychiatric evaluation was made by physicians who had had no special training in psychiatry but who were corralled for the job. Many were sensible men who did quite well. Others did not. At one large station, it was several weeks before the authorities caught up with an examiner whose method of psychiatric evaluation consisted of suddenly approaching the nude man standing before him and slapping him very hard on the abdomen; he then purported to assess the man's emotional state on the basis of how high he jumped. Many selectees reported that the sole question they were asked by the examining psychiatrist was, "Do you like girls?"

In addition to the overwhelming pressure of time, the psychiatrists were further handicapped by the necessity to evaluate a man's future performance without any idea of the orders of stress that he would encounter in his military career. The psychiatrists knew that whether a man would eventually break depended in part on whether he would have to serve in combat or spend most of his time with a quartermaster battalion at a safe outpost in the Caribbean. The examiner had to make an assumption that all would serve in combat.

To further compound the screening difficulties, frequent directives from Washington modified the existing criteria without making clear the reasons for the change. These were processed and interpreted as they passed through the headquarters of the nine Service Commands into which the country was divided and under which the Armed Forces Induction Stations operated. There was little uniformity in practice especially before the War Department reorganized the induction stations in 1943. Moreover, the number of induction stations and their territorial jurisdiction underwent sudden alterations with resulting changes in policy and direction. Early in 1941 there were 75 stations in operation; by February, 1942, there were only 37; but in April the number stood at 108, only to decline next month to 94.

In any military organization, the local commander has tremendous power. Although the doctors were in charge of the medical examining procedures, final responsibility rested with the commanding officer. To quote another respondent to our earlier inquiry: "When someone got hell for not meeting the quota the buck was passed all the way down along the line. There were days in which four of us psychiatrists sitting at a Board would reject a man; the man would be kept around until 4:30 or 5:00 o'clock in the afternoon, and the Major in charge would induct him himself." [6]

It is not surprising that many civilian psychiatrists "soon quit in frustration. I could not in all fairness judge who was fit for duty when I had only a few minutes . . . I could not use my psychiatric tools." [7] There were frequent disagreements among the experts, between the psychiatrists and line officers, and above all between the Armed Forces and the leaders of the community. There were many intelligent and devoted laymen who gave unsparingly of their time and effort to serve on their local Selective Service Boards. These men found it difficult to understand a procedure which rejected a strong, healthy young bachelor of twenty-four who was getting ahead very well in his job and who was known to his friends and neighbors as a solid citizen, with the notation "neurotic potential" or "diffuse anxiety," with the result that they had to forward in his place a portly man of thirty-four, father of three. Since the local Board had the right to forward for a second and a third time a selectee who had been previously rejected, some men were bounced back and forth with resultant disruption to their lives and further burden to the already overloaded administrative machinery.

A major objective of this book is to explore in some detail the major consequences for manpower utilization arising from the fact that during the course of World War II the Army rejected almost one million men on the ground that they were emotionally unfit to serve. While, as the war progressed, the Army found that it had to lower many of its screening standards to get the numbers it required, it never gave up the doctrine that all who gave evidence of being, or becoming, emotionally unstable should be rejected. Here was a policy born of a marriage of military expediency and psychiatric enthusiasm that was not successfully challenged until the end of the war.

Chapter Three: ASSIGNMENT, TRAINING, AND UTILIZATION

IT WOULD REQUIRE several volumes to relate the major developments in the assignment, training, and utilization of the more than 10 million enlisted men who saw active service in the Army during World War II. All that can be ventured here is to call attention to a few of the outstanding developments, especially in manpower policy. This will help the reader to appreciate how manpower policies influenced the performance of soldiers and to understand why so many failed.

The net additions to the work force in manufacturing industries in the United States during a period of expanding business such as in 1955 averaged 46,800 per month. In contrast, during the last four months of 1942 the net growth of the Army averaged 417,000 enlisted men per month.

The rate of growth is only one of the significant differences between the experience of the Army and civilian industry. We have pointed out that no civilian is adequately prepared to assume the role of soldier immediately upon entering active duty. Even the policeman or the FBI agent requires a period of time to adjust to a military type of organization and to master the weapons with which few civilians are acquainted. The typical Army recruit has much more to learn. Although the Army sometimes created unnecessary problems for itself, such as when it insisted that neurosurgeons take part in field maneuvers with the result that many tore their hands, the Army had little option but to require most men to undergo rigorous training. This was essential in order to convert soft civilians into hard soldiers within the shortest possible time.

Many large corporations have indoctrination programs for junior executives. Some stretch over a three-year period. Three years after the large inflow of men into the Army late in 1942 the war was over. A real complication was that the Air Corps, to which this country looked to strike not only the first but perhaps the decisive blow against the enemy, had to grow from an even smaller base than the Ground or Service forces. When Hitler's legions marched into Poland, the aviation industry in the United States was embryonic. In the two years prior to our own entrance into the war, our aviation industry expanded very rapidly but not rapidly enough to provide the Air Corps with enough trained men. Those it did train were required for its own continuing expansion. A week before Pearl Harbor the Air Corps numbered 300,000; a year later its strength was 1,500,000. Almost all of this increase consisted of men who had no knowledge of, or experience with, any phase of the aviation industry. Even today the Air Force estimates that less than 5 percent of its new recruits have skills that are directly usable; the remainder must be trained or retrained before they can be assigned.

The Army Service Forces were best able to make direct use of men with civilian skills. Within the limitations of the classification and assignment system, men with experience in railroading or shipping were likely to be sent to the Transportation Corps; those from the medical professions to the Medical Department; men with experience in telephone, telegraph, and other sectors of the communications industry to the Signal Corps; those with buying or warehousing experience to the Quartermaster; those with experience in the chemical industry to the Chemical Warfare Corps; those with experience in construction or engineering to the Corps of Engineers; those with experience in heavy manufacturing to the Ordnance Department; and those with white collar skills to one of the Administrative Services. However, even if the system had worked perfectly, the seven Technical Services and the eight Administrative Services would still not have been able to establish a proper balance between their requirements and the men made available to them.

There were many difficulties attendant on operating the assignment system. We have already noted that the manpower planners had not been able to develop a complete list of requirements so the Army was unable to estimate its own needs, either in gross numbers or in terms of skills. The absence of such data meant that a man fluent in French might not be noticed when he passed through a reception center, while the next week the Army might circularize all posts, camps, and stations for candidates to attend a foreign language school. A more subtle difficulty—but one that cost the Army dear—was the absence of good tables of conversion. There was no ready way to classify a man whose record showed that he had a master's degree in mathematics. The reception center might well give him a military occupational specialty of "clerk." Again, a young man who had developed a high order of skill as an amateur radio operator might go unnoticed when the Army was in dire need of capable men for communications because the interviewer forgot to ask him his hobbies.

There was no more serious weakness in the entire system than the lack of experience and competence in the enlisted men and officers responsible for routine personnel operations. Most of them were given a short course and put to work, only to be reassigned themselves after they gained a little experience, to be followed by other novices who, upon acquiring a modicum of competence and skill were also likely to be reassigned. There was nothing unusual in this procedure. It was characteristic of all assignments within the continental limits of the United States. Unless men were clearly disqualified for foreign service, they were left in an assignment only until they could be reassigned as individuals or as members of a unit scheduled for overseas service. The Army did this deliberately, because it had to use all physically qualified men in overseas assignments, primarily in combat or combat support operations.

The assignment system was also made inefficient because it was very difficult to retain even relatively small numbers of men at a reception center until a demand for their skills was forthcoming. Housing was one facet of the problem. In the last four months of 1942, approximately 1,765,000 enlisted men were taken into the

Army. This meant a daily average of about 14,500. At this time there were 38 reception centers in operation. Since it required a minimum of three days to process a man, there was very great pressure on all reception centers to move men out just as quickly as possible in order to make room for new recruits.

Not until the end of the war did the Army finally develop a system whereby it was able to keep men with high ability and skill in a special pool until suitable assignments could be found for them. The pressures to get men into training or duty positions were always very great. It was impossible in 1942 when the inflow was overwhelming. It was much easier for the Army to sort men by gross characteristics, such as age, physical condition, and intelligence score, and to ship them out to units in large groups. This meant that on any one day, unmet requirements determined to what unit a man would be sent. Once it was determined that a recruit could meet the minimum performance standards of the unit he was to join, no further questions were asked. Pressure and speed resulted in frequent errors. Older men, in a flabby condition, were sent for infantry training; young athletes with low intelligence scores were sent to Signal Corps units where men with a flair for numbers or gadgets were needed.

It was not until early 1944, too late in the war to affect most recruits, that the Army adopted the system of profiling men which had been instituted much earlier in the Canadian and British armies. This system was based on a rough estimate of a man's physical, mental, and emotional characteristics. The profile was known in the American Army as PULHES, the letters referring to Physical condition, Upper extremities, Lower extremities, Hearing, Eyes, Stability (emotional). The major objective of the procedure was to assign men in accordance with their strengths and weaknesses so that they could better meet the performance demands of the unit they were joining.

The profiling system could work properly only if the performance requirements of all duty assignments had been worked out in advance and if those responsible for personnel decisions understood the system and were willing to use it. By the time the system was introduced it was too late to properly indoctrinate medical and personnel officers, so that it never gained more than limited support. Throughout most of the war the Army differentiated among men on physical grounds only to the extent of classifying some as fit only for "limited service," thereby indicating that they were not to be assigned to arduous duties. But even this limitation proved so cumbersome that the Army made strenuous efforts in 1943 to release all who were so classified.

Since so few recruits had directly usable skills, the Army's success in quickly building up strong forces depended primarily on the ability of the men to absorb training. Thus the crux of the assignment problem during World War II was the allocation and use of men with better than average learning ability. A man's score on the Army General Classification Test (AGCT) became the key. This test, administered to all recruits when they were processed at a reception center, sought to determine their abilities to absorb both basic and advanced training. For administrative simplicity the Army divided all men into five classes. Classes I and II were composed of men who scored above average (110 or above); Class III was average (90–109); Classes IV and V were composed of men below average (89 and below).

In general, the top third, those in Classes I and II, were able to cope with any training program, even the most difficult. Those in the middle third, Class III, could meet most training requirements, other than those that required ability to deal with mathematics and other abstract forms of reasoning. Men in Class IV were expected to absorb basic training and even some of the simpler types of advanced training, but this was not true about the more than 750,000 recruits in Class V. Men in the lowest class were definitely handicapped and could be expected to meet minimum performance standards only if they were given special training, such as a preliminary course to prepare them for basic training, or a prolongation of basic training itself.

Throughout the war there was a never-ending competition

among the Army Ground Forces, Army Air Forces, and Army Service Forces for a greater share of men in the upper classes and a smaller share of those in Classes IV and V. The scramble for high-scoring men was also a source of conflict between the Army and the Navy. Until December, 1942, the Navy was permitted to rely on volunteers to secure its manpower. With the draft pressing them, many men preferred to take their chances with the Navy, where conditions of service were more congenial and their chances of survival better. The Navy took the best of those who applied, leaving the rest to enlist in or be inducted into the Army. Despite his love of the Navy, the President finally responded to the insistent pressures of both the Army and the Director of the Selective Service System and put an end to this basic inequality in manpower procurement by banning enlistments of draft-eligible men into any Service.

During 1943 the Army processed more than 2½ million men. The Army Ground Forces included the infantry, coast and field artillery, armored, cavalry, anti-aircraft, and tank destroyer branches; these ground combat arms were allotted 40 percent of the total. The service branches, most of which were in the Army Service Forces, were allotted 37 percent, and the Army Air Forces, 23 percent. Table 9 presents the distribution of the recruits assigned to each by their AGCT scores.

It shows that the Air Forces were definitely favored: more than two out of every five men assigned to the Air Forces were in Classes I or II; only about 1 in 4 was below average. Less than 30 percent of the men assigned to the Ground Forces were in Classes I and II; and more than a third were in the lowest two classes. The Army Service Forces fared better than the Ground Forces, but not as well as the Air Forces.

It was no accident that the Air Forces received more than their share of able men. Early in the war a definite decision was made to favor the Air Forces in this regard. The assumption was that the Air Forces' need for men able to absorb advanced technical training was greater than that of the other Services and that it should therefore receive a disproportionately larger number of men with high AGCT scores. As early as February, 1942, the War Department directed that 75 percent of all white soldiers forwarded to the Air Forces should have an AGCT score of 100 or better—in short, that 3 out of every 4 men should be average or better. This ruling was violently protested by General McNair and General Somervell. As a result of these protests by the commanding generals of the Ground and Service forces, the directive was rescinded, only to be followed shortly thereafter by

Table 9. ENLISTED MEN INDUCTED INTO THE ARMY AND ASSIGNED DURING 1943, BY AGCT CLASS AND BY MAJOR BRANCH ASSIGNMENT

MAJOR BRANCH ASSIGNMENT	AGCT CLASS *I & II*	*III*	*IV & V*	TOTAL
	NUMBER OF MEN[a]			
Ground Forces	308,200	345,700	382,600	1,036,500
Service Forces	348,600	271,700	334,300	954,600
Air Forces	247,100	185,500	159,300	591,900
Total	903,900	802,900	876,200	2,583,000
	PERCENT OF FORCE TOTAL			
Ground Forces	29.7	33.4	36.9	100.0
Service Forces	36.5	28.5	35.0	100.0
Air Forces	41.8	31.3	26.9	100.0

[a] Palmer *et al.*, table 3, p. 18.

the War Department's acting favorably on a recommendation of General Arnold to provide that 50,000 of the 70,000 monthly quota of the Air Forces be composed of men who had scored 100 or better on both the AGCT and the mechanical aptitude test.

The new formula substantially improved the quality of men assigned to the Air Forces since only one-third of all men scored above 100 on both tests. Continuing protests by the other services led to a further revision late in 1942 so that thereafter the Air Forces received only 55 percent of its monthly quota in men who scored 100 or better on both tests. The advantage of the Air Forces was actually greater, for aviation cadets, who had to have a better than average AGCT score, were not included in the quota; moreover, properly qualified men initially assigned to the Ground Forces could volunteer for flying and, even if they washed out, were retained by the Air Forces. This policy remained in effect until June, 1943, when the Army, and particularly the Air Forces, were approaching their peak strengths.

It was the Army Ground Forces that paid the price for the preferential treatment accorded the Air Forces. The Army Service Forces, as we noted earlier, were able to make use of many civilian specialists with only a little conversion. Moreover, the Army Service Forces operated the reception centers, so that they were able to skim off some of the cream. So it was that the Army Ground Forces were penalized by the system of "residual allocation." Not only did they get a much smaller proportion of "high quality" men and a much larger proportion of "low quality" men, but further inroads were made on even their limited number of men in Class I and II. During 1942 such men were able to apply for commissions outside of the combat arms and many did. To illustrate: in one division where 1,200 enlisted men were accepted for officer training, 800, or two out of three, chose training in the quartermaster, finance, or medical administration branches. Some of these were later reassigned to the combat units, but many good men were lost to the Ground Forces by this route before the regulations were changed.

Another serious drain on the pool of able men resulted when many were withdrawn from the Ground Forces so that they might participate in the Army Specialized Training Program, which was established in 1942 for such diverse purposes as to provide the Army with requisite numbers of college-trained specialists, prevent the complete cessation in the training cycle of such important professions as medicine, and provide some students for hard-pressed colleges, many of which would have been in serious financial difficulties unless they were afforded an opportunity to participate in training servicemen. Only men with at least a high-school education, and usually below the age of twenty-two with a score of

115 or better on the AGCT, were selected. Of the 216,000 who entered the program during the two and a half years that it was in existence, a high percentage came from the Army Ground Forces. Small wonder, therefore, that the program was bitterly fought by the Ground Forces every inch of the way from inception until its dramatic emasculation in the early spring of 1944. The Army Ground Forces were convinced that the War Department was in error in failing to recognize its need for a relatively large number of intellectually able men, especially to meet its requirements for noncommissioned officers.

There was no way for the War Department to determine objectively the relative strength of the claims of the three Forces for preferred numbers of capable men. Its backing and filling was the inevitable consequence of the absence of a firm basis for determining manpower requirements and resources. That such a basis is hard to develop is suggested by the effort made by the Department of Defense in 1950–51 to develop valid criteria for allocating manpower among the respective Forces. The project came to naught and recourse had to be taken to an arbitrary allocation system.

Even if the system of allocation had been on a firmer base, difficulties in training and utilization would still have proved a serious challenge. It is characteristic of civilian as well as military organizations to assume that personnel difficulties always arise from shortages of qualified people, rather than from faulty training or poor utilization. If the supply is deficient, management is free of blame. On the other hand, it must accept responsibility for failures in training or utilization. Small wonder, therefore, that most organizations stress the former in explaining why they are encountering intractable manpower problems. It is admitted that errors in allocation that resulted in overassigning men contributed to their eventual breakdown, and underassigning men contributed to lowered morale and poor performance. But difficulties on the training front must not be minimized. Many who failed might have been salvaged had more caution been exercised in the crucial period when they were being converted from civilian to soldier.

Attention was called in the preceding chapter to the additional problems that the Army faced during its rapid expansion because it had to rely so greatly on inexperienced officers and noncommissioned officers to command and supervise the training of new recruits. Many draftees encountered great difficulties in adjusting to military service. Some found the separation from home very painful, while others were confused and harassed by the multiple demands that were constantly made on them. Many lost their bearings and their balance. When they had the good fortune to be assigned to a unit under the command of a wise old sergeant or a mature lieutenant, they could be helped over the hump; but if their supervisors themselves were insecure and unsettled, their situation was likely to worsen to the point where they became totally ineffective.

The Army was further burdened because it had not made provision for helping the large numbers of handicapped persons whom it was forced to draft. It was not until June of 1943 that the Army established special training units at reception centers where illiterates could receive preliminary instruction to help them cope successfully with basic training. But before these special training units were established thousands of poorly qualified men, left to their own devices or given only makeshift support, failed to make a go of it.[8]

During World War II, 91 divisions were activated: 36 in 1940 and 1941, 38 in 1942, and 17 in 1943. By the war's end only 2 of the 89 divisions (the 2d Cavalry was twice activated and inactivated during the war) had not been committed to combat. The Army originally proposed to train men in divisional organizations, on the assumption that this would help build unit morale. But early in the war it had to modify these plans. The excessive stripping of partially trained divisions to provide cadres for newly activated ones made it impossible for many organizations to complete their training cycles and be readied for overseas shipment. For instance, the 30th Division declined from a strength of 12,400 in June, 1942, to 3,000 only two months later. Divisions frequently had to maintain multiple training programs to accommodate replacements who had been shipped in at different points in time. This put an excessive strain on the limited training personnel with the result that older members of the division were often forced to repeat part or all of the training cycle.

The following excerpt from the official history of *The United States Army in World War II*, detailing the experiences of the 65th Division, provides a vivid picture of the great difficulties that were encountered in training men during World War II.

The 65th Division was activated on 16 August 1943. But because at that time inductions were lagging behind mobilization requirements, the complete quota of fillers was not received until the end of the year. . . . Individual training began early in January 1944. The division made a good showing. . . . In the latter part of May, while infantry units were engaged in company exercises and taking the AGF Platoon Proficiency Tests, an order came down from higher headquarters to begin furloughing infantry privates in preparation for their movement to overseas replacement depots. Even though furloughs were staggered over a period of several weeks, the disruption to training was great. One battalion was so badly depleted that some of its platoons numbered only fifteen or twenty men when they took the platoon tests. . . . By the end of July the division had lost about 7,000 men. . . . Officer losses for overseas replacements during the period April–July inclusive exceeded 250. These and other withdrawals almost cleaned out the division's infantry lieutenants and captains. . . . About the same time the division G-1 reported a 100-percent turnover in regimental and battalion commanders since activation, and a 50-percent turnover in general staff officers. . . . Shipping out of men and officers was interspersed with the reception of replacements. The processing of incoming and departing men placed a heavy burden on the dwindling corps of experienced officers and NCO's.

The first large batch of replacements was the 1,100 Air Corps cadets who came to the division in May. . . . Most of them made excellent soldiers. In July the division received a thousand-odd 18-year-olds from replacement training centers in exchange for a like number of soldiers of age nineteen and over which the division sent to a replacement depot. These boys were somewhat inferior to the Air Corps cadets. About 3,000 other replacements from miscellaneous sources trickled into the division in June and July, bringing the total influx of enlisted men during the period May–July to something over 5,000. A substantial portion of the miscellaneous group came from disbanded anti-aircraft artillery and tank destroyer units. About 700 were men sent back from overseas. . . . The division G-1 [stated] "Overseas commanders send their 'eight-balls' to us under the rotation plan. Most of the men are very bitter. They feel like they have done their share. They are a bad influence on the other men." More than 300 of the replacements were "infantry volunteers." Of these the G-1 observed: "In every case . . . [they] have been men who were dissatisfied in other branches—men who did not like their commanding officers, who wanted a change of station, or who were falling down on their jobs. . . ." Because the division was overstrength when the ASTP was curtailed, it did not receive an allotment of this choice personnel. Of replacements in general, except those from the Air Forces, the Division G-1 reported: "As they come along the line they are picked over. When they get to us they're a sorry lot."

. . . .

An attempt was made to continue the regular program of unit training concurrently with the process of POR (Preparation for Overseas Replacements) for departing men and the instruction of replacements. But the depletion of personnel and the heavy burden of running a multi-level program made progress difficult. Unit training was completed after a fashion early in July, but some of the battalion exercises were held with less than 200 men, and the few regimental problems that were undertaken were not deserving of the name. In July the Infantry and Artillery went through the motions of combined training for a period of approximately two weeks, but strength was so low and many of the officers so inexperienced that the regimental combat team exercises bore little resemblance to the real thing. The operations were so limited, indeed, that when, later, the division's final status report was submitted none of the personnel was credited with any combined training. Late in July, having reached approximately 80 percent of its T/O strength, the division initiated the 6-week program of modified individual training. . . . Even after retraining was initiated the division continued to lose men. Withdrawals of infantrymen were lighter than formerly, but drafts on specialists of other branches were heavier. Enlisted losses in all categories during August totaled 1,173.

From 3 September to 14 October the division participated in modified unit training. During the fourth week of this period word came from Second Army that the division had been placed on alert status with readiness dates of 3 January 1945 for equipment and 18 January 1945 for personnel. This news came as a bombshell, for until the alert the division had no indication that overseas movement was likely before the summer of 1945. . . . The alert, together with the change about the same time of War Department regulations concerning physically deficient personnel, made it possible for the division to drop about a thousand "cripples." The worst cases were discharged. Those capable of service in noncombat capacities were transferred to the Air Forces or the Fourth Service Command. The division was pleased to be relieved of this dead weight, but the postponement of housecleaning until the eleventh hour gave another setback to the development of teamwork. All in all, the division received more than 2,000 replacements in the three months preceding embarkation. The prior training of many of the last-minute replacements left much to be desired. Moreover, a considerable number of men originally received in response to emergency requisitions were disqualified by physical defects. This caused additional disruption and delay.

Another startling bit of news came on 13 October in the form of a telephone call from the Second Army stating that, because of pressing overseas needs, the division had to prepare its infantry regiments for movement to port by 13 November. Organizational equipment was to be ready by 28 October and packing was to begin immediately. This notice prevented the beginning of modified combined training. . . . On 24 October the regiments completed the packing of their organizational equipment and began to load the boxes on freight cars. The next day a telephone call from Second Army directed that all loading cease as the movement order had been temporarily suspended. Several days later, instructions were received moving the personnel readiness date back to 24 December and the equipment date to 10 December. . . . Mortars, heavy machine guns, and other essential equipment were borrowed in considerable quantities from nondivisional units stationed at Camp Shelby, but, in spite of such emergency measures, the division had to go through the heartbreaking task of unpacking some of the equipment that had been so carefully processed and stored away in the shipping boxes. . . . The last element of the division left Camp Shelby on New Year's Eve. . . .

The 65th when it moved overseas in 1945 might have been the most battleworthy of the long line of divisions produced by the Army Ground Forces. For into the planning of the organization, training, and equipment of this unit was poured the accumulated experience of four years' intensive effort. But, mainly because of personnel exigencies . . . , the 65th was about the least ready for combat of all divisions trained in World War II. Its regiments had never worked with their supporting battalions of artillery in field exercises. The division commander had never maneuvered his command as a unit; in fact, the division had never been together, except for reviews and demonstrations, and its composition had changed greatly from one assembly to another. In the infantry regiments only one man in four had been with the division for a year, and almost every fourth man had joined his unit in the past three months. The division was more of a hodgepodge than a team.[9]

There were many other training practices that had an adverse effect. In 1944 when large numbers of replacements were required for the European Theater, new recruits were hurried through basic training, sometimes of only 6 weeks duration, shipped overseas, and fed into the line after only the shortest period of additional training. The casualty rate among these individual replacements was appallingly high.

Many men failed because they had been poorly assigned. A thirty-five-year-old lawyer was likely to fall by the wayside if he were forced to keep up with the rigorous training schedule of the combat engineers, but had he been given a chance to attend a Quartermaster or Medical Department training center, his record might have been outstanding. Some who failed at their initial assignments were given a second chance but many were not.

Without a firm basis on which to plan their training programs, the technical services and combat arms fluctuated between feast and famine, and this led to a serious wastage in manpower resources. To illustrate: Late in 1944 the War Department ordered the shipment overseas of 65 engineer combat battalions no matter what their current state of training. This precipitous action made it impossible for almost 2,000 specialists who were undergoing advanced school training to rejoin their outfits in time. The organizations that were shipping out received many replacements who were untrained and ill suited for their new assignments. When the specialists completed their training, they were sent to new units, many of which had no way of utilizing them effectively. It is not necessary to spell out the decreased morale and performance resulting for both specialists and their replacements.

Among the most spectacular illustrations of the difficulties which resulted from the Army's inability to gear its training programs to future requirements is the experience of the Army Specialized Training Program, to which reference has already been made. It was not until the winter of 1943–44, not quite a year after the program had been inaugurated, that the complaints of the Army

Ground Forces finally found a sympathetic ear in the Pentagon. At that point the Chief of Staff became convinced that the Army had to choose between disbanding 10 divisions and 29 tank and anti-aircraft battalions and cutting back the ASTP to the bone. Those in favor of cutting back the ASTP argued that, in addition to the overall need for manpower, these specially selected soldiers were required for "sweetening" the Ground Force units which were short of men qualified to serve as noncommissioned officers.

The decision was made to interrupt all but a few of the ASTP programs under way. Of the original 216,000 who entered the program, only 73,000 completed their course. But instead of being eagerly absorbed by the Ground Forces, thousands of these high quality men sat around for months awaiting reassignment, and when they arrived at their new units they were not appointed as noncommissioned officers. In the first place, others held these assignments; and the newcomers, no matter how great their potential ability, did not have the specific combat training required. Many of them were therefore assigned as riflemen, which has led an outraged critic of the War Department to conclude that the disbanding of the ASTP was a plot to place the best brainpower in the country in the most vulnerable positions, where the largest number were likely to be killed.

An example of a different kind of difficulty that the Army encountered in fitting the right men into the right positions is the experience of the Fourth Army in the fall of 1944. In one of its dramatic reversals in personnel policy, the War Department permitted the Army Ground Forces to rid itself of men who were below minimum physical standards either by transferring them to the Air Forces or the Service Forces or by discharging them to civilian life. Although many units were in an advanced stage of training, ready to leave for overseas within the next few months, the Fourth Army rid itself of 30,000 physically handicapped men. But no provision had been made for replacements. They were not available.

It is easy to see at this date the many shortcomings in the assignment, training, and utilization practices followed by the Army during World War II. But it is not so easy to appreciate the pressures that the Army was under at the time and to which it had to respond. Expanding from under 200,000 men to over 8 million in less than five years forced the Army to handle men as a mass, not as individuals. Victory was the goal even at a high cost. When Task Force A (for the invasion of North Africa) was about to embark, men trained as machine gunners joined units as riflemen, even though they had never fired the basic weapon—the M-1 rifle. The Army was constantly forced to meet situations which it had not foreseen. More and better planning would have helped. But the exigencies of war would have wreaked havoc with even the best of plans. Throughout, the Army had to allocate men as they became available, train them as rapidly as possible and utilize them in accordance with pressing requirements that were largely determined not by the Army but by a resourceful enemy.

Much that transpired during the war with respect to the Army's assignment, training, and utilization of its personnel resulted in manpower waste. Some of the difficulties can be placed at the doorstep of poor planning and faulty administration. But much was the inevitable waste that war brings in its wake. Great as was the cost to the individual, the end of military policy is victory for the nation.

Chapter Four: THE MAGNITUDE OF SEPARATIONS

WORLD WAR II brought significant changes in our national life, and their full impact has not been completely realized even after a decade and a half. The postwar concern with mental illness is an illustration. Even while the war was still under way the first alarms were being sounded by those who had become acquainted with the mounting casualty figures which reflected soldiers' breaking down with one or another type of psychiatric disability. These data were not released to the public for fear that they would enable the enemy to glean useful information from them about the state of our manpower resources and the morale of the Armed Forces. Nevertheless, a considerable number of prominent psychiatrists became alarmed from the few figures that were released, and from their own limited experience with the screening of selectees and the treatment of veterans.

Among the distinguished leaders of the psychiatric profession who sounded the alarm were many who had long suspected on the basis of their private practice that for every patient whom they saw, there were ten others who, though in need of help, had never consulted a doctor. The war seemed to prove their point. The scattered evidence pointed to the pervasiveness of mental illness in the American population. Further, the large-scale manpower losses from psychiatric disability underscored the national as well as the individual wastes involved.

The public became alerted in the immediate postwar years when many psychiatrists who had had firsthand experience with the large-scale psychiatric problems of the Army and the Navy published their evaluations and criticisms. Moreover, the wartime restrictions on the release of official data were lifted, so that many startling facts and figures became available to the public for the first time.

Although more than a decade has passed since the end of the war, those who continue to crusade for a higher level of mental health rely heavily on the experience of World War II to drive their point home. They seek to prove the high incidence of emotional disorder in the population by reference to the data on screening and separation of military manpower during World War II. Although there have been many excellent reports of individual segments of the war experience, except for one large-scale investigation [10] no major effort has been made to examine critically what in fact did happen during the war. Yet generalizations about the mental health of the American public continue to be based on the uncritical use of the data of World War II.

Table 10 summarizes the total number of Armed Forces enlisted male personnel released to civilian life for all causes and establishes the framework within which the following analysis of those separated for ineffective performance can be viewed in perspective. This framework in turn sets the statistical limits within which the evaluation of ineffective performance can proceed. The table emphasizes that more than 2.3 million servicemen were returned to civilian life before the end of hostilities. There are important differences in the claims to which veterans in these major discharge categories were entitled. Those who were separated for medical reasons were honorably discharged and entitled to all veterans' benefits, and they also had a presumptive claim on an initial disability compensation award. Those who were separated for inaptitude and unsuitability also received an honorable discharge, but they had no claim to disability compensation. Those who were separated for undesirability or bad conduct received discharges "without honor," which limited their claims to veterans' benefits and otherwise made more difficult their readjustment to civilian life. Various state and local governments as well as the Federal

Civil Service gave preference to veterans who were separated with a medical discharge, and many employers simply refused to hire men who had not been honorably discharged.

Table 10. WARTIME SEPARATIONS OF ENLISTED MALE PERSONNEL FROM THE ARMED FORCES TO CIVILIAN LIFE, BY SERVICE AND BY REASON FOR SEPARATION, 1942–1945

REASON FOR SEPARATION	NUMBER OF SEPARATIONS				ARMY PERCENT OF TOTAL
	Army [a]	*Navy* [b]	*Marine Corps* [c]	*Total*	
Medical	956,000	258,000	52,000	1,266,000	76
Inapt and unsuitable	122,000	90,000	14,000	226,000	54
Other than honorable	73,000	37,000	5,000	115,000	63
Overage, and other administrative, Jan. 1942—June 1945	663,000	75,000	9,000 *	747,000	89
Total wartime separations	1,814,000	460,000	80,000	2,354,000	77
Overage, surplus, and other administrative, July–Dec. 1945 †	668,000	58,000	3,000 *	729,000	92
Demobilization	3,204,000	479,000	120,000 *	3,803,000	84
All separations	5,686,000	997,000	203,000	6,886,000	83

* Estimated distribution of 132,000 separations.

† Many of these separations, although not strictly "demobilization," reflect the deliberate release of surplus personnel by the Armed Forces in view of the greatly reduced manpower requirements following the termination of hostilities.

[a] Medical: *Health of Army*, vol. 1, report 2, p. 21; Inapt and unsuitable: AG, Stat. & Acctg., unpub. worksheets; Others: *Strength of Army*, STM-30, pp. 86–89.

[b] Medical: Navy, *Annual Report of SG: 1942*, table 4, pp. 343–65; *1943*, table 6, pp. 176–206; *1944*, table 6, pp. 225–87; *1945*, table 6, pp. 235–312; Others: NAVPERS-15115, tables 87 and 91, pp. 103 and 107 (1945 data: Navy Records, unpub. tables 172 and 179).

[c] Medical: Navy, *Annual Report of SG: 1942*, table 4, pp. 343–65; *1943*, table 6, pp. 176–206; *1944*, table 6, pp. 225–87; *1945*, table 6, pp. 235–312; Others: NAVPERS-15115, tables 87 and 91, pp. 103 and 107 (1945 data: Marine Corps, unpub. summaries; also Armed Forces, *Demob.*, p. 178).

Although the nomenclature varied among the Army, Navy and Marine Corps, partly because of differences in the conditions of service and the administrative practices followed in evaluating men whose performance was ineffective, it has been possible to develop Table 11 that compares the experiences of the three services during World War II.

Since the average strength of the Army during World War II was two to three times that of the Navy and Marine Corps combined, it is not surprising that the Army, together with the Air Corps, accounted for the largest number of men separated prematurely for emotional and related causes.

Table 11. SEPARATIONS OF ENLISTED MALE PERSONNEL FROM THE ARMED FORCES FOR INEFFECTIVENESS, BY SERVICE AND BY STATED REASON, 1942–1945

	NUMBER OF SEPARATIONS			
STATED REASON FOR SEPARATION	*Army* [a]	*Navy* [b]	*Marine Corps* [c]	*Total*
Medical disability—psychiatric *				
Psychoneurosis	256,000	39,000	12,000	307,000
Psychosis	55,000	10,000	2,000	67,000
Other psychiatric †	21,000	37,000	6,000	64,000
Total psychiatric	332,000	86,000	20,000	438,000
Inaptitude and unsuitability	122,000	90,000	14,000	226,000
Undesirability and bad conduct	50,000	36,000	4,000	90,000
Grand total	504,000	212,000	38,000	754,000

* Excludes epilepsy and other diseases of the nervous system.
† Includes "personality" disorders.
[a] Medical Disability-Psychiatric: *Health of Army*, vol. 1, report 2, p. 22; Others: AG, Stat. & Acctg., unpub. worksheets.
[b] Medical-Psychiatric: Navy, *Annual Report of SG: 1942*, table 4, pp. 343–65; *1943*, table 6, pp. 176–206; *1944*, table 6, pp. 225–87; *1945*, table 6, pp. 235–312; Others: NAVPERS-15115, tables 87 and 91, pp. 103 and 107 (1945 data: Navy Records, unpub. tables 172 and 179).
[c] Medical-Psychiatric: Navy, *Annual Report of SG: 1942*, table 4, pp. 343–65; *1943*, table 6, pp. 176–206; *1944*, table 6, pp. 225–87; *1945*, table 6, pp. 235–312; Others: NAVPERS-15115, tables 97 and 91, pp. 103 and 107 (1945 data: Marine Corps, unpub. summaries). Also Armed Forces, *Demob.*, p. 178.

Table 12 presents the rates of premature separations by major cause experienced by each of the services during World War II.

Some interesting findings are suggested by this table. The first is that the Navy and Marine Corps together had an "ineffective rate" approximately 21 percent higher than that of the Army.

In this connection it is well to bear in mind that because the Navy was able to rely exclusively on volunteers until the beginning of 1943, it secured a better "cut" of manpower than was true for the Army, which from the start had to depend heavily on the draft. Further, as we pointed out elsewhere, the order of danger, as measured by casualty rates, to which soldiers were exposed was much greater than obtained for Navy personnel.[11]

Table 12. RATE OF SEPARATIONS OF ENLISTED MALE PERSONNEL FROM THE ARMED FORCES FOR INEFFECTIVENESS, BY SERVICE AND BY STATED REASON, 1942–1945

	RATE OF SEPARATIONS PER 1,000 [a]			
STATED REASON FOR SEPARATION	*Army*	*Navy*	*Marine Corps*	*All Services*
Medical disability—psychiatric *				
Psychoneurosis	25.4	10.9	21.4	21.6
Psychosis	5.4	2.8	3.6	4.7
Other psychiatric †	2.1	10.4	10.7	4.5
Total psychiatric	32.9	24.1	35.7	30.8
Inaptitude and unsuitability	12.1	25.3	25.0	15.9
Undesirability and bad conduct	5.0	10.1	7.1	6.3
Grand total	50.0	59.5	67.8	53.0

* Excludes epilepsy and other diseases of the nervous system.
† Includes "personality" disorders.
[a] Data in Table 11 divided by each service's enlisted male strength as of 31 Dec. 1941 (Army: *Strength of Army*, STM-30, p. 51; Navy and Marines: NAVPERS-15115, p. 10), plus enlisted male accessions 1942–1945 (Table 5) in thousands.

Without discussing at this time the relation between stress and failure, it can be postulated here that the two are positively correlated. Hence one would expect on both counts—better initial selection and less stress—that the Navy's rates would be below those of the Army. The fact that the reverse was true suggests that the Navy, conditioned to operating with more selective personnel, moved speedily to discharge those found lacking. Conditions on ships made it more difficult for the Navy to provide the special adjustments for handicapped personnel that the Army, operating on land, found possible if not always practical.

Naval recruits were examined by psychiatrists upon their arrival at training centers and doubtful cases were either hospitalized immediately for detailed evaluation or marked for careful observation during their initial weeks of training. Those found unsuitable were quickly discharged. As the following chapter will try to make clear, the Army did not follow such a well-defined policy leading to the early separation of those who were unsuitable.

Table 12 highlights another aspect of how the services dealt with the problem of ineffectiveness. The rate of separation of men from the Army with a diagnosis of psychoneurosis was more than double that of the Navy. In contrast, the Navy's rate of separation under the headings of "inaptitude" and "undesirability" was more than twice that of the Army's. Without entering into a detailed evaluation of the medical and administrative procedures used by the two services in evaluating and separating men for ineffective performance, we can point out that from the start the Navy was reluctant to undertake medical surveys of men who could be separated more easily under administrative procedures. Only in the presence of demonstrable clinical symptoms did the Navy undertake a medical survey of a man and separate him with a psychiatric diagnosis.

Now that we have set out, at least in brief compass, the scale of premature separations from the three services during World War II, we will concentrate on the Army, whose experience forms the foundation of this study of ineffective performance. Of the more than 10 million men who saw service, just under 2½ million were separated during the period 1942–1945, excluding those demobilized on the basis of point scores. Table 13 provides a picture of the major causes for separation. It should be noted that the 668,000 men who were separated after July, 1945, because they were overage or for other honorable reasons, were released even though they had not earned sufficient credits to be demobilized because the Army no longer needed so many men. If these are excluded, approximately one out of every five men was prematurely separated.

In view of the thorough physical examination that men re-

Table 13. WARTIME SEPARATIONS TO CIVILIAN LIFE OF ARMY ENLISTED MALE PERSONNEL, BY REASON FOR SEPARATION, 1942–1945 *

Reason for Separation	*Number of Separations*	
Dishonorable [a]		23,000
Other than honorable (blue) [b]		50,000
Undesirable habits and traits	37,000	
Other	13,000	
Inaptitude [b]		122,000
Certificate of disability [c]		956,000
Psychiatric	332,000	
Physical	547,000	
Limited service, Sec. II	77,000	
Limited service, Sec. X [d]		211,000
Overage [e]		569,000
Jan. 1942—June 1945	222,000	
July–Dec. 1945 †	347,000	
Other reason, honorable [f]		551,000
Jan. 1942—June 1945	230,000	
July–Dec. 1945 †	321,000	
Total		2,482,000

* Excludes demobilization.

† Many of these separations, although not strictly "demobilization," reflect the deliberate release of surplus personnel by the Armed Forces in view of the greatly reduced manpower requirements following the termination of hostilities.

[a] Army Other than Honorable discharge data from Table 10 less Undesirability and Bad Conduct discharge data from Table 11.

[b] From Table 11. This breakdown between Undesirable Habits and Traits and Other Blue discharges was made on the basis of unpublished AG worksheets detailing the month to month separations of enlisted men by specific cause within the Other than Honorable category. SGO files, based on other, undifferentiated AG data, show 40,657 men to have been discharged for Undesirable Habits and Traits.

[c] From Table 11 except Physical: Total Medical (from Table 10) less Psychiatric and Limited Service, Sec. II. Physical includes and Psychiatric excludes epilepsy and other diseases of the nervous system.

[d] AG, Stat. & Acctg., unpub. worksheets. These Limited Service men received administrative discharges for the "Convenience of the Government." During the period when most of them were discharged, Sec. X of AR 615–360 (later made into a separate AR) applied.

[e] *Strength of Army*, STM-30, pp. 86–89.

[f] Jan. 1942—June 1945: Miscellaneous Honorable from Table 10 less Overage and Limited Service, Sec. X; July–Dec. 1945: Miscellaneous Honorable from Table 10 less Overage.

ceived prior to entering the Army, it is surprising to learn that very large numbers had to be prematurely separated for a physical disability in addition to the 77,000 limited service personnel. Included in the 624,000 total were tens of thousands of battle wounded and substantial numbers of men who sustained nonbattle injuries. But the majority who were released had not suffered any injury.

Some slipped by the screen and others developed a disease or condition that made their retention in the service inadvisable. But in the case of many who were separated for disease or injury, emotional and motivational factors played a role. As every doctor knows, the level of performance that a person can reach in the face of a former or current disability will be determined only in part by the disability itself. A major determinant will be a man's desire, or lack thereof, to continue to meet the standards of the organization to which he belongs. Almost 100,000 men were prematurely separated because of a muscular-skeletal defect or because of bad feet. If a soldier kept reporting to the dispensary and the hospital, if he refused to do duty because of "pains in his back," both his commanding officer and the medical officer might finally still their scepticism and separate him even though they suspected that the pain, if it existed, was emotional in origin, or that the soldier was actually a malingerer.

More than 60,000 were separated because of gastro-intestinal symptoms, of which the vast majority were ulcers. Here the emotional factors predominated. It would be venturesome to risk an estimate of how many of the 624,000 who were separated for physical reasons might have served longer if the Army had been harder pressed for manpower or if the soldiers had been more strongly motivated. But no informed person can question that the proportion would be very considerable indeed. Late in the war men wounded in action were permitted, if they so desired, to remain on active duty even though their disability brought them below minimum standards. Many who elected to remain—and who continued to perform effectively—had much more severe disabilities than others who were separated.

On the basis of its experience with older men, the Army decided at the end of 1942 not to call up any more men over thirty-seven years of age. Having reached this decision the Army felt obligated, though not legally compelled, to release those already in the service who were above the new maximum age. Nearly 200,000 were released. The Army might have decided to screen the overage group and to release only those who were clearly ineffective. But having decided that men over thirty-seven were a liability, the Army found it easier to separate the entire group. The fact that an older soldier was performing satisfactorily in a clerical assignment in the Zone of Interior was surely no guarantee that he would have the stamina to cope with an overseas assignment, especially in or near combat. And the Army kept its eyes focused on its combat mission.

No one who recalls the "old man" of forty in a barracks with eighteen- and nineteen-year-olds will question the difficulties of mixing younger and older men in the same unit. The older the man, the more difficulty he encountered in meeting strenuous training and duty assignments. But if the Army had found it as necessary as our Allies did to conserve manpower, most of these men could have made the grade, despite their age, if appropriate adjustments had been made. It is conducive to neither individual nor group morale to have an eighteen-year-old sergeant or a twenty-year-old lieutenant command a group composed of much older men. Effective group performance usually requires some limitation on the age range of its members and particularly in the age structure of superiors and subordinates.

Another group that should be considered in the present context were men designated as fit for "limited service" who were accepted in one period, only to be released in another. Many entered the service with minor handicaps and others developed them while in the service. No fewer than 288,000 limited service men were separated prematurely because of some physical limitation although only 77,000 of them received a medical discharge. The others were separated administratively; the difference was that military service had presumably not changed their condition while those whose condition had been aggravated were given a medical discharge. For no other group of men was motivation more likely to determine whether they would serve effectively until demobilization or be prematurely separated. Although sweeping Army directives forced some out who wanted to remain, and although others were discharged late in the war because the Army no longer had suitable assignments for them, many of those who remained made no effort to compensate for their disabilities. In fact, they did the opposite: they exploited their handicaps, made a nuisance of themselves, and almost asked the Army to release them.

Figure 3. GROSS SEPARATIONS OF ARMY ENLISTED MALE PERSONNEL, 1942–1945

(Excludes personnel separated to enlist in the regular Army (Aug.–Dec. 1945)

Source: *Strength of Army*, STM-30, pp. 86–89.

The relative importance of the various groups who were separated prior to demobilization is shown by Figures 3 and 4.

The question might well be asked why we concern ourselves in detail only with the 1 in 5 who was separated for some psychiatric disability, for inaptness, or a behavior defect, rather than with the entire group of approximately 2½ million. The answer is simple: Concerned as we were with the relations between personality and performance, there seemed little to be gained by broadening our sample to include the large numbers whom the Army separated for reason of age or physical disability. The remaining categories promised a richer yield.

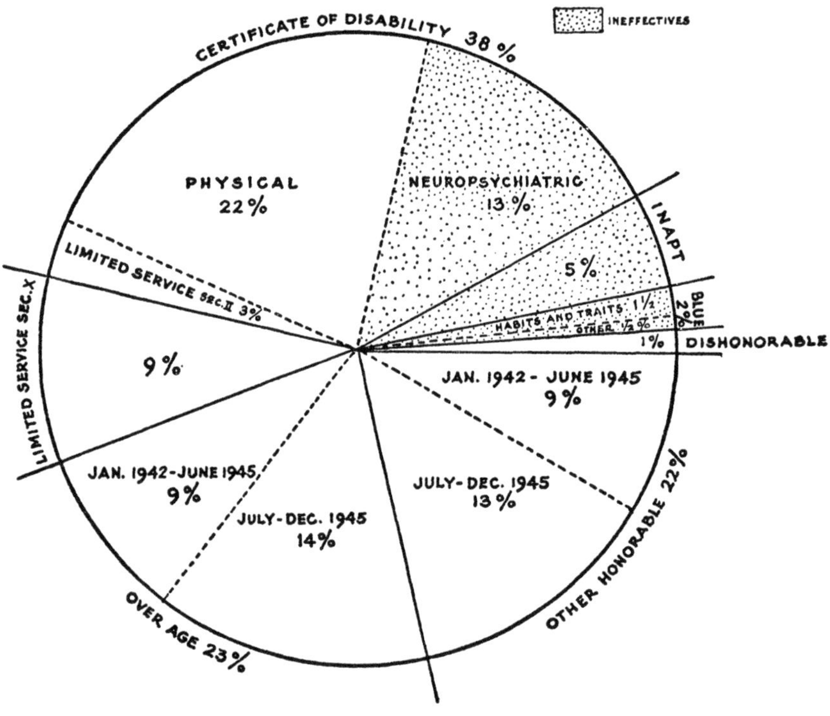

Figure 4. WARTIME SEPARATIONS TO CIVILIAN LIFE OF ARMY ENLISTED MALE PERSONNEL, SHOWING REASON FOR SEPARATION, 1942–1945

(Excludes demobilization)
Source: Calculated from data in Table 13.

The magnitude of premature separations can be understood only in terms of the assumptions and objectives that guided the Army's manpower policies during the course of the war. The assumption of inexhaustible manpower reserves was so deeply ingrained that no adequate consideration was paid to the warning signs. At the end of 1942, with only one tenth of the registrants still unclassified, approximately 2¼ million had been rejected while only 5 million had been accepted. Although 16 million had been deferred for a variety of reasons and the prospective yield from this large group looked very promising at the time, it actually turned out differently. During the latter months of 1942 approximately 4 out of every 10 men examined were rejected, and in some of the Southern states the rejection rate exceeded 50 percent.

The Army followed the same liberal policy in discharges as in selection. It held on to the good men and let the others go, hoping to replace them with better men. If the basic assumption of an inexhaustible manpower supply had been correct, this approach would have been logical for an Army that was short of supervisory and trainor personnel and that was fighting against time to get its divisions ready for combat. It seemed wasteful to attempt to train an emotionally upset or educationally handicapped soldier if better replacements could be obtained.

This exchange theory was particularly attractive to the local commander who was under relentless pressure from Washington to get his unit into shape. As long as the replacements which he received were superior to the soldiers whom he discarded, he stood to gain. He could save time and scarce training personnel by discharging the laggards rather than by making an added investment which might still not bring them up to a satisfactory level of performance. As long as good replacements were available, the local commander could see little point in establishing outpatient clinics to provide psychiatric services for those who were encountering difficulty in adjusting to military life. Moreover, he did not want to assign his best noncommissioned officers to teach the alphabet and sums to illiterate inductees who, even if they profited from the instruction, might never be able to perform at more than a minimum level.

The same logistical considerations that motivated the unit commander were reflected in the War Department's disinclination to establish, as had our British allies, Pioneer Battalions to which the emotionally unstable and the educationally deprived could be assigned and which facilitated the use of marginal personnel. Our General Staff balked at the idea, first on the ground that even such handicapped soldiers would be counted against its strength authorization. Moreover, a high proportion of this handicapped group were Negroes and it would have been difficult, if not impossible, to explain to the public why so many Negroes were deliberately restricted to laboring jobs. And even aside from the racial issue, it is questionable whether the American public would have accepted having some soldiers labeled "second class" and treated accordingly.

As we shall see in Chapter Five, the Army eventually recognized that the manpower supply was limited. But this recognition came slowly, and not until large numbers of soldiers had been separated. It was not only this more realistic appraisal of the manpower pool that was responsible for altering Army policy. The changes inherent in the course of the war itself were also determining. It was one thing to separate men for ineffectiveness shortly after they had been inducted and while they were in the early stages of their training. It was quite a different matter to follow the same liberal separation policy with regard to a soldier whom the Army had trained for two years and whose division was about to enter combat.

Finally, the Army learned as it went along. It took time for the evidence to accumulate that psychiatric screening at induction was falling far short of what had been claimed for it. Despite the large-scale rejections, many who had been accepted proved ineffective. And it took time for the Medical Department to learn that the diagnostic and therapeutic approaches of civilian psychiatrists were not necessarily suitable for men who broke down in the Army. And even more time was required for the staff officers to learn how their directives setting out the conditions for discharge could, by unfortunate wording, precipitate an outflow of tens, or even hundreds, of thousands of soldiers.

The paramount importance of manpower policy on separation rates came to be appreciated only late in the war. The original assumption that underlay policy was that ineffectiveness in the Army was a direct consequence of the selectee's emotional weakness; hence, the best course was to reject those with unstable personalities. But the war showed that one key determinant to performance lay elsewhere—in the policies and procedures that the Army followed in dealing with its manpower. Certainly the personal characteristics of men accepted for military duty had significance for their performance, but the margin between effective and ineffective performance frequently was found in the realm of personnel policy.

The aim of our large-scale statistical investigation is to facilitate the appraisal of the complex factors that influenced the performance of the more than 10 million men who served in the Army during World War II. The following chapter sets out the alterations that occurred in the separation rates subsequent to each significant shift in personnel policy. There is no direct counterpart to this experience in civilian life, where men usually try to hold on to their jobs. Yet the experience of World War II has clear relevance for industry. There are many examples in the civilian sphere which would prove that faulty personnel policy, even if introduced and carried out with the best of motives, can lead to such unsettlement of the work force and attendant declines in its efficiency that it may take months or even years for a company to recoup the losses sustained therefrom.

There is, however, one important difference between the two environments, civilian and military. Industry makes a major effort to preserve continuity in policy. Changes are carefully evaluated before they are introduced, since management seeks to avoid major disruptions that new policies may bring in their wake. But during World War II the Army had to improvise as it went along and had to risk acting first and evaluating later. Time did not permit otherwise. The Army had only one recourse to correct errors when it discovered them—to promulgate a new policy. And if after the passage of time the new policy was still off target, the Army had no option but to try again. Chapter Five sets out the efforts that the Army made during World War II to develop improved separation policies appropriate in time and place to the manpower resources of the country and its own changing requirements.

Chapter Five: SEPARATION POLICY

DURING the first two years of mobilization, and especially in the period after Pearl Harbor, the primary aim of Army manpower policy was to take in the maximum number of men and to make them battle-ready as quickly as possible. The policy also aimed at rejecting all who gave any indication that they might prove ineffective. This was the period when the Army established and maintained high standards of acceptability on multiple fronts—physical, emotional, educational, moral—giving way only slightly with respect to physical standards during the latter months of 1942. Throughout this period the Army gave little thought to separation policy, for there was no evidence that any significant number of soldiers would have to be sent back to civilian life because of their failure to perform effectively.

At the end of 1942 Army strength was just under 5½ million. Discharges at this point were negligible, as indicated by the separation figures for December. Approximately 250 soldiers were separated without honor with the notation of undesirable traits of character; about three times that number were discharged on the ground that they were inapt; under 4,000 were judged by the psychiatrists to be emotionally unstable, some of whom were seriously deranged; and only approximately 8,000, were found to be suffering from a physical disability that made their further retention in service unwise. There were others, but the foregoing accounts for the vast majority who were separated.

As Figure 5 makes clear, the following months saw the separation rate rise with unbelievable rapidity to reach totally unexpected heights. By late summer, instead of monthly separations of the approximately 13,000 that had prevailed in December, the monthly separations were in the neighborhood of 65,000 even disregarding the losses that the Army was then sustaining as a result of the release of men thirty-eight years of age or over. In March, 1943, separations from this cause alone reached 89,000. In total the Army

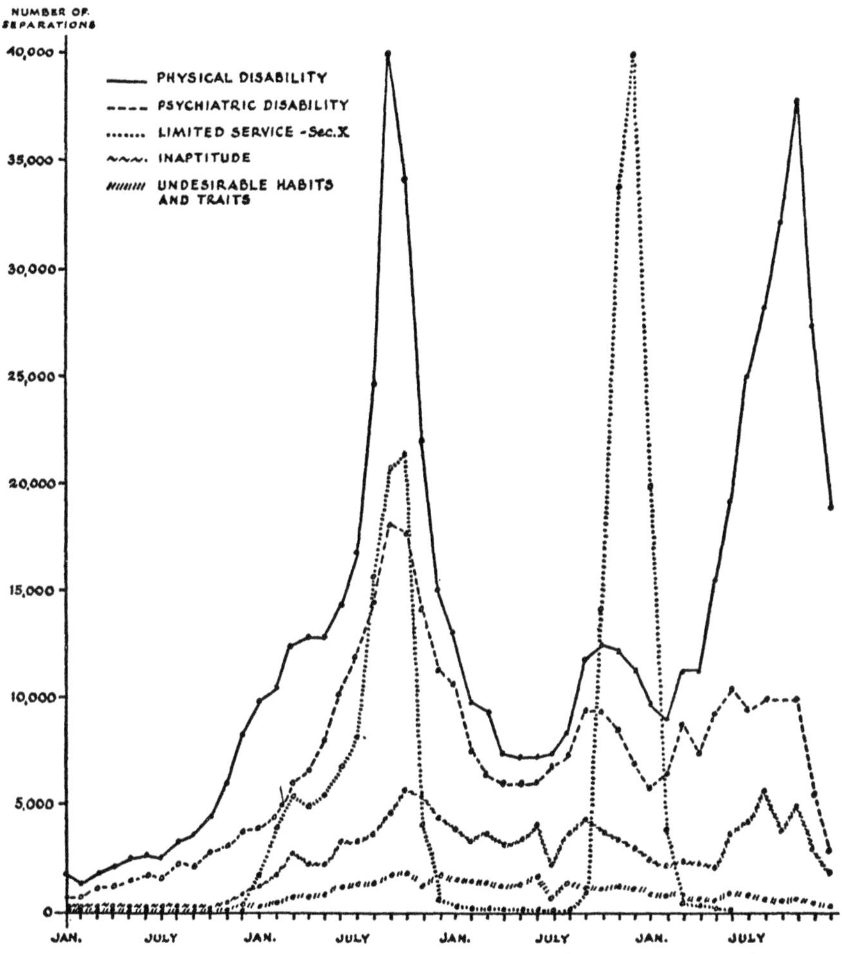

Figure 5. PREMATURE SEPARATIONS OF ARMY ENLISTED MEN, BY SELECTED CAUSE, 1942–1945

Source: AG, Stat. & Acctg., unpub. worksheets; and SG, unpub. worksheets.

lost just under 200,000 men over thirty-eight at about this time. Any older man who could prove that he would be employed after discharge in an essential civilian activity was let out on his own request. While some increase in separations was to be expected as a result of gains in total strength and heightened stress, these factors could not possibly account for the fivefold increase within a nine-month period.

An inspection of the chart reveals that just as the separation rates shot up during the first part of 1943, so they catapulted downward during the last quarter of that year when the Army changed its personnel policies radically. They continued to decline until the second half of 1944 when another change in policy took place in anticipation of a fall victory in Europe. A significant rise began but when the German failed to capitulate, the trend was reversed. Separations declined during the late part of that year. And then, as might have been anticipated, the rates rose once again in 1945 as the end of warfare in the European Theater approached and the Army recognized that it could cut back its strength even while bringing Japan to heel.

The chart also makes clear that while the numbers separated for different causes varied greatly, they moved together, with only a month or two lead or lag between them. There is no better introduction to this chapter, which will seek to trace the impact of personnel policy on the scale of separations, than to note this parallelism. When Washington gave the go-ahead sign, commanders in the field rushed to rid themselves of troublesome soldiers by whatever routes were most convenient. When policy was reversed, and the Army ordered manpower to be conserved, relatively few men were separated through any route. But it is necessary to study the details for the picture to become clear.[12]

The story begins in September, 1942, which inaugurated the first period of easy discharges. At that time Circular Letter 99 from the Surgeon General's Office directed discharging from Army hospitals all seriously disturbed patients. Medical officers had been disinclined to send such patients home for fear that if they became suicidal or, worse, homicidal, the doctors would be personally held to account. The postwar tragedy at Camden, New Jersey, when many innocent people were killed by a veteran who went berserk, was proof that this fear, if exaggerated, was not totally unwarranted. If mental patients were not to be sent home, the only practical alternative was to find a place for them in a Veterans Administration hospital. But these hospitals, which had lost so much of their professional staff to the Army, were poorly prepared to handle an increased patient census, which helps to explain why the Army doctors were disinclined to transfer their patients.

Circular 99 also called attention to the desirability of speedily assessing and disposing of all other types of mental patients in Army hospitals. There were many line officers as well as some medical officers who saw little point in differentiating too sharply among psychiatric patients. If a man was a "mental case," unable to perform effectively, the specific diagnostic label was unimportant. He should be separated; the method was a matter of indifference.

That in this early period most medical officers frequently did not differentiate between the occasional manic patient, who was able singlehanded to break down a wing of an Army hospital, and the much larger numbers who were suffering from anxiety, phobias, or just simple maladjustment, is revealed by the following. All psychiatric patients, including those suffering from a mild psychoneurosis were kept on "locked wards." In evacuating patients from overseas, all psychiatric patients were kept in the ship's hold; ships' captains feared that if they permitted them on deck, they might set the vessel on fire. In light of this commingling of the mildly upset with the seriously ill, it is not surprising that all psychiatric patients, not only those suffering from a psychosis, were affected by Circular 99 and separated more quickly.

Before the end of the year a new War Department Circular (395, December, 1942) authorized the discharge of limited service personnel who did not have usable skills or the physical or intellectual capacity to acquire such skills rapidly. Some had slipped through the screen; others had developed minor disabilities while in the service. The War Department facilitated the separation of these soldiers by authorizing that they could be discharged administratively. As the chart indicates, by late summer of 1943 more than 20,000 men were being separated monthly in this one category.

Aside from the small numbers who were fighting in the Pacific, the first major campaign involving considerable numbers was the invasion of North Africa at the end of 1942. It was not long before many soldiers who broke down at or near the front were passed backward until large numbers accumulated in rear areas. Shortly thereafter they were on ships heading back to the United States. After months or even years of training, after being transported overseas, they broke down without firing a shot or after only the briefest encounter with the enemy. The War Department received urgent pleas not to send unsuitable soldiers abroad, "unsuitable" being a term which was used to cover those suffering from a psychoneurosis, mental deficiency, or a psychosis; as well as those classified as constitutional psychopaths. In a memorandum of March 25, 1943, the War Department stressed that great care should be exercised by all concerned to see that such men should not be sent overseas since they are "disturbing to the morale and discipline of a unit" and present "a problem and an unnecessary burden to the unit commanders." The memorandum explicitly stated that the detection of "mentally abnormal cases" before their shipment out of the country was "an extremely important duty of each medical officer."

A month later the War Department, recognizing that many soldiers were breaking down both at home and abroad, directed medical officers at induction stations to do everything possible to keep out of the service individuals predisposed to or suffering from psychoneurosis, mental deficiency, constitutional psychopathic state, psychosis, or related conditions, or having a proven history of such conditions. Pointing out that there was "no classification for duty of military personnel with such diagnoses," the memorandum went on to urge all concerned with the assessment of soldiers to "increase their efforts" to detect individuals with these conditions "with a view to the discharge of those who cannot be expected to render full military duty."

By these several actions the Army reaffirmed its adherence to the doctrine that ineffective men could be spotted before they actually broke down despite the accumulating evidence to the contrary. Its solution was to tighten screening still further and to reject still larger numbers. Moreover, it was opening the floodgates in speeding the separation of all who, having been accepted, gave evidence of ineffective performance in service.

At the end of July, 1943, the War Department issued another memorandum that further reinforced the directives of March and April, emphasizing again that there was "no classification for duty of military personnel with such mental diagnoses as psychoneurosis"; and going on to state that individuals with such diagnoses who were not capable of performing general military service should be separated from the service, except for "those relatively few cases" of psychoneurosis or acute psychotic reaction incident to the service who, in the opinion of the medical officer might be returned to duty in the continental limits of the United States.

But it was War Department Circular 161, July 14, 1943, that really opened the floodgates. Under this directive all men who were classified limited service and whose records showed that they did not meet the current physical or mental standards for induction were to be reassessed and if the examination was confirmatory, they were to be immediately discharged. An exception was made for men physically qualified to perform their *present jobs* provided their commander desired to retain them. A fortnight later this circular was superseded by yet another, 176, that provided two routes for the discharge of these men: they could be separated with a certificate of discharge for disability, or administratively, for the "convenience of the government."

The chart leaves no doubt about the avidity with which commanders in the field responded to this permissive, in fact encouraging, attitude of headquarters to unload troublesome soldiers. By September the numbers being separated for physical reasons had jumped from a beginning-of-the-year figure of about 10,000 to 40,000; and in this same month the number separated administratively because they were limited service, which had been zero ten months earlier, passed the 20,000 level. And during the same period those separated on psychiatric grounds jumped from about 4,000 to about 18,000 monthly.

The manpower accounting data for September, 1943, shows that in that one month, the Army lost 112,500 enlisted men; exclusive of battle casualties and those released to accept a commission, 92,000 were separated. During that same month it inducted 118,600. At this rate the Army had to induct 100 to secure a net increase of 5 enlisted men! The Director of the Selective Service System, General Hershey, had questioned the easy separation policy almost from the start on the grounds that the men in the manpower pool from which he had to draw were no better, and possibly a little worse, than those the Army was separating. When the September data became available, he was finally able to convince the Army. The Army suddenly realized that it was still accepting some men who did not meet general duty standards and who could not be assigned to combat training at the same time that it was releasing men with the same disabilities.

The first indication of the Army's realization that its discharge policy might be too easy was a War Department memorandum of August 26, which stressed that it had not been the intent of the earlier directives to require the examination of *all* limited service men or to discharge *all* who did not meet minimum standards for induction. It noted that commanders were authorized to, and should, retain soldiers who were performing effectively. This clarifying memorandum left to commanders the decision whether a soldier was performing adequately. His discharge did not require action by a board of officers. But by simplifying the discharge procedure in this manner, the net effect of the memorandum was to accelerate separations still more. It was not until November 11 when War Department Circular 293 was issued that a new and drastically revised policy was put into effect. By that time the Army was well on the way to running up a total of 821,000 separations for the calendar year 1943.

Slowly but surely, the Army had come to realize that there

were limits to the exchange theory on which it had been operating —which held that when a man gave evidence of malperformance, the best thing to do was to send him back to civilian life and get another in his place. But by late 1943, the manpower pool was no longer able to support a policy which cost the Army about three quarters of a million men within twelve months. As is usual in very large organizations, shifts in policy must be accentuated to be quickly effective. Nuances will not be noted, and certainly not acted upon. Only clear signals will be effective. Circular 293 sounded an alarm that all could hear. The Army had suddenly decided to conserve manpower. It was "imperative" that every man be assigned to a position where he could render maximum service.

According to the new policy if a man did not have the physical or other qualifications to perform effectively in his current assignment, command was not to separate him, but should find him a duty position within his competence. A new criterion was set forth: only men "unable to perform a reasonable day's work for the Army" were henceforth to be separated. All others were to be retained. Senior officials in Washington, through speeches and formal inspections, let it be known that every commander in the field would be held personally responsible for conserving manpower. So much pressure was put behind the new line that some commanders interpreted the criterion to mean that if a man was capable of doing one day's work per month, he was not to be separated!

Many adjustments were made to reinforce the new policy. Finally recalling what it had first learned in World War I, the Army set about treating men who broke down emotionally at the front at an aid station so that they might be encouraged and helped to rejoin their unit immediately and re-enter the fight. The assumption was that if, as in North Africa, they started the trek to the rear through the hospital chain, widening the distance between themselves and the front, there was little prospect of ever salvaging them for combat or even for noncombatant duties. They had too much to gain by holding on to their symptoms.

The Surgeon General, through a letter from his office, warned that the neuropsychiatric criteria for service had probably been interpreted "too strictly" and that men "were being separated from the service who could be of value were they retained." The letter went on to state that henceforth no individual was to be separated merely because he had a psychoneurosis or similar psychiatric condition. It emphasized that under stress any man might develop such a condition but that with proper treatment he could be expected to recover. The letter also made the important, but up to then largely neglected, point that many individuals developed psychiatric symptoms as a result of poor motivation. Henceforth, such individuals were to be retained, not separated.

Other circulars called attention to the fact that hospital admissions for neuropsychiatric reasons were excessive and reflected a failure on the part of command to maintain the mental health of their troops. In the future, this index would be used in appraising leadership. At about this same time, early in 1944, the Army Service Forces established developmental training units to help rehabilitate patients suffering from a psychoneurosis, and special assignment procedures were introduced to insure that recovered patients were properly utilized.

The extent to which the Army altered its basic approach is suggested by the following excerpts from a technical bulletin on the treatment of psychiatric patients issued in April, 1944, by the War Department. The introduction stated that the acute need for manpower made it imperative "to salvage every possible soldier for further duty." The bulletin emphasized that the widespread practice of considering patients suffering from psychiatric illnesses as "merely a matter of diagnosis and disposition" was faulty. The role of stress in precipitating anxiety was emphasized and a warning was issued against the widespread misconception that every person who suffered from a psychoneurosis was a "weak" individual, who should be slated for discharge as soon as he was admitted to a psychiatric ward.

The bulletin went on to alert medical officers to the danger of the "infectious virulence" of the old attitude that admission to a hospital was a way station to discharge. The need for such a warning is indicated by the experience of one hospital on the West Coast that was on an embarkation post for troops shipping out to the Pacific. An inspection team found a sergeant on a neuropsychiatric ward holding classes, admission to which cost five dollars, where he taught new patients how to simulate psychiatric disorders, thereby insuring their being retained within the continental limits of the United States and assisting them towards gaining their discharge.

As Figure 5 makes clear, this major effort of the Army to turn itself around and close the various discharge routes through which so many had poured several months earlier started to take effect late in 1943 and continued until the summer of 1944, a period of approximately nine months. Separations for physical causes plummeted from 40,000 to approximately 7,000 monthly, a decline of over 80 percent at a time when increases in strength and stress might have been expected to bring about a further rise in the rate. Separations for neuropsychiatric reasons dropped from a high of about 18,000 to about 6,000 monthly, a decline of 67 percent. One route which had resulted in the release of substantial numbers in 1943—discharge because of limited service classification—was almost closed completely.

The Army succeeded in accomplishing its aim. But once again it appeared to overshoot the mark. Just as in the period of easy separations it had failed to appreciate how great an exodus might follow a lowering of the criteria for separation, so it had no perception of the full impact of its new stringent regulations. Not until evidence began to accumulate that many divisions getting ready for overseas shipment were carrying large numbers of ineffectives, that commands were retaining men in excess of their authorized strength, that the number of assignments in the Continental United States for handicapped persons was decreasing since most units had shifted to overseas theaters—not until sufficient time passed for these undesirable consequences to come forcibly to the attention of headquarters was the stage set for a new shift. The old policy had resulted in the retention of too many ineffective soldiers; now it became clear that the new policy had to be made more liberal.

The renewed willingness of the War Department to liberalize separation procedures was predicated on the need to rid the Army of soldiers who performed little useful service, particularly in the Zone of the Interior, and it was reinforced by the widespread conviction held by many of the senior officers in the Pentagon that the war with Germany would be won before the snow fell. There was no point in retaining such men since they would surely not be needed in the war against Japan. New War Department and Army Service Forces circulars were formally issued in September, 1944, which stipulated that while "psychoneurosis, mild" was not to be considered an adequate basis for separating a man with a certificate of disability discharge, he could be declared "surplus" if no acceptable assignment could be found for him, and separated for the convenience of the government. As Figure 5 makes clear, the numbers separated administratively increased spectacularly until the total reached 40,000 monthly.

The decline late in 1944 in the numbers separated for psychiatric disabilities probably reflects a preference for the new route that was opened up—a preference which the neuropsychiatrists in the Surgeon General's Office strongly supported. The parallel decline in the number separated for physical causes probably reflects the evacuation policy followed by General Hawley, the Chief Surgeon in the European Theater, who held on to most of his battle casualties during the fall because he had sufficient hospital beds and because he wanted to return the more seriously wounded to the United States only by hospital ships of which there were a limited number. Only when it became clear that the Germans would not capitulate by Columbus Day nor by Thanksgiving nor by Christmas, did Hawley step up his evacuations. On New Year's Day, 1945, there were more patients in Army General Hospitals in the United States and on ships en route to the United States than there were beds to care for them. The crisis was met by placing certain types of patients on furlough, transferring all psychoneurotic patients to newly opened convalescent hospitals, and by sending Air Corps personnel to their own hospitals for convalescent care.

Heavy fighting in the European Theater of Operations during the winter of 1944–45 resulted in some tightening of separation policy, at least for troops within the Theater. One medical officer in charge of a rehabilitation center far back of the lines relates how he responded to a sudden call for replacements. He lined up a large number of Army trucks against a temporary shelter in which he had assembled 200 convalescent psychiatric patients. At a given signal the trucks backfired. All men who remained on their feet were declared well enough to be sent to the front!

By March 1945, it was clear that the war with Germany was in its last stages. The liberalizing of separation policy that had been instituted in the middle of 1944, then temporarily halted though not reversed in early 1945, was now accelerated. President Roosevelt had informed the Secretary of War several months earlier that no patient was to be released to civilian life until he had had the benefit of rehabilitative services. Although the Army spared no effort to establish a group of convalescent centers with excellent facilities and enthusiastic personnel, experience disclosed that many soldiers failed to profit even from a three months' stay. The Army came to realize that many would not recover unless they were discharged. They had had their fill of military service. In soldiers' language, "they wanted out."

In March, 1945, the War Department issued what came to be recognized as the definitive document on the handling of ineffective personnel—Circular 81. After years of trial and error, the War Department was able to codify its procedures for discharge. Psychoneurosis was to be considered an illness only if the disability was of some duration. The mere presence of psychiatric symptoms without impairment of an individual's ability to perform did not justify a diagnosis of psychoneurosis; soldiers temporarily disabled from combat should be designated as suffering from "operational fatigue" or "exhaustion."

The circular went on to define many causes of ineffectiveness other than sickness, such as, for instance, inaptness, misassignment, defective attitude, and lack of physical stamina. A warning was issued against attributing noneffectiveness to coexistent medical conditions such as flat feet or lumbar-sacral strain when actually these defects were not in themselves disabling. Above all, the circular stressed that medical channels were to be used only to separate individuals who were sick or injured and that noneffective soldiers who were not disabled were to be discharged through administrative channels with responsibility resting on command, not on the Medical Department. And so the see-sawing of separation policy was finally faced and resolved—but never really tested, for the war was almost over.

The major implications of this summary review of Army separation policy during World War II should be made explicit so that their bearing on the utilization of manpower in large organizations, military and civilian, can be more clearly perceived. Although the prevailing opinion at the outset of the war held that only men with deficiencies in personality or character would become ineffective, experience proved that the personnel and medical policies promulgated by the Army had an important effect on the numbers who were eventually discharged as lacking the ability to perform effectively as soldiers.

Hidden beneath this finding was the emerging realization that ineffectiveness is not solely or even primarily a function of the qualities that characterize a man nor of the order of stress with which he is faced. For there were no significant changes early in 1943 in the quality of military manpower or in the conditions of the war, yet the numbers designated as ineffective increased three- and fourfold over the preceding year. The reason for these great manpower losses therefore must be found in changes in policy. Certainly, some men failed because of their own inadequacies; and others could not cope with the stress and strain of prolonged fighting. But the sudden and spectacular changes in the numbers declared to be ineffective could only reflect changes in organizational policy and procedures.

Such radical fluctuations require further consideration. Management's ability to determine whether a man is or is not effective or whether he will become ineffective in the future is extremely limited. Obvious failures can be spotted. But it is difficult to decide whether a man's limitations will or will not interfere with his capacity to perform effectively. The vigilance with which organized labor seeks to delimit management's freedom to use tests and other measuring devices to select workers for training or promotion grows out of its conviction that available techniques are not sufficiently reliable and can therefore cloak arbitrary action.

Every personnel action has indirect as well as direct consequences. When the Army made it easy for men with minor defects to be separated while the war was still under way, many others who were finding military service difficult and disagreeable but who had been attempting to adjust suddenly lost spirit and looked for escape. This is what lay back of the warning to medical officers to beware of "infectious virulence." Many psychiatrists never learned the lesson, or learned it only very late, that every evaluation that they made had to be tested not only against the needs of the individual soldier but also in terms of its probable impact on his barracks mates. For if one soldier with a mild psychoneurosis could be separated with a certificate of disability, many of his companions would seek a similar discharge.

Throughout the war there was a never-ending struggle between the line and the medical officer. Clearly, the screening, preventive, therapeutic, and rehabilitative policies of the Surgeon General's Office had a major impact on manpower logistics. The closer the coordination between the medical officer and command, the better the outcome. The relations between the two remained unclear until virtually the end of the war—until Circular 81 was issued in March 1945; but by then there was too little time remaining to test whether or not the resolution of the problem embodied in that circular would in fact have proved successful. Its objective was to leave the sick to the doctor, the inapt and the poorly motivated to command. Unfortunately, it is frequently difficult to make such a clear-cut distinction, because among other reasons the nervous man may also be inapt and poorly motivated. And in the midst of war such subtleties may appear less important than the end—to facilitate or impede discharges.

Moreover, the psychiatrist could conserve manpower only if he knew how the personnel officer would assign recovered patients. Psychiatry differs from medicine and surgery in that the patient's motivation plays a much more important role in his illness and recovery. There was no satisfactory resolution of the relations of the psychiatrists to command throughout World War II because the former found themselves involved in problems of manpower utilization far beyond the limits of their professional competence. It is no disparagement of the psychiatrist to say that his clinical training did not equip him to be a good logistical officer. That some became excellent staff officers and were able to contribute substantially to the maintenance of the morale and effectiveness of their units reflects their individual strengths, not their professional training.

There is another lesson worth extracting from this study of the influence of separation policy on the utilization of military manpower during World War II. As the record unfolded we noted the difficulties that the Army encountered in balancing troop requirements with available manpower. A shift in personnel policy resulted either in overshooting or undershooting the target. Too many men were released, or too few were let go. In either case, the efficiency of the Army was impaired. In this regard the written word, no matter how much care is taken to make it clear, has inherent limitations. A directive, passing through several headquarters, was repeatedly interpreted before reaching the field where implementation took place. Those who had to act were likely to proceed cautiously, unable to believe that so radical a change in policy was intended. But as days turned into weeks and weeks into months and their actions were not criticized or countermanded by higher headquarters, they grew bolder. And before long they were operating without restraint under the new directive. In a large organization the full implications of such enthusiastic support become clear only in time. When the policy makers finally learn what is happening, they are likely to move quickly to reverse the policy. This then starts another cycle.

Small wonder, therefore, that large business organizations try to avoid sharp changes in policy. They are in a more fortunate position than the Army for they can usually plan ahead and, what is more, can better control the rate of change. If the Army's manpower planning had been better, it would not have been forced to rely on improvization in developing its separation and other personnel policies. But the ebb and flow of the war would still have forced it to move first in one direction and then in another. The main challenge that the Army faced was not consistency in policy but an overriding commitment to its objective—to win the war as quickly as possible. It needed flexibility. However, flexible tactics require a sound strategic framework. In large measure this was missing on the manpower front.

Chapter Six: PERFORMANCE RECORDS OF INEFFECTIVE SOLDIERS

THE PRECEDING chapters have dealt with the problem of ineffectiveness in terms of the numbers of men rejected for military service or prematurely separated from the Armed Forces, with particular reference to the experience of the Army, during World War II. Up to now, our analysis has accepted the decision of the Armed Forces induction stations to reject a man or the decision of an administrative or medical board to discharge a soldier as prima facie evidence of his ineffectiveness. No attempt was made to go back of these operational decisions and inquire into their validity or to raise questions about whether a soldier, prior to being prematurely separated, had given useful service to the Army.

No one who has ever participated in mass selection, especially under pressure of time, will doubt that mistakes are inevitable. But a man who was rejected for service early in World War II because a medical examiner decided that a particular defect or disability was sufficiently serious to make him a poor risk was not necessarily safe from induction for the duration. It depended on when such a determination was made and, more particularly, on the pressure later exerted on his draft board to provide additional selectees. A man rejected early in the war who was registered with a board that later had difficulty in meeting its quota was likely to be forwarded, as we have seen, not once but several times for reexamination, especially if the board members felt that he was able to serve and saw no reason why he should not. Within the standards set by the Armed Forces to judge a man's suitability for service, no large numbers escaped through errors on the part of the examining physicians. The draft boards saw that apparently healthy men, unless deferred on occupational grounds, were examined a second or even a third time.

The determinations made within the Army about whether a soldier should be retained or discharged were more complicated. We have seen in the preceding chapters how Army policy alternated between opening and closing the sluices controlling discharge. If a recruit having trouble adjusting to military service came to the attention of his commanding officer in the summer of 1943, the odds were good that he would be back in civilian life within a matter of a few weeks. But if the same soldier was drafted in the late fall of that year, when the policy had veered to retaining men at almost any cost, he may well have served until demobilization.

No single definition of ineffectiveness can adequately cover the many different groups of soldiers who performed poorly and the fluctuating standards that the Army developed to assess performance. Any criterion of ineffectiveness must inevitably be justified by its operational usefulness. Civilian industry in its great expansion during the war also encountered serious personnel difficulties. When the shipyards, aircraft factories, and munitions plants were desperately in need of personnel, they hired almost indiscriminately all who came looking for a job, and frequently sent out recruiters to bring in young girls, married women, and old men who were then not working. In the attendant confusion, nobody was able to take the time to assess whether the newcomers could do the work and at what cost. When the initial rush had subsided and management got a better idea of its future requirements, various efforts were made by foremen and the personnel departments to sort out the acceptable from the unacceptable and to discharge the latter since actually they cost more than they produced.

During the past decade and a half, the mass statistics of ineffectiveness in the Army have been given wide currency and many important proposals have been advanced and responded to on the basis of these figures. It is surely significant that approximately 500,000 men "failed" in the Army in that they were separated before the fighting was over because they were inapt, emotionally disturbed, or presented disciplinary problems. But before we can draw too many conclusions, we will have to consider what lay back of these discharges. For example, the mentally deficient soldier who slipped through the induction screen and was discharged within his first month of service was labeled as inapt, and so was the soldier who, after two and a half years of adequate performance including sixty combat missions in the air, balked at a reassignment.

Four major categories comprise all of the men included in our study of the ineffective soldier who were separated prematurely for reasons of a mental, emotional, or behavior defect. Our first step toward understanding ineffective performance will be a review of the circumstances which determined that a soldier was to be classified under one rather than another of these discharge categories.

A man discharged as inapt or lacking adaptability for military service may have slipped through the screen though he was a true mental defective, which precluded his being able to make a contribution to the Army no matter how great an investment was made in training him. On the other hand, he may have been a man who encountered initial difficulties because his modest education and background handicapped him in adjusting to the new. In the latter case his performance might have been significantly influenced by the effort which the Army was willing to make to train him. And even if the Army did give him special training, the quality of his performance would depend on whether he was assigned, for example, to the combat engineers, in which case he would probably fail, or to a laundry unit, in which case he would probably prove effective.

A discharge as inapt was supposed to apply to men who could not readily learn the simplest military skills, either because they were mentally deficient or, more typically, because their educational background was exceedingly meager. However, the category "inapt" was also used, as we have noted, for other groups as a matter of convenience and compromise rather than of logic. Enuretics were so classified. So were a considerable number of men with good overseas records who were returned on rotation to the United States towards the end of the war. Many were Air Corps men who had served the required number of missions, which alone made them eligible for rotation. In many instances, they represented only a small fraction of their original unit; the others had been lost in action or killed. Having done their part and survived, they felt that they were entitled to special consideration. Since the Air Forces did not have suitable assignments for most of them, they became restless and "wanted out."

The Air Forces were disinclined to take disciplinary or punitive action against veterans who had proven themselves in combat, especially since most of the available assignments were not suitable for these medal winners. With its manpower situation beginning to ease in late 1944 and early 1945, the Air Forces adopted an easy policy and separated these men as "lacking in ability to adapt to military service." Most of them were not seriously upset emotionally and consequently did not warrant a medical discharge, and they certainly did not deserve a discharge without honor. As we will later show, the number of battle-decorated veterans discharged as inapt accounted for only a small part of the total category.

Medical discharges were given to two groups who were diagnosed as suffering from a psychiatric illness. By far the larger number were those with a "psychoneurosis," a term used to cover a wide range of emotional disturbances varying from temporary reactions to situations of acute stress to chronic emotional instability expressed in diffuse anxiety, phobias, compulsions or somatic disturbances such as inability to sleep or retain food, excessive sweating, or rapid breathing.

The second group, much smaller but still substantial, were those diagnosed as psychotic. This classification included the men who became so disoriented that they lost contact with reality and could therefore no longer be held responsible for their actions. Although most of the men suffering from a psychosis could be sharply differentiated from those suffering from a psychoneurosis, the onset, duration, and outcome of their illness showed great variability.

Most patients in civilian life suffering from a psychosis are afflicted with a chronic condition, although in many instances they may be free of pronounced symptoms for longer or shorter periods of time. Psychotic disturbances of an episodic rather than a chronic nature are known to civilian psychiatry, but they account for only a minority of the cases. Under Army regulations, individuals with a prior history of hospitalization for mental disease were to be rejected for service, on the assumption that even if the disease were currently in remission, the patient might have a relapse.

The same assumption underlay the policy of discharging men who developed a psychosis while on active duty. The rule was to discharge them for treatment, usually to a Veterans Administration hospital near their home. In the early years of the war the Army did not consider itself obligated to treat these patients since they were not to be returned to duty and they frequently required hospitalization for months or even years. Later in the war the Army realized that many soldiers appeared to be suffering from a psychotic episode rather than a chronic condition and would respond well to treatment that sometimes included shock therapy. The Army therefore instituted an active therapeutic program, and many psychotic patients were sent home rather than to a Veterans Administration hospital at the end of 90 or 120 days of treatment in an Army hospital.

In addition to the inapt, the psychoneurotic, and the psychotic, a fourth group of ineffectives was discharged from the service for "undesirable habits or traits of character." These men were given so-called "blue" discharges (from the color of the discharge paper) which meant that they were separated under conditions other than honorable. Included in this category were men who had been in serious trouble with the Army because they were frequently absent without leave, were alcoholics, used drugs, were homosexuals, stole, or were guilty of other serious infractions of Army discipline. Whatever the root of their aberrant behavior, the Army found them guilty of serious breaches of discipline and since they were mentally responsible for their actions, they were punished—at least to the extent of being discharged without honor.

Many of these men were given repeated opportunities to make good before they were finally separated from the service. Others, such as the homosexuals, were separated as soon as their deviating behavior came to the attention of a responsible officer. The punitive nature of the blue discharge derived from the fact that it did not entitle the veteran to many of the benefits available to those who were honorably discharged. Yet a blue discharge was frequently a boon to the soldier in that, had the Army decided to hold him for a general court martial, he would probably have been convicted, which could have carried with it loss of the right of suffrage and a prison term.

Although some men discharged for inaptitude or psychoneurosis might more properly have been separated for undesirable behavior, the reverse was also true. Some who were given a "blue" discharge were of such limited intelligence that they could not understand the regulations; others were so disturbed emotionally that their behavior may have been a manifestation of their illness. By recognizing that every category scheme has inherent limitations, medical and line officers did their best to deal justly with the soldiers whom they had to assess for discharge. Table 14 can be considered to reflect correctly gross differences among those who were prematurely separated from the service.

The figures in this table are the base data to which the percentages given in subsequent tables in this and the following two chapters should be applied. The percentages in these subsequent tables are derived from sample data pertaining to premature separations for reasons of psychoneurosis, psychosis, undesirable habits and traits, and inaptitude, and exclude ineffective personnel separated for other psychiatric (21,000) and other "blue" (13,000) reasons. (See Tables 11 and 13.) Thus, they cover 470,000 of the Army's 504,000 premature separations for ineffectiveness.

How ineffective were these soldiers? The preceding discussion implied, but did not make explicit, variations in the performance of these soldiers prior to their separation. If a man became psychotic on the train between the induction station and the reception center, as some did, he would clearly be a total loss to the Army. But what of the soldier who served for two and a half years before he broke down? Or again, there were men who after a week or two of living in close relations with thirty-nine other men went to see the chaplain or the medical officer to explain that although they had hoped to be able to control their homosexuality, they felt unable to do so and asked to be removed before something happened.

Table 14. SEPARATIONS OF ENLISTED MALE PERSONNEL FROM THE ARMY FOR INEFFECTIVENESS, BY MAJOR REASON, 1942–1945

MAJOR REASON FOR SEPARATION	SEPARATIONS *Number*	*Percent of Total*
Psychoneurosis	256,000 [a]	54
Psychosis	55,000 [a]	12
Undesirable habits and traits	37,000 [b]	8
Inaptitude	122,000 [b]	26
Total	470,000 [b]	100

[a] *Health of Army*, vol. 1, report 2, p. 22.
[b] AG, Stat. & Acctg., unpub. worksheets.

But there were others, overt homosexuals, who had no difficulty in performing their assignments well over a two- or three-year period and who came to the attention of the military authorities only after one of their partners had denounced them.

Length of service is clearly one important factor in assessing the contribution that a soldier made prior to his being discharged, but by itself it can be misleading. Men can get lost in large organizations and unless management is alert to weed out all who fail to perform, they may survive for a long time before their ineffectiveness is uncovered.

Since the Army could win the war only by carrying the fight to the enemy in North Africa, Western Europe, the Pacific, and elsewhere, the value of a soldier was much greater if he could serve overseas than if his disabilities necessitated his being restricted to duty within the United States. Since it was Army practice to screen men again prior to shipping them out of the country, "overseas duty" was a second important criterion for assessing a soldier's effectiveness. Most useful perhaps was a soldier's rank. While it is true that many were promoted on the basis of seniority, and those who served overseas were likely to be promoted more rapidly because of the losses which took place in combat, the Army was not likely to promote men to the rank of corporal or higher—and to retain them in their higher rank—unless they were reasonably efficient. Although the promotion system did not insure that the best man would be advanced, it did guarantee advancements usually only for those who could cope with additional responsibility.

Length of service, overseas service, and rank are crude criteria, but they do provide a first approximation of the effectiveness which characterized various groups of soldiers who were prematurely discharged. In our two companion volumes many more factors are considered, including the number of days a soldier was in the hospital or in confinement, his medals or courts martial, his efficiency ratings, and other relevant facts about his Army service. Since a separation card was punched on each soldier at the time of his discharge which contained information about his length of service, overseas service, and rank, we can apply these selective criteria to the entire group. And when we deal with actual case records we can make use of the more elaborate indices of military performance.

Table 15 summarizes the length of service of the half million soldiers who are included in our analysis of ineffectiveness.

It is striking that almost 1 out of every 3 soldiers eventually released because of ineffectiveness served for at least two years and that 1 in 7 actually served for at least three years. Less than half were in the Army for under one year. Although length of Army service included the time that a man spent in the hospital or in confinement—which, in the case of the psychotic patient or the soldier who received a "blue" discharge, might have totaled between four to six months—the finding that so many served for such a considerable period is presumptive evidence that all of them were not completely ineffective. Even among those who served less than a year, many were discharged before they had been adequately tested, since in 1943 the General Staff encouraged commanders in the field to release any soldier who gave any evidence of emotional instability or other handicap.

Other soldiers were doubtless kept on active duty long after they became ineffective either because the regulations in effect at the time made it difficult to separate them or because, since their units were far from home, their commanders did not want to let them go knowing that they would not be replaced. Further understanding about this criterion of effectiveness can be accumulated by analyzing and comparing the several discharge categories by length of service. The appropriate data are given in Table 16.

Table 15. PERCENT DISTRIBUTION OF ENLISTED MALE PERSONNEL SEPARATED FROM THE ARMY FOR INEFFECTIVENESS, BY LENGTH OF SERVICE, 1942–1945

Months of Service	*Percent Serving* [a]
Less than 12	44
At least 12 but less than 24	25
At least 24 but less than 36	17
36 or more	14
Total	100

[a] Calculated from data in special tabulations of a 5% sample, AG, Stat. & Acctg., CHR.

Several findings emerge. A considerable proportion of the two major groups of ineffective soldiers—the psychoneurotic and the inapt—served for less than six months, which means that they were truly ineffective as far as rendering useful service to the Army in World War II. As has already been suggested, some of these men might have eventually been able to perform effectively had they been given more of a chance, but if they were inducted in late 1942 or early 1943, and very large numbers were then taken in, they were unlikely to have had such a chance for, at that time the Army was pursuing an easy discharge policy. It should be recalled in this connection that while the Army began to accept large numbers of illiterates during this period, it had not as yet instituted the special training units at reception centers to which illiterate and poorly educated soldiers could be sent for special instruction immediately following their induction. These came into operation only during the second half of 1943.

Table 16. PERCENT DISTRIBUTION OF ENLISTED MALE PERSONNEL SEPARATED FROM THE ARMY FOR INEFFECTIVENESS, BY MAJOR REASON AND BY LENGTH OF SERVICE, 1942–1945 [a]

	MAJOR REASON FOR SEPARATION			
MONTHS OF SERVICE	*Psychoneurosis*	*Psychosis*	*Undesirable*	*Inaptitude*
Less than 6	20	12	9	41
At least 6 but less than 12	19	16	20	28
At least 12 but less than 18	13	14	20	13
At least 18 but less than 24	11	14	14	7
At least 24 but less than 36	20	24	23	7
At least 36 but less than 48	12	14	9	3
48 or more	5	6	5	1
Total	100	100	100	100

[a] Calculated from data in special tabulations of a 5% sample, AG, Stat. & Acctg., CHR.

In an earlier study [13] we showed that of the 300,000 who attended the special training units, only 30,000 were discharged from these units for inaptitude and less than 10,000 "graduates" were ultimately separated for this reason. Hence the majority—about 2 out of every 3—separated for inaptitude never had the advantage of the special training furnished by these units.

To continue the analysis of the inapt group: 4 out of 5 had less than eighteen months' service. This relatively short service can be explained by the comparative ease of identifying such men and the further fact that a commanding officer could declare a soldier, early in his service, inapt and discharge him through administrative channels without reflecting on his own leadership.

Quite a different picture is presented by the undesirable group, whose service on the average was considerably longer. Aside from the fact already mentioned that many spent considerable time in the stockade or in disciplinary barracks, their relatively longer term of duty can best be explained by the effort that the Army made in most instances to give a man a second or even a third chance before taking definitive action to separate him under punitive conditions. The indulgence of the Army was particularly marked in the case of alcoholics, who were given repeated chances to reform, especially if they were pleasant fellows or performed well when sober.

As far as the psychotics are concerned, the most significant finding is that so many served for so long before breaking down. More than 2 out of every 5 had more than two years of service. Only about 1 out of 4 served for less than a year; 1 out of 8 for less than six months. These figures suggest that the majority who manifested a psychosis in the service were not men who had managed to sneak past the examining physician at the induction station, although a few did. One psychiatrist recalls a selectee whom he had accepted asking whether the Army cared that he had been a patient in five different mental hospitals. Upon checking, the medical officer found this to be true. However, despite this and other alarming examples, the data suggest either that most psychotics first broke down on active duty, or that many were able to perform more or less satisfactorily for long periods of time until their aberrant behavior became sufficiently pronounced to attract the attention of their commander.

With regard to the largest group, the psychoneurotics, the figures indicate that almost 2 out of every 5 served for two years or more, and that 6 out of every 10 served for more than a year. This suggests that most of these soldiers were able to perform more or less satisfactorily for some time before they broke down. Although some could not adjust to the demands made on them during their training cycle, most of them spent over a year in training in the United States before being shipped overseas. However, many who were somewhat disturbed already experienced mounting anxiety as their units prepared for overseas shipment. Some broke down at that time. Others were able to get up the gangplank with the "help" of the medical officer, the chaplain, or military police. It was only after exposure to combat—or after assignment to an isolated outpost—that they actually broke down.

In three of the four categories about 40 percent of all men separated for ineffectiveness served for more than two years. The exception was the inapt. Even making allowance for the fact that the Army was deliberately or inadvertently slow in making a final judgment on the performance potential of the men in the other three categories, their serving for more than two years suggests that they were able initially to meet prevailing standards and that the shortcomings which led to their separation developed only after the passage of considerable time. Another reason might have been that, as the Army's manpower needs eased, those who were performing marginally could be more readily released.

To be sent overseas a man had first to complete his training, which was frequently both extended and arduous, including infiltration courses in which live ammunition was used and ending with extended maneuvers. Even if he was trained as an individual replacement—and consequently hurried through his training—he still had to demonstrate a reasonable proficiency as a soldier, including an ability to adjust to military life. Moreover, as we noted earlier, commanders were frequently permitted to cull their ranks of the unstable and the troublemakers as their units neared the time of overseas movement. Hence a man who was sent overseas passed two additional screens beyond induction—his training and a screening prior to embarkation.

There was a small group, however, whose presence overseas reflected not their strength but their weakness. If a man once cleared for shipment overseas jumped ship and was apprehended, the prevailing practice was not to punish him by incarceration in the United States but to get him on the next ship in order to force him to fight. Hence in a small number of cases overseas service cannot be accepted as clear evidence of satisfactory performance up to that point in time, but these undoubtedly accounted for a small fraction of the total.

Table 17 presents the percentage of soldiers who were separated for ineffectiveness who served overseas.

The table shows that more than 2 out of every 5 of these men served overseas. There are striking differences, however, among the different discharge categories. Three out of every 5 psychoneurotics and more than half of the psychotics had service overseas. But only a relatively small percentage of the inapt or the undesirable ever

Table 17. PERCENT DISTRIBUTION OF ENLISTED MALE PERSONNEL SEPARATED FROM THE ARMY FOR INEFFECTIVENESS, BY MAJOR REASON AND BY LOCATION OF SERVICE, 1942–1945 [a]

	MAJOR REASON FOR SEPARATION				
LOCATION OF SERVICE	*Psychoneurosis*	*Psychosis*	*Undesirable*	*Inaptitude*	*Total*
Overseas	62	55	15	8	42
Zone of Interior only	38	45	85	92	58
Total	100	100	100	100	100

[a] Calculated from data in special tabulations of a 5% sample, AG, Stat. & Acctg., CHR.

left the United States. We noted earlier that most of the men who were separated for inaptitude served for only a short time. And those who eventually got into disciplinary trouble with the Army apparently gave early warning of their aberrant behavior so that if they were not separated during their training cycle, they were left at home when their unit got ready to move overseas.

There are two further observations that must be borne in mind in interpreting these figures. As we have seen, a few men with good and sometimes outstanding records overseas were eventually discharged as inapt because the Army and particularly the Air Forces did not want to give them a discharge without honor despite their unsatisfactory behavior late in the war. This attitude also explains the disinclination of the Surgeon General to permit any combat veteran to be separated from an Army General Hospital with a "blue" discharge.

The percentage of ineffective soldiers who served overseas must be compared to the Army as a whole, for not all effective soldiers served overseas. It is estimated that about 75 percent of all enlisted personnel of the Army had overseas duty at some time during World War II. Hence the fact that 60 percent of those eventually

Table 18. PERCENT DISTRIBUTION OF ENLISTED MALE PERSONNEL SEPARATED FROM THE ARMY FOR INEFFECTIVENESS, BY MAJOR REASON AND BY GRADE AT SEPARATION, 1942–1945, AND AN ESTIMATED GRADE DISTRIBUTION OF MEAN ENLISTED MALE STRENGTH

		MAJOR REASON FOR SEPARATION [b]			
GRADE	MEAN ENLISTED MALE STRENGTH [a] *	*Psychoneurosis*	*Psychosis*	*Undesirable*	*Inaptitude*
Top three grades (M/Sgt., T/Sgt., S/Sgt.)	9	5	3	†	†
Sergeant	12	7	5	†	†
Corporal	18	10	9	1	1
Private, first class	22	20	19	3	5
Private	39	58	64	95	94
Total	100	100	100	100	100

* Based on grade distribution of Army enlisted male strength, quarterly 1942–1945.

† 0.5 percent or less.

[a] Calculated from data in *Strength of Army*, STM-30, p. 61.

[b] Calculated from data in a special tabulation of a 5% sample, AG, Stat. & Acctg., CHR.

separated for psychoneurosis served overseas suggests that there was some selective screening on the way which kept some of the emotionally unstable at home. But the fact that so many did get overseas suggests that their eventual breakdown may have been a result of the stresses they encountered there, especially in combat. Our companion volumes throw more light on this relationship.

There were seven grades for enlisted men in the Army. The two lowest grades—private and private first class—accounted for approximately 60 percent of the total strength; the remaining five grades of corporal, sergeant and staff, technical, and master sergeant—the noncommissioned officers group—accounted for 40 percent of the total. Table 18 sets out the grade attained by the ineffectives in each of the specific discharge categories in comparison to the grade distribution for the Army as a whole.

The earlier data have revealed that the ineffective soldier served for a shorter period of time than the average soldier and that he was less likely to serve overseas. Both of these factors militated against his attaining as high a grade as the average. It is striking that despite these handicaps, 22 percent of the psychoneurotics and 17 percent of the psychotics became noncommissioned officers.

It is not surprising that so few of the inapt ever reached even the grade of private, first class. But the data on the undesirable require a word of elaboration. The separation card which was punched on each soldier noted his grade at the time of discharge, not his highest grade. Some of those who were eventually given "blue" discharges—how many it is impossible to say—were "broken" from higher grades because of infractions in discipline.

The analysis which we have presented in terms of the major discharge categories and the major indices of performance shows that it would be misleading to deal with ineffective soldiers as if they were a homogeneous group. The inapt, with few exceptions, were almost a total loss to the Army: they served for only a short time; only a few got overseas; they seldom advanced beyond the grade of private. A quite different assessment emerges from an evaluation of the psychoneurotic—the largest group among the ineffectives. Approximately half served for at least eighteen months; over 60 percent of the entire group saw service overseas; and 22 percent attained noncommissioned officer status. More than half as many psychoneurotics as soldiers in the Army as a whole were promoted to one of the three top noncommissioned grades. Thus, in considering the problem of the ineffective soldier, it is essential to differentiate these men from the inapt and the undesirable.

Perhaps the most significant finding of all is the performance of soldiers who eventually had to be separated because of a psychosis. Their record prior to breakdown was much better than would have been expected on the basis of civilian experience. Almost 60 percent served for eighteen months or more; 55 percent served overseas; and 1 out of 6 became a noncommissioned officer.

Chapter Seven: CIVILIAN BACKGROUND AND MILITARY PERFORMANCE

AS General Snyder has stated in his Foreword, a major objective of General Eisenhower in establishing the Conservation of Human Resources Project was to investigate the rich personnel data of World War II in the hope that research could uncover why so many men were ineffective. Corrective social action can only follow an understanding of the factors responsible for ineffectiveness. Two earlier publications of the Project [14] have illuminated the parts played by education (or more correctly, the lack of it) and race (specifically, the Negro minority status) in the large-scale ineffectiveness characteristic of World War II.

This chapter will describe our further efforts to discover the extent to which such factors as age, marital status, education, and race played a significant part in the premature separation of approximately half a million soldiers. In contrast to the approach used in the accompanying volumes, the present analysis is delimited primarily to information available on the separation card itself. On the basis of these data, we will seek to discover whether significant differences can be found between the soldiers who were prematurely separated and those who successfully served until the end of the war. We will further explore whether significant differences can be found among the major discharge categories. We know that even if significant differences are found between the ineffective and other soldiers and between different groups of ineffective soldiers, the results will not provide definitive answers to the causes of ineffectiveness. But such findings will advance our understanding of the complex phenomenon of ineffective performance and serve as a link in a chain that we hope will lead to corrective policy.

AGE

Except for sex, age has been the principal criterion used to determine who shall serve in the Armed Forces in times of mobilization. In the nineteenth century young people who were tall for their age were able to join the colors as early as twelve and in exceptional cases even younger. During the Civil War the recruiting sergeant placed more importance on what he saw than on what the birth certificate might reveal. This is less surprising when we recall that there are men alive today who first started working at the age of nine!

Although recourse was had to the draft during the Civil War, it was not until World War I that the call-up of manpower was placed on a formal and systematic basis. Since then age has played a major role in military manpower policy. Congress determined both the age below which a young man could not be drafted as well as the age above which men were exempt. Since in a major war the Armed Forces must depend primarily on manpower secured through the draft, these age limitations were highly significant. Considerations of both equity and efficiency have played a part in determining the age limits. Prevailing social attitudes hold that young men should not be taken into the Armed Forces until they are mature, which has come to be set at about eighteen, though there is always a vocal minority that insists that twenty should be the minimum. The Armed Forces have been willing to accept volunteers in their seventeenth year in the conviction that young men are easiest to train and have the greatest potential for fighting.

With regard to the upper end of the scale, the public has been reluctant to see married men with major family and business obligations forced to don a uniform. It has been less concerned with protecting the single man. Early in World War II, the Army believed that it would gain flexibility if it were permitted to call men to duty up to the age of forty-five. But as the Army acquired experience with older men, it quickly decided that as a group they were more of a liability than an asset and gave them an opportunity to return to civilian life, which almost 200,000 took. From 1943 on, the Army drafted only men below thirty-seven and at a later stage of the war (summer, 1944) when only infantry replacements were required, it concentrated on those below twenty-six.

The factor of age is closely associated with physical characteristics—the younger men have much lower rates of physical disability. This is not completely true, however, with respect to psychiatric disorders which disabled the majority of the ineffective soldiers. It has been argued that older men are likely to be less well motivated for military service, first because their roots are more deeply imbedded in civilian life; secondly, because they are less flexible and adaptable in new situations. But as an offset, older men will have the advantage of greater skills, experience, and judgment—which should help them adjust to a new and demanding environment.

While young men have greater stamina, flexibility, and enthusiasm, the very young are likely to be less stable emotionally. At eighteen or even nineteen many will still be struggling with unresolved problems of adolescence. At best they will have had little opportunity to test themselves in the adult world and to have learned about their strengths and weaknesses. Industry has long been aware that the late teens are likely to comprise a period of exploration and testing for many men and that they will settle down only in their middle twenties.

The data show that young men in their late teens did have a somewhat higher rate of rejection than men in their early twenties. But with this single exception all the other associations were in one direction—the older the group, the higher the rejection rate. One analysis showed that for men between the ages of thirty and thirty-seven the rate was about twice that of the eighteen to twenty-five year group. Those over thirty-eight had a rate nearly three times that of the youngest age group.

Age likewise played a significant part in the Army's premature separations, particularly among soldiers who were diagnosed as suffering from a psychoneurosis. In analyzing the Army data it is important to bear in mind that men over thirty-eight were released as a group without prior evaluation, and consequently no significance can be placed on the rates for these older men.

Table 19. PERCENT DISTRIBUTION OF ENLISTED MALE PERSONNEL SEPARATED FROM THE ARMY FOR INEFFECTIVENESS, BY MAJOR REASON AND BY YEAR OF BIRTH, 1942–1945, AND A DISTRIBUTION OF ENLISTED MALE ACCESSIONS BY YEAR OF BIRTH

YEAR OF BIRTH	ENLISTED MALE ACCESSIONS, FISCAL 1941–1945 [a]	MAJOR REASON FOR SEPARATION, 1942–1945 [b]			
		Psychoneurosis	*Psychosis*	*Undesirable*	*Inaptitude*
1907 or earlier	8	16	18	21	28
1908–1912	12	34	36	39	29
1913–1917	22	25	24	20	21
1918–1922	36	17	15	13	15
1923–1927 *	22	8	7	7	7
Total	100	100	100	100	100

* Includes a small number (less than 0.7%) of Undesirables and Inapts for 1945 whose year of birth was 1928.

[a] Calculated from data in AG, Stat. & Acctg., unpub. worksheets.

[b] Calculated from data in special tabulations of 5% sample, AG, Stat. & Acctg., CHR.

Table 19 shows the age distribution of all enlisted men who entered the Army between July, 1940, and July, 1945, compared with the age distribution of soldiers separated prematurely because of ineffectiveness during 1942–1945.

Although a strict comparison between the age of the ineffective group and the rest of the Army is complicated by such factors as the mass release of the thirty-eight-year-olds, the emphasis on the induction of younger men late in the war, and the effort to select more stable and mature men for officer training, the foregoing table tends to support the following conclusion. Those separated for psychiatric reasons (the psychoneurotic and psychotic groups combined) were substantially older than the average soldier, while the administrative separatees (the inapt and the undesirable) were even older than the psychiatric separatees.

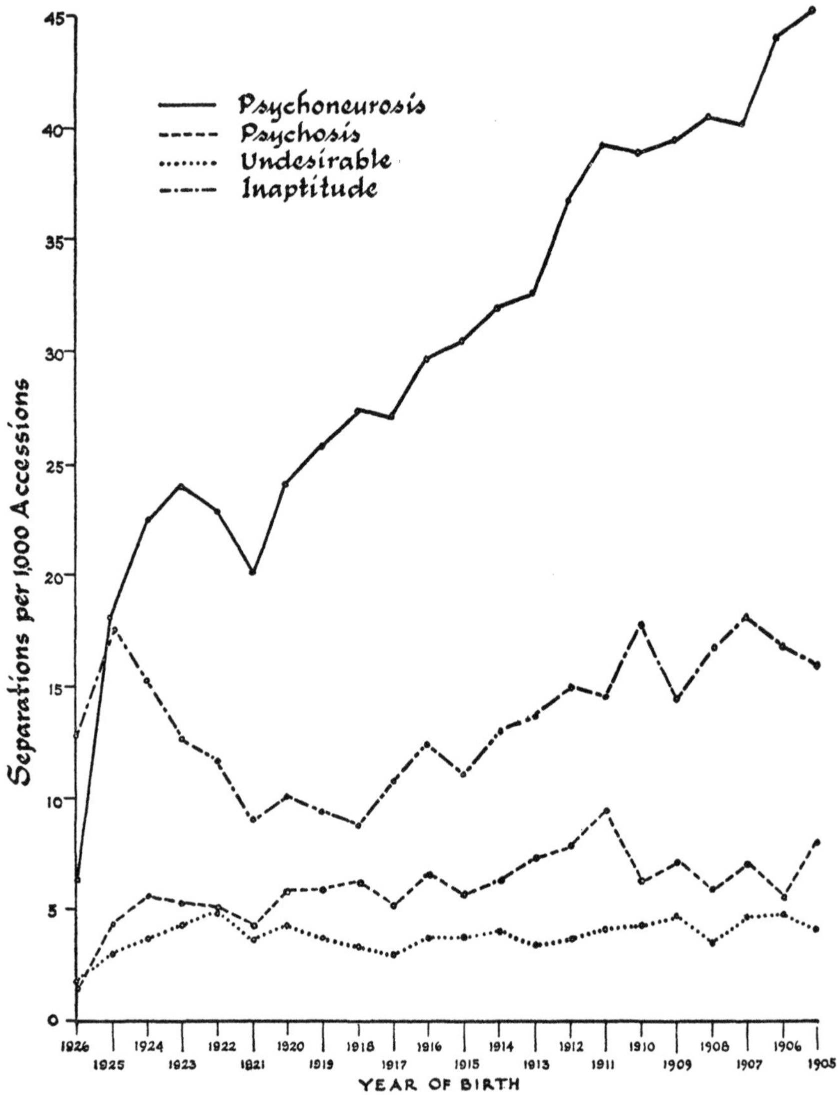

Figure 6. RELATIONSHIP BETWEEN YEAR OF BIRTH AND RATE OF SEPARATIONS FOR INEFFECTIVENESS, BY MAJOR REASON, ARMY ENLISTED PERSONNEL, WORLD WAR II

Source: AG, Stat. & Acctg., unpub. worksheets; and SG, unpub. worksheets.

Figure 6 shows the relationship between age and premature separation. It is based on men who entered the Army from mid-1940 through mid-1945 who had to be separated for ineffectiveness during 1942–1945.

The most striking finding is the extent to which the separation rate for psychoneurosis rises with age. Between the youngest men —eighteen- and nineteen-year-olds—and the oldest group—thirty-six and seven—the rate increases from just over 6 per 1,000 to over 45 per 1,000, or sevenfold. The curve rises steadily and sharply. For men separated because of psychosis the rate rises with age, but the increase is less pronounced. Among the undesirables there appears to be little systematic relationship between the rate and age.

The curve for the inapt is more difficult to explain since higher separation rates obtained for both the younger and the older groups. To consider first the higher rates among the older men: Starting with some doubt as to whether an older man could cope with the physical demands of service, the Army moved quickly to separate one who gave indication of limited capacity to learn. Since there has been a more or less steady improvement in the quantity and quality of schooling over the past half century, the older men were more likely to be educationally deprived. Furthermore, as General Hershey once remarked, "The older man was discharged or crushed at times because he was trained for what he could never be by methods he was too old to endure."

But what about the relatively higher separation rate for inaptitude among the youngest group? It is likely that induction station examiners were willing to take a chance on a healthy looking young man even though they may have had some doubts about his intellectual capacity to make the grade. For the young and robust, the examiners lowered the educational screen. But since some of these recruits were immature, they were unable to cope with Army life.

Stouffer, in his detailed study of *The American Soldier* [15] found that men hospitalized for psychoneurosis in 1944 were considerably older than a comparable sample of the total Army enlisted group. A comparison between Stouffer's data and our sample of men separated for psychoneurosis during 1944 is shown in Table 20.

Both Stouffer's data and our own—which differ in that he dealt with soldiers hospitalized in the United States for psychoneurosis

Table 20. AGE AND PSYCHONEUROSIS: A COMPARISON BETWEEN THE FINDINGS OF STOUFFER AND CONSERVATION OF HUMAN RESOURCES PROJECT (IN PERCENT)

STOUFFER[a]

AGE IN 1944	ENLISTED CROSS SECTION, FEB. 1944[b] *Privates*	ENLISTED CROSS SECTION, FEB. 1944[b] *NCOs*	PSYCHONEUROTIC PATIENTS IN STATION HOSPITALS, FEB. 1944[c]
30 or over	20	23	40
25–29	20	32	25
20–24	42	42	28
19 or under	18	3	7
Total	100	100	100

CONSERVATION OF HUMAN RESOURCES PROJECT

AGE IN 1944	ARMY ENLISTED MALE STRENGTH, 30 JUNE 1944[d]	ENLISTED MEN SEPARATED FOR PSYCHONEUROSIS, 1944[e]
30 or over	25	37
25–29	29	31
20–24	40	28
19 or under	6	4
Total	100	100

[a] Stouffer, *et al.*, *The American Soldier*, Vol. I, p. 114.
[b] Res. Br., Inf. & Ed. Div., US Army, Survey S-95, as reported in Stouffer.
[c] Res. Br., Inf. & Ed. Div., US Army, Survey S-99, as reported in Stouffer.
[d] Calculated from data in unpub. report, AG, MRBr., STN-94.
[e] Calculated from data in special tabulations of a 5% sample, AG, Stat. & Acctg., CHR.

while we considered only those separated for this cause—demonstrate clearly the higher incidence of psychoneurosis among older soldiers. This is especially marked in the above-thirty age group. Some question might be raised whether the data for a single year—1944—are truly representative of the entire war. Table 21 shows that the age distribution of psychiatric separatees in 1944 paralleled the distribution for the entire period 1942 to 1945. The sharp increase in the rate for those under twenty in 1943 was due to the substantially heavier induction of younger men which began to get underway late in 1942.

Our findings are also in general accord with the careful study of the age factor made by Brill and Beebe in which they found high hospital admission rates for psychoneurosis among older soldiers in the Zone of the Interior in 1944 as well as a higher in-

Table 21. RATE OF SEPARATIONS OF ENLISTED MALE PERSONNEL FROM THE ARMY FOR PSYCHONEUROSIS, BY YEAR OF BIRTH, WORLD WAR II

	RATE OF CALENDAR YEAR SEPARATIONS PER 1,000 FISCAL YEAR ACCESSIONS (CUMULATIVE) [a]			
YEAR OF BIRTH	*1942 ÷ Fiscal 1941–1942*	*1942–1943 ÷ Fiscal 1941–1943*	*1942–1944 ÷ Fiscal 1941–1944*	*1942–1945 ÷ Fiscal 1941–1945*
1912 and earlier	7.5	20.8	27.0	34.5
1913–1917	4.4	17.2	23.5	30.1
1918–1922	3.2	11.5	16.3	23.5
1923–1927	1.5	14.4	16.2	18.4
Average, all ages	4.5	15.2	20.2	26.0

[a] Separations per calendar year from special tabulations of a 5% sample, AG, Stat. & Acctg., CHR, divided by accessions per fiscal year from AG, Stat. & Acctg., unpub. worksheets.

cidence among older soldiers assigned to overseas noncombat organizations.[16] Included among the interesting findings of these authors, on which our data do not enable us to comment, is the lack of significance of age in the breakdown of men in active regimental combat. The authors suggest that older men are cleared for combat units only after they have been very carefully screened. While we cannot corroborate this finding specifically, an analysis of our materials in the accompanying volumes on *The Ineffective Soldier* shows that among men in the ground combat arms overseas, those under twenty-four accounted for the highest percentage of psychoneurotic breakdowns.

The Army experience was not unique. The Navy, for example,

has reported that in World War II the incidence rates for "diseases of the mind" increased steadily with age from a low of 9 per 1,000 for white personnel under twenty in the Navy and the Marine Corps to 21 per 1,000 for the thirty-five to thirty-nine-year-old white group.[17]

It is easier to see that age is definitely associated with psychoneurotic breakdown in the Armed Forces than to understand the reasons for it. The most challenging finding is that the rates increase with age quite rapidly even for men in their twenties. There is nothing in civilian life that suggests a parallel. And the figures have been sufficiently well controlled so that we can be sure that age does not mask different orders of stress, such as exposure to combat. But it may well mask a more subtle factor—motivation to perform.

Possibly older men felt that war was for the young and that it was unfair of the Army to induct them in the first place, especially when many younger men were being deferred on what seemed to be irrelevant or flimsy grounds. Many married men—and this would include a considerable number in their middle and late twenties—had come to center their lives around their wives and children. Although they were uprooted and transported far from home, their ties remained strong. They could not therefore throw themselves into the war with the same enthusiasm as did younger single men, many of whom found in the Army a meaningful center for the first time in their lives. It may be that age is closely associated with emotional commitment; we can explore this relationship by considering the influence of marital status on the rate of separations for ineffectiveness.

MARITAL STATUS

To begin with, let us emphasize the close relation that is likely to exist between age and marital status, for as a man grows older, the probability increases that he will be married. Since we have already found that the rate of psychoneurotic breakdown in the Army is higher among older men, we must anticipate that the same will be true for married men compared to single men. Brill and Beebe noted this fact but ascribed the phenomenon completely to age.[18] Stouffer, however, after controlling his data for age, found that married men generally had a higher rate of breakdown than single men.[19]

Unfortunately there are no data that permit a test of the relationships between age, marital status, and ineffectiveness for the entire war period, but selective information is available which permits an exploratory if not definitive analysis.

The following three tables show the separation rates for psychoneurosis by marital and dependency status during 1943, which was approximately the middle of the war.

Table 22. RATE OF SEPARATIONS OF ENLISTED MALE PERSONNEL FROM THE ARMY FOR PSYCHONEUROSIS, BY MARITAL AND DEPENDENCY STATUS, 1943 [a]

Marital and Dependency Status	*Rate of 1943 Separations per 1,000 Enlisted Male Strength on 31 Dec. 1943* *	
Single		10.9
With dependents	5.9	
Without dependents	14.2	
Married		29.1
Broken Marriage †		43.1
With dependents	37.8	
Without dependents	49.5	

* Army enlisted male strength 31 Dec. 1943: 6,739,000.
† Separated, divorced, widower.
[a] Separations calculated from data in special tabulations of a representative sample, AG, Stat. & Acctg. Rep. Sample, CHR divided by strength in thousands from data in unpub. report, AG, MRBr., ETN-43.

Table 22 shows that married men had a notably higher separation rate than single men and that men with marriages broken by divorce, separation, or death had a still higher rate.

In both the "single" and "broken marriage" categories, men with dependents show somewhat lower rates than those without dependents. With respect to the single men this is probably because the presence of dependents means that the soldier had been willing to assume some responsibility for his parents or siblings and thereby attest to his somewhat greater stability. At the other extreme, a soldier with a broken marriage and no dependents was probably a man who had more than his share of personal distress and who was likely to be disturbed in a way that made it more difficult for him to adjust to the Army. Among those with broken marriages, men who were separated from their wives but not divorced had by far the highest rates.

Tables 23 and 24 indicate that marital status itself was an important factor contributing to ineffectiveness.

Table 23. RATE OF SEPARATIONS OF ENLISTED MALE PERSONNEL FROM THE ARMY FOR PSYCHONEUROSIS, BY MARITAL STATUS AND BY YEAR OF BIRTH [a]

	RATE OF 1943 SEPARATIONS PER 1,000 ENLISTED MALE STRENGTH ON 31 DEC. 1943 *		
YEAR OF BIRTH	*Single*	*Married*	*Broken Marriage* †
1907 and earlier	15.0	87.0	51.9
1908–1912	12.1	64.6	45.6
1913–1917	10.9	47.0	43.6
1918–1922	9.3	17.6	28.1
1923–1927	12.4	8.0	30.2
All years	10.9	29.1	43.1

* Army enlisted male strength 31 Dec. 1943: 6,739,000.
† Separated, divorced, widower.
[a] Separations calculated from data in special tabulations of a representative sample, AG, Stat. & Acctg. Rep. Sample, CHR divided by strength in thousands from data in unpub. report, AG, MRBr., ETN-43.

Table 23 sets out the rates of separation for psychoneurosis of married and of single men within each of five separate age groups. Since these data apply to the early war period, when older married men and married men with families were not generally being inducted, the age distribution of the nearly one million married men in service at that time was practically identical with that of single men. In spite of this parallelism, married men were 2½ times more likely to be separated for psychoneurosis than single men. The highest separation rates were among the older married men. Men with broken marriages, though likely to be somewhat older than the average soldier, had a separation rate significantly greater than one would have expected on the basis of their age difference alone.

The significance of marital status in a man's emotional adjustment to military service can also be seen by considering those separated for psychosis, the rates for which are shown in Table 24. With some important variations, the experience of the psychotic group parallels that of the psychoneurotic group. In both, men with dependents had higher separation rates than those without dependents and men with broken marriages higher rates than either single or married men. On the other hand, the rate for married men separated for psychosis was relatively low. Very disturbed men frequently do not marry and if they do, their marriage is not likely to be permanent.

Table 24. RATE OF SEPARATIONS OF ENLISTED MALE PERSONNEL FROM THE ARMY FOR PSYCHOSIS, BY MARITAL AND DEPENDENCY STATUS, 1943 [a]

Marital and Dependency Status	*Rate of 1943 Separations per 1,000 Enlisted Male Strength on 31 Dec. 1943* *	
Single		7.7
With dependents	2.4	
Without dependents	11.2	
Married		7.0
Broken marriage †		17.9
With dependents	15.8	
Without dependents	20.3	

* Army enlisted male strength 31 Dec. 1943: 6,739,000.
† Separated, divorced, widower.
[a] Separations calculated from data in special tabulations of a representative sample, AG, Stat. & Acctg. Rep. Sample, CHR divided by strength in thousands from data in unpub. report, AG, MRBr., ETN-43.

EDUCATIONAL LEVEL

In an earlier chapter attention was directed to the loss which the nation suffered as a result of the more than 700,000 young men rejected for military service because they were illiterate or of such limited intelligence that the Armed Services could not readily transform them into effective servicemen. These men were not "failures" in the sense that they were tried and found wanting; the Services refused to take a chance on them in the first place. It was believed that a man who was below the minimum standard of intelligence or education would not be able to acquire the necessary military training and discipline. And those who were accepted were presumed to be able to absorb training and to serve effectively.

To adapt to a new situation a man must be able to learn new skills and during a war he must be able to learn them rapidly. In today's complex world ability to learn depends in considerable measure on what one has learned before—that is, on a man's educational achievement. Learning to be a soldier means more than learning how to fire a rifle. Soldiers have to learn how to live in a highly specialized society, the Army, with its many rules and regulations.

There is good reason, therefore, to investigate the relationship between educational background and separations for ineffectiveness. The fact that 122,000 were discharged for inaptitude is presumptive evidence that lack of education was a significant element in their ineffectiveness. But no such presumption can be made about the other categories of men prematurely separated for psychoneurosis, psychosis, or for unsuitable behavior. The relationship must be investigated. Table 25 sets out the distribution of men in major categories in terms of their level of education and in comparison with the educational level for the Army as a whole.

As we have already suggested, the inapt had conspicuously less educational background than the Army as a whole. Less than 1 out of 4 had gone beyond grammar school. The fact that 7 percent in this category were high-school graduates or had attended or graduated from college is largely a reflection of the special use that was made of this category to separate a few good soldiers who were unable to adjust to new assignments late in the war.

The undesirables also showed a much lower than average educational level, though not as low as that of the inapt. More than half never went beyond grammar school and only 1 out of 6 had graduated from high school or gone to college. In contrast, 2 out of 5 of the total enlisted strength were at least high-school graduates. There were undoubtedly a considerable number of soldiers who ran into difficulty because they were "dumb." General Elliot Cooke tells about a group of soldiers who ended up in the East Coast Processing Center at Camp Edwards, Massachusetts, the col-

Table 25. PERCENT DISTRIBUTION OF ENLISTED MALE PERSONNEL SEPARATED FROM THE ARMY FOR INEFFECTIVENESS, BY MAJOR REASON AND BY LEVEL OF EDUCATION, 1942–1945, AND A DISTRIBUTION OF ENLISTED MALE ACCESSIONS BY LEVEL OF EDUCATION

	MAJOR REASON FOR SEPARATION [a]					
LEVEL OF EDUCATION	*Psychoneurosis*	*Psychosis*	*Undesirable*	*Inaptitude*	*Total*	TOTAL ENLISTED MALE ACCESSIONS FISCAL 1941–1945 [b]
Grammar school or less	40	40	53	77	51	32
Some high school	31	30	31	16	27	28
High school grad.	20	20	11	5	15	26
College, including grad. and post-grad.	9	10	5	2	7	14
Total	100	100	100	100	100	100

[a] Calculated from data in special tabulations of a 5% sample, AG, Stat. & Acctg., CHR.
[b] Calculated from data in AG, Stat. & Acctg., unpub. worksheets.

lection point for "boat jumpers" on their way to Europe, who reported that their captain, wanting to lose them, gave them permission to go to town on the night their unit was embarking.[20]

Although a higher level of educational attainment was no safeguard against emotional disturbance in the Army, the lower the educational level, the higher the incidence of serious emotional difficulties. Several hypotheses suggest why this relationship exists. If education facilitates adjustment, especially to a new and complex organization such as the Army, men who are handicapped in learning are likely to become upset by their failure.

Inadequate education and emotional instability may have been reinforcing each other for a long time. A disturbed childhood is likely to be reflected in learning difficulties; children who do poorly in school are likely to develop emotional problems. Hence the problems of adjustment that many encountered in the Army were frequently a projection of long-established difficulties. Finally, it is possible that some men who were unable to adjust because of mental deficiency were incorrectly diagnosed as psychoneurotic by inexperienced or sympathetic medical officers.

Table 26. RATE OF SEPARATIONS OF ENLISTED MALE PERSONNEL FROM THE ARMY FOR INEFFECTIVENESS, BY MAJOR REASON AND BY LEVEL OF EDUCATION *

LEVEL OF EDUCATION	MAJOR REASON FOR SEPARATION [a]				
	Psychoneurosis	*Psychosis*	*Undesirable*	*Inaptitude*	*Total*
Grammar school or less	32.8	7.1	6.2	30.0	76.1
More than grammar school	22.8	4.9	2.6	4.2	34.5
Some high school	28.9	5.9	4.2	7.1	46.1
High school grad.	19.9	4.2	1.6	2.3	28.0
College, including grad. and postgrad.	16.1	4.1	1.4	1.8	23.4

* Rate of 1942–1945 separations for ineffectiveness per 1,000 fiscal 1941–1945 accessions.

[a] Separations per calendar year from special tabulation of a 5% sample, AG, Stat. & Acctg., CHR, divided by accessions per fiscal year from AG, Stat. & Acctg., unpub. worksheets.

The important relationship between education and ineffective performance can be seen even more clearly in Table 26, which sets out the separation rates per 1,000 accessions for each major discharge category by educational level.

From Table 25 we learned that approximately half of all ineffective soldiers had no more than a grammar-school education, whereas less than a third of the total Army's enlisted strength was at this same low level. The present table emphasizes the marked differences in the rates of ineffectiveness between those with less and those with more than a grammar-school education. This table makes it clear that the poorly educated man was much more likely to become ineffective and to be prematurely separated than the average soldier. The more education a man had, the better was his chance to escape breakdown. For the two psychiatric categories, psychoneurotics and psychotics, the poorly educated had a separation rate almost 1½ times that of the better educated; among the undesirables the poorly educated had a rate over twice that of the better educated; and as one could anticipate, in the case of the inapt, the poorly educated had a separation rate 7 times as great as the better educated and 13 times as great as high school graduates.

Unfortunately, the data available from Army tabulations do not permit refinements within the category "grammar school or less," which makes it impossible to ascertain what the rates were for those with the least education, those with less than four years of schooling. It is likely that the same differentiation found to exist in the available data between the less and better educated would be discernible among those with more or less grammar-school education, since there seems to be a well-defined progression of the rate of ineffectiveness from the lowest educational level.

To ascertain that important differences found to exist on the national level were not due to disproportionate numbers of cases from a particular region, the data were examined accordingly. The relationships found to exist on the national level held within each region and for each diagnostic category. In other words, it did not matter from what part of the country a man came: if he was poorly educated, he was more likely to prove ineffective and be prematurely separated than a man with more education.

In spite of the roughness of these measures, which are the only ones available, it is clear that lack of adequate educational background contributed significantly to the Army's manpower problem in World War II. The difficulties encountered are underscored when one recalls that substantial numbers had to be rejected for service—over 700,000—and that among those inducted 300,000 received additional training in the Special Training Units set up in mid-1943.

RACE

The last demographic factor which we will consider is that of race. * In 1940 the total Negro male population was just over 9.5 percent of the total U.S. male population. During the war the

Table 27. PERCENT DISTRIBUTION OF ENLISTED MALE PERSONNEL SEPARATED FROM THE ARMY FOR INEFFECTIVENESS, BY MAJOR REASON AND BY RACE, 1942–1945 [a]

RACE	MAJOR REASON FOR SEPARATION: *Psychoneurosis*	*Psychosis*	*Undesirable*	*Inaptitude*	TOTAL
DISTRIBUTION BY RACE					
Negro	9	10	27	40	17
White	91	90	73	60	83
Total	100	100	100	100	100
DISTRIBUTION BY MAJOR REASON FOR SEPARATION					
Negro	28	7	12	53	100
White	60	13	7	20	100

[a] Calculated from data in special tabulations of a 5% sample, AG, Stat. & Acctg., CHR.

Army accepted Negroes for enlistment or induction in numbers almost identically proportionate to their ratio in the population. In this process many more Negroes than whites were examined—the respective rejection rates were 47 percent and 27 percent, which

* Throughout this book the term "Negro" refers strictly to the negroid race. The term "white," on the other hand, refers to all races other than negroid, e.g. white, Indian, Japanese, Chinese, Asiatic Indians, etc. This results from the practice of the Armed Forces and the Selective Service System in publishing their data on a Negro—Nonnegro racial basis. The U.S. Census, however, limits the term "white" to the Caucasian race. Therefore, for the few references to Census data the terms "white (white only)" and "nonwhite" will be used.

These racial groupings are essentially comparable for the purposes of this book due to the dominance of the white and negroid races. No state has more than 4% of its total population made up of races other than white or negroid except the states of Arizona and New Mexico which have 9.2% and 6.3% respectively; 36 states have less than 1% of their total population composed of races other than white or negroid.

reflected primarily the much higher proportion of Negroes who were unable to pass the educational screen. Almost one third of all Negroes were rejected essentially on educational grounds while the corresponding figure for whites was under 10 percent. Despite the heavy screening out of poorly educated Negroes, the separation rate for ineffectiveness during 1942–1945 among Negroes accepted for duty in the Army was 86 per 1,000 accessions during 1941–1945 or more than double the white rate of 40 per 1,000.

As Table 27 shows, Negroes were not separated within the major discharge categories in the same proportions as whites.

Table 28. PERCENT DISTRIBUTION OF MALES AGED 18–34, BY LEVEL OF EDUCATION AND BY RACE, 1940[a]

RACE	LEVEL OF EDUCATION IN PERCENT: *Eight Grades or Less*	*Some High School*	*High School Grad.*	*College, Including Grad. & Post-Grad.*	*Unknown*	*Total*
Non-white	74	14	7	3	2	100
White (white only)	36	24	25	14	1	100

[a] Calculated from data in U.S. Census, 1940, Vol. IV.

Negroes were markedly overrepresented among the inapt and among the undesirables; in the two psychiatric categories they were, however, represented proportionately to whites. The extent to which the two racial groups differed can be seen in the following comparison: 60 percent of all white ineffectives were psychoneurotic; 53 percent of all Negro ineffectives were inapt.

Since the poorly educated predominated among those separated for inaptitude, it is not surprising, considering the comparatively low level of education among Negroes, to find so many in this category.

Table 28 shows that three-fourths of all nonwhites liable for military service during World War II had only a grammar-school education or less—compared to one-third of the whites (white only). Although there are no comprehensive data available on Army accessions by race and education, a personnel survey in mid-1944 revealed that the proportion of Negro enlisted men with only a grammar-school education was twice that of white soldiers—54 percent compared to 26 percent.

Handicapped as they were by insufficient education, Negro soldiers were further handicapped by the fact that so many had been born and raised in the southeastern part of the United States where they had attended segregated schools, were limited occupationally largely to farm or menial labor, and lived their lives in a

Table 29. MINIMAL EDUCATIONAL ACHIEVEMENT OF MALES AGED 18–34, BY RACE, SOUTHEAST AND REMAINDER OF U. S., 1940 [a]

RACE AND REGION	PERCENT HAVING COMPLETED *3 Grades or Less*	*6 Grades or Less*	*8 Grades or Less*
Whites (white only)			
Continental U.S. other than the Southeast	2	7	33
Southeast U.S.*	6	26	50
Non-whites			
Continental U.S. other than the Southeast	8	30	58
Southeast U.S.*	28	70	86

* Ala., Ark., Fla., Ga., Ky., La., Miss., N.C., S.C., Tenn., and Va.
[a] Calculated from data in U.S. Census, 1940, Vol. IV.

rigid culture which constantly emphasized and reinforced their inferior status. The extent to which the Southeast in 1940 was a disadvantageous region for both white and Negro is brought out in Table 29.

These figures would lead us to anticipate that since separation for inaptitude was found to be so largely a function of poor educational achievement, Negroes from the Southeast would have a much higher discharge rate than those from other regions. This is verified by Table 30.

These gross comparisons, while revealing the educational disadvantages of the Negro, hide the extent of his handicap. As Table

29 made clear, about one third of the Southern Negroes with no more than a grammar-school education had not gone beyond the third grade, while in the case of whites in other regions this was true of only about 5 percent of those who had only a grammar-school education. Moreover, as we have shown in an earlier study [21] the quality of education received by the Southern Negro was notably inferior. The effects of these handicaps are revealed in Table 31 by the distribution of scores received on the Army General

Table 30. RATE OF SEPARATIONS OF ENLISTED MALE PERSONNEL FROM THE ARMY FOR INAPTITUDE, BY RACE, SOUTHEAST AND REMAINDER OF U.S., WORLD WAR II [a]

Race and Region	*Rate of Separations for Inaptitude (1942–1945) per 1,000 Accessions (Nov. 1940–June 1945)*
White	
Continental U.S. other than the Southeast	7
Southeast U.S.*	20
Negro	
Continental U.S. other than the Southeast	36
Southeast U.S.*	52

* Ala., Ark., Fla., Ga., Ky., La., Miss., N.C., S.C., Tenn., and Va.

[a] Separations from special tabulations of 5% sample, AG, Stat. & Acctg., CHR, divided by an estimate of accessions in thousands based on data in *Strength of Army*, STM-30; AG, MRBr., XTQ-13; and SSS, Monograph 10, Vol. II, table 55, pp. 113–14.

Classification Test by Negro and white soldiers on active duty in mid-1944 and early 1945, a period subsequent to the large-scale separations of ineffective soldiers. It should be recalled that the test was designed to measure a man's ability to learn as well as his general adaptability for military service.

The striking finding is that 3 out of every 4 Negroes scored in groups below average in learning ability, while this was true of only slightly more than 1 out of every 4 white soldiers. This is a much greater variation than one could expect from differences in educational achievement alone.

The markedly higher ineffective rate among Negro soldiers—about twice that of white soldiers—was largely, but by no means exclusively, the result of their inferior educational background. Men who grow up in a segregated world which considers them inferior from the day of their birth cannot develop normally. Recognizing early that their opportunities are severely restricted, their ambition is likely to be stunted. Treated by many whites as only a grade or two above an African native, they see no point in

Table 31. PERCENT DISTRIBUTION OF ARMY ENLISTED MALE PERSONNEL, BY RACE AND AGCT CLASS, 30 JUNE 1944 AND 31 MARCH 1945

	30 JUNE 1944 [a]		31 MARCH 1945 [b]	
AGCT CLASS	*Negro*	*White*	*Negro*	*White*
I	1	6	1	6
II	5	31	6	32
III	12	31	14	32
IV	42	23	45	23
V	31	4	28	3
Unknown	9	5	6	4
Total	100	100	100	100

[a] Calculated from data in AG, MRBr., ETN-104.
[b] Stouffer, *et al.*, *The American Soldier*, I, 492. Data based on a 2% sample of the Army conducted by the office of the Adjutant General in March 1945.

attempting to live up to the standards of the white community. Staying out of trouble, even if one must feign "dumbness," appears to be more rewarding than seeking to win the respect and admiration of men who deny that you are, or ever can be, their equal. To make matters worse, the Northern Negro who grew up and lived in a society that was at least legally desegregated was subjected in the Army to the full weight of segregation not only during his duty hours but also—since most training camps were located in the South—in his off-duty hours.

While many Negroes saw military service as an opportunity to prove their individual worth and to help raise the prestige of their group, thereby striking a blow against segregation, many others failed to do their best. They could not free themselves from the crippling experiences which had been theirs from earliest childhood— "as a man is treated, so he is likely to respond." The Army in turn was greatly handicapped in making effective use of Negro manpower. Segregation interfered with the optimal training and assignment of Negroes with high potential; it led to a serious imbalance of skills and aptitudes in Negro divisions; and it was reflected in serious weaknesses in the leadership of Negro units.

In the face of the handicaps which they brought with them into the Army and the barriers which they encountered once they were in uniform, the remarkable finding is that the vast majority of Negroes performed satisfactorily, not that they accounted for a disproportionate number of ineffectives.

Chapter Eight: SITUATIONAL STRESS

THE PRECEDING analysis has sought to correct certain misconceptions about why so many men proved ineffective in discharging their responsibilities during World War II. We have seen that these men—both those who were not selected for service and those who after being selected were unable to perform effectively as soldiers—were not a homogeneous group. Among those rejected for military service were the seriously deranged or mentally deficient men who had sometimes spent many years in a mental hospital or who had been unable to learn to read and write. At the opposite extreme were some individuals who had served on active duty with distinction for two or three years, who had been promoted to the top enlisted ranks, and whose combat records were so distinguished that they had received medals or commendations. Between these two extremes were the largest number of men, and their performance varied from poor to adequate or good, but all of them developed defects before the end of hostilities which led the Army to separate them.

In our attempt to discover the reasons why so many men proved ineffective, we considered initially the standards which the Army used during World War II for both the selection of soldiers and the separation of ineffectives. This review underlined the significant role of manpower policy. When, as in early 1943, the Army decided to send back to civilian life all men with minor defects, thousands—in fact, hundreds of thousands—were suddenly made "ineffective" by the directive. Had the separation criteria remained unchanged, many of these men would have served out the war. Thus ineffectiveness cannot be considered only in terms of personal limitations and shortcomings. It may and frequently does reflect operational decisions.

The second determinant of performance with which we have been concerned is the individual himself. The preceding chapter has analyzed some of the factors likely to contribute to a man's ineffectiveness. No matter what personnel policy an organization pursues, it will have to separate men who become severely disturbed, especially if they do not respond readily to treatment. When men are given firearms and are trained for combat, it is that much more important to protect the individual and the group from the aggressive and disruptive behavior that sometimes accompanies mental illness.

Included in the group who had to be discharged for personal failings were a considerable number who never would have been accepted in the first place had they been properly screened. As soon as their deficiencies were noted, which was usually quite early after induction, they were forthwith separated.

In addition to organizational policy and the personal qualities of individuals a third determinant significantly influences effective performance—that is the amount of stress to which people are subjected. The Army situation was unique in this regard. From the day of his induction until his discharge every man had to face the likelihood that he would be exposed to danger and the consequent possibility of being wounded or killed. This threat continued on top of the other pressures which he might face: being assigned to a unit with an unpleasant and punishing sergeant, being forced to undergo rigorous training on a time schedule so compressed that until his body hardened he was a bundle of aches and pains, having to live in an outpost in unfinished barracks with little protection from the heat or cold. All of these and many more stresses were part and parcel of an Army at war. It is a lasting testimonial to the flexibility of young men that the vast majority were able to adjust. Their "griping" apparently gave them sufficient release. But no soldier ever becomes acclimated to war. No matter how brave he is, no matter how deeply he believes in the righteousness of his country's aims, the passage of every day wears thinner his protective armor so that the time may come when he can no longer face the morrow.

Thus, our framework for the study of ineffectiveness must provide for the role of personnel policy and the characteristics of the individual and also for the orders of situational stress. There is an old adage that misfortune hardens a man and there is truth in it. Challenge is a spur. But misfortune can overwhelm a man—and it frequently does.

There is no simple index of stress that will indicate what an individual soldier experienced during his military service, or the great range of stress faced by different soldiers. Ignoring for the moment the personality differences which made it relatively easy for one man to cope with barracks life while the next found it difficult to meet its demands, we will note the marked objective differences in the strain and danger of different assignments. It was very much a matter of luck whether a man inducted into the Army would eventually find himself in situations of great or only moderate stress. Among the earliest troops to leave the United States for the Pacific were two contingents, one of which found itself in Guadalcanal while the other occupied Christmas Island. Men in the former had to fight to the last ounce of their strength; men in the latter never heard a shot fired. But the next step in the island-hopping campaign might have reversed the positions of the two groups.

Differences in situational stress cannot be easily determined from the available gross data. In fact, even the extensive use of case materials on which the companion volumes are based does not permit us to determine accurately the differential orders of stress that soldiers experienced. While the case studies indicate that one man was in active combat for 60 days while another was in the line for only 16 days, it is impossible to reconstruct the intensity of the fighting that each encountered. And even if a rough estimate of the fighting could be made, it would not be possible to know whether one man was a member of a company which had excellent officers while the other had only a green lieutenant and a weak sergeant on whom to lean. Thus the concept of stress turns out to be more complex than is generally assumed and a precise use of it would have to take account of at least three aspects: differences in quality, in intensity, and in duration. Since our case materials cannot capture the many ramifications of this factor, the mass data must be an even less satisfactory basis for assessing the role of situational stress. Yet a first approximation can be ventured.

One key to the study of the stress a soldier encountered is the nature of his assignments. But such an analysis here is restricted by the fact that a soldier was likely to have had a series of assignments during the course of his military service, and only his last would be noted on his separation card. One soldier might be transferred from one branch to another because he possessed special skills. And another might be transferred because he had no skills and his company commander attempted to unload him in the hope of gaining a better replacement. Another complication from the point of view of analysis derives from the fact that many men when separated had no branch assignment. In the majority of such cases the men had not been in the Army long enough to have completed their processing and initial training. But there were others who for reasons of illness or on other grounds were separated from their regular units and were in a pool without a branch assignment prior to being discharged.

Despite these many limitations, the data on assignments can be used as a rough criterion of stress. Soldiers assigned to the Ground Forces were likely to be in combat and to have been subjected to a more strenuous training program. Those assigned to service units were more likely to serve behind the lines and while occasionally exposed to a bombing raid or enemy breakthrough were less exposed to injury or death. As a matter of fact fatalities in the Arms were ten times those in the Services and twelve times as many were wounded in the Arms as in the Services. And most of the serious casualties in Service troops were among the medical aid men and the combat engineers. In the Air Corps the vast majority of enlisted men were in relatively safe assignments on the ground while the minority who flew had among the most demanding and dangerous of all assignments. In addition to these differences in branch assignments which can be roughly correlated with differences in exposure to combat and can be used as a crude criterion of stress, some assignments such as the Aleutians, Iceland, and isolated islands in the Pacific were usually safe as far as direct contact with

Table 32. PERCENT DISTRIBUTION OF ENLISTED MALE PERSONNEL SEPARATED FROM THE ARMY FOR INEFFECTIVENESS, BY MAJOR REASON AND BY BRANCH ASSIGNMENT, 1942–1945, AND AN ESTIMATED ASSIGNMENT DISTRIBUTION OF MEAN ENLISTED MALE STRENGTH

	MAJOR REASON FOR SEPARATION [a]					
MAJOR BRANCH ASSIGNMENT	*Psychoneurosis*	*Psychosis*	*Undesirable*	*Inaptitude*	*Total*	MEAN ENLISTED MALE STRENGTH [b]
Ground Arms	46	38	32	35	34	36
Services	34	40	43	28	41	38
Air Corps	16	17	18	10	15	22
No branch assignment or detached list	4	5	7	27	10	4
Total	100	100	100	100	100	100

[a] Calculated from data in special tabulations of a 5% sample, AG, Stat. & Acctg., CHR.

[b] Based on mean of Branch strengths as of March 1942, 1943, 1944, and 1945. Ground Arms and Services: derived from Total Strength in *Strength of Army*, STM-30, less Air Corps strength, resulting figure apportioned between Ground Arms and Services according to personnel surveys in Stouffer, *et al.*, *The American Soldier*, I, 494; Air Corps: *Army Air Forces Stat. Digest*, p. 20.

the enemy was concerned, yet they proved exceedingly onerous to many men who could not stand the climate, the isolation, or the boredom. More than one soldier walked out of his hut during one of the long winter days in Alaska to stretch his legs, never to return, the victim of a sudden blizzard.

Table 32 presents the percentage distribution of Army ineffectives by major discharge categories by branch of service. The data refer to the last assignment of the soldier prior to discharge.

Several interesting generalizations are suggested by the foregoing. The Air Corps had a lower percentage of ineffective soldiers both in total and in each of the major discharge categories than was true of the Services or the Arms. Proportionately more separations for ineffectiveness occurred in the Arms than in the Services. Since divisions leaving for overseas cast off men whom they did not want and many were released to civilian life after a period of time with a service unit, the percentage that proved ineffective in the Arms was actually larger than is shown in the table. Most of those without a branch assignment separated for inaptitude were probably men who failed early in training.

The proportions separated for different reasons from the major branches also prove revealing. A high proportion of the psychoneurotics were separated from the Arms. Since we know from earlier analysis that about 3 out of every 5 psychoneurotics saw overseas service, this higher proportion probably reflects the fact that more men in the Arms were exposed to the rigors of combat. There are many special studies based on the experience of World War II which show a substantial increase in incidence of psychoneurotic breakdown with the prolongation and intensification of combat.[22] As might have been expected, the distribution of soldiers who had to be separated for psychosis parallels, except in the case of the Air Corps, the distribution of enlisted strength among the major branches since psychosis is seldom induced primarily by external stress.

Those separated as undesirable were slightly overrepresented in the Services and underrepresented in the Arms, reflecting in large measure the weeding-out process referred to earlier that the combat units engaged in prior to embarkation. It must be recalled that only 1 in 6 of the men who were separated as undesirable ever got overseas. Some men with serious behavior problems did well as long as the fighting was on, but ran into trouble once it was over. Shortly after the war ended one could find in the stockades in the Pacific and in Europe men who had committed the most serious offenses, many of whom had performed very well during the many grueling months of combat.

A disproportionately high percentage of those separated for inaptitude had no branch assignment. It should be recalled in this connection that 41 percent of all those discharged for inaptitude had less than six months service; only 1 out of 12 ever got overseas. This suggests that most of these men were unable to make even an initial adjustment to the Army. The fact that proportionately more of those reported as inapt had been assigned to the Arms than to the Services is easy to understand in view of the much tougher training cycle of the combat units and the fact that certain service units such as quartermaster and transportation were able to provide more assignments for soldiers of limited capacity. Once again the Air Corps is conspicuous: with 22 percent of the enlisted strength, it was responsible for only 10 percent of the soldiers who had to be separated as inapt.

Although the data do not permit the development of clear-cut separation rates because of the lack of information about interbranch transfers, an approximation can be ventured which will at least suggest the comparative experience of the major branches.

Table 33 reinforces the conclusions which have been derived from the analysis of the gross data. Once again, the Air Corps reveals a much more favorable experience with the ineffective soldier than either the Arms or the Services. This is particularly true of two largest discharge categories—psychoneurosis and the inapt.

Table 33. ESTIMATED RATE OF SEPARATIONS (PER 1,000) OF ENLISTED MALE PERSONNEL FROM THE ARMY FOR INEFFECTIVENESS, BY MAJOR REASON AND BY BRANCH ASSIGNMENT, 1942–1945 [a]

MAJOR BRANCH ASSIGNMENT	MAJOR REASON FOR SEPARATION			
	Psychoneurosis	*Psychosis*	*Undesirable*	*Inaptitude*
Ground Arms	32	6	3	12
Services	23	6	4	9
Air Corps	19	4	3	6

[a] Separations calculated from data in special tabulations of a 5% sample, AG, Stat. and Acctg., CHR, divided by an estimate of total enlisted male personnel in thousands serving in each major Branch (from data in *Strength of Army*, STM-30, pp. 52, 84, and 85) distributed on basis of Branch of assignment percentages derived from Table 32.

How can one explain this consistently better record of the Air Corps? Some observers argue that the Air Corps had many clearcut advantages—it had the best morale because it succeeded in convincing itself and the public as well that victory in the war depended on it. Being the youngest of the branches and having grown very rapidly, it was less encrusted with customs and traditions which many citizen soldiers found unduly burdensome. Its rapid expansion resulted in rapid promotions—an important reinforcement of morale. Although men who flew had a high mortality, the vast majority of the Air Corps enlisted personnel had little to fear by way of injury or death. It was a relatively safe service. Each of these explanations has merit and together they carry much weight in explaining why the rates for ineffectiveness in the Air Corps were considerably below those in other branches.

But there is more to the story. We noted in an earlier chapter that the Air Corps had secured a much higher cut of manpower in terms of educational background and that to a lesser degree the Services had the edge over the Arms. Since we found earlier that the lower a man's educational background, the more likely that he would become ineffective, the differences that have just been noted between the branches cannot be explained solely by differences in situational stress. They also reflect differences in the quality of men assigned to the several branches.

Table 34 summarizes the distribution among the branches in 1943 when over 2½ million men were processed and assigned.

Table 34. PERCENT DISTRIBUTION OF ENLISTED MEN INDUCTED INTO THE ARMY AND ASSIGNED DURING 1943, BY AGCT CLASS AND BY MAJOR BRANCH ASSIGNMENT

MAJOR BRANCH ASSIGNMENT	AGCT CLASS [a] I & II	III	IV & V	TOTAL
Ground Arms	29.7	33.4	36.9	100.0
Services	36.5	28.5	35.0	100.0
Air Corps	41.8	31.3	26.9	100.0

[a] Table 9.

Such a distribution must have exercised a considerable influence on the branches' later experience with ineffectiveness. The Air Corps had a marked advantage over the Arms and Services in two regards: it received a higher proportion of men in the top mental grades and in turn it received a considerably smaller proportion of those with limited capacity. The Services had the edge over the Arms in one respect: they had a higher proportion of able men who could more readily assume positions of responsibility and leadership. Since ineffective performance is frequently a composite result of a man's personal handicaps and his failure to receive support when he needs it, the disadvantage under which the Arms had to operate can be seen. They had the highest percentage of personnel in the lowest mental groups, and they had the smallest number of people capable of assuming leadership positions.

The foregoing analysis shows that the differential experience of the branches with ineffectiveness which might be interpreted as reflecting varying degrees of stress must be modified at least to the extent of recognizing that the three major branches did not have soldiers who were equally immune or prone to breakdown. The Air Corps was in the most favored position, the Services the next, and the Arms was in the least favored. There is something almost paradoxical that the men assigned to the Arms, who were most likely to encounter the severest stress, were the very ones whose lack of various personal qualifications made them most prone to break down.

The study of assignments was undertaken to illustrate that men of equal strength, subject to the same personnel policies, will not respond alike if they are subjected to vastly differing orders of stress. One may collapse while the other will be able to perform at a consistently high level. Or to make the same point even more forcibly: Some men were inducted even though it was recognized that their emotional stability and intellectual competence were at best marginal. Yet many received assignments with which they could cope and if lucky enough to serve under good officers were able to meet the demands placed on them. Others, who were their superiors in every respect, may have been poorly assigned or poorly led with the result that they reached a point where they could no longer serve effectively.

In the companion volumes special attention is devoted to the way in which stresses in the environment contributed to breakdown. But it may be helpful at this point to illustrate briefly how differently two men inducted on the same day may have fared. One may have been sent to a combat unit far advanced in its training where maximum pressure was being exerted on the men so that the unit could be sent overseas, where no provision was made to help the slow learners, and where no tolerance was shown the man who slowed down the group. The other inductee may have been sent to a quartermaster or medical replacement training center where there was no special pressure of time, where formal provisions had been made to assist slow learners, and where the slow and the inapt were tolerated.

A second major difference might have related to their duty assignment. One might have been directly related to the man's former work, such as if a laboratory technician in civilian life were assigned to a similar job in an Army hospital. But the second might have been the assignment of a farm boy as a cook. More significant was whether a man's job was dangerous, such as a machine gunner, or relatively safe, such as a clerk.

Still another difference would result from where a man was stationed. A Negro born in the North, who was sent for training to Mississippi, encountered difficulties which he would have escaped if he had been sent to Wisconsin. Some men spent the war years assigned to a unit in the Caribbean while others fought in North Africa, Sicily, and France. Even men who were assigned to combat units were exposed to quite different orders of stress. To be pinned down at Anzio for many weeks and then to fight one's way to Rome was a different experience from being a member of the Ninth Army which for the most part engaged the enemy only when it was able to catch up with him during his retreat across France and Germany.

A more subtle but still important difference was in the type of leadership which soldiers encountered. The senior noncommissioned officer of one unit may have been a tower of strength who welded his troops into a force with high morale, while another, insecure in his own position, was a martinet insisting on blind conformity to the rules and being especially hard on men who in civilian life had held good jobs and of whom he was envious.

It is not possible to set out the entire range of circumstances that might significantly affect the order of stress to which soldiers were exposed. One soldier received supportive letters from home; another heard nothing from his wife for many weeks and then learned from a short note that she was planning to divorce him. Some soldiers had the good fortune to be stationed in Florida during the winter months both for their basic and advanced training. Others had to take their basic training in Mississippi during the summer months and advanced training in northern New York in the winter. Some men were stationed in overseas bases where they could have no effective relations with the native population and where there were very few amenities on the base. Others spent most of the war years in England.

For the outsider the Army was a specific environment, war a unique order of stress. But from the viewpoint of the more than 10 million men who served in the Army this was not so. As they saw it, there were many different "armies" and many different "wars." Some soldiers were better off than they had been in civilian life, and others reached a point of exhaustion where they no longer feared death. No study of ineffective behavior can ignore the impact of these vastly different orders of stress on men's performance.

Chapter Nine: SCREENING: EXPECTATIONS AND RESULTS

AN ORGANIZATION is always more effective if it attracts and holds a larger number of capable people. The Civil Service Commission is constantly seeking ways of strengthening the incentives and rewards for government personnel; the Armed Services have recently received additional funds from the Congress to provide extra compensation for enlisted men who possess special skills so that they will remain in the services; business is spending ever larger sums on its personnel programs, particularly its executive training programs, in order to develop stronger leadership. Schools and colleges are attempting to encourage a larger number of talented people to prepare for and enter teaching. Each sector is looking to improve its manpower resources and thereby raise its efficiency.

Improved selection and improved training and utilization of personnel are the keystones to a more efficient manpower program. At the beginning of mobilization in 1940 the Armed Services sought to avoid a large number of potential manpower difficulties by rejecting for service men who, they felt, could not be readily converted into effective soldiers. Since time was at a premium the Armed Services placed great stress on the screening process. Selection became the anchor of military manpower policy and continued to be crucial throughout World War II.

However, since the Army alone had to release prematurely more than half a million men because of a mental or emotional disability and since the total separated prematurely from the Armed Forces for these causes approximated three quarters of a million, it is clear that the expectations about the efficacy of screening were not realized. This large gap between the expectations and the results of the screening process suggests the desirability of reviewing critically the theory and practice of personnel selection for the Armed Forces during World War II.

Since, as we have noted, screening remains a cornerstone of personnel policy in most large organizations, civilian as well as military, a critical evaluation of the largest personnel screening operation in the history of the United States should prove constructive. Moreover, before entering upon a detailed appraisal of the selection experience of the Army in World War II we will examine the major parallels and differences in the civilian and the military sectors.

Typically, an employer, even a large employer, does not increase his work force very rapidly within a short period of time. Only when a company opens a new plant, or when it starts production of a new line does it expand its work force significantly. But even then the differences between civilian industry and the Armed Services are substantial. In the civilian arena, there are usually many men with skill and experience who are looking for a better job. They seek out the employer who is expanding. Even those with little skill or experience must also take the initiative and present themselves at the hiring gate.

During the war, some men with experience and skill volunteered for military service, but the number was not large, particularly among enlisted personnel. A high proportion of those who enlisted did so to beat the draft and thereby to improve their choice of assignment. For the most part the Armed Services got their manpower through compulsion. Men were notified to appear for examination to determine their eligibility for service. This is the most striking difference between civilian and military experience. The civilian job-seeker looks to improve his circumstances; the man who dons a uniform must reconcile himself to following Army orders.

Another difference between the two sectors lies in the selection process. When a civilian employer considers a new man for a job, his major question is whether the prospective employee can handle the job. Many men are hired after only a brief interview and an inspection of their record. Others have to undergo a physical examination and still others may be asked to take a series of aptitude tests. In general, a civilian selection technique is geared to ascertain whether a man can function in a specific job.

The Armed Services were faced by much more difficult considerations in deciding whether a selectee should be accepted or rejected. The war could be won only on the battlefield and the Army therefore had to assess whether a man's physical condition and stamina would enable him to keep the pace of the training schedule and later on withstand the stresses and strains of combat. The Army also believed that it had to consider the man's emotional stability. Could he face the threat of injury or death without buckling under the strain?

Time pressed the Armed Services. The war was under way. It had to be won as quickly as possible. It would be too costly to induct a man, train him for a year or more, send him overseas, and then discover that he could not fight. If screening could avoid this wasteful expenditure of time and effort, it had everything to commend it, even if some men who might have made the grade were lost to the Army in the process. As long as the manpower supply was adequate the Armed Services had every reason to reject those who appeared to be bad risks.

The interest of the Armed Services in developing an effective screening mechanism was heightened by their recollection of the experience in 1918 when sizable numbers of the American Expeditionary Forces broke down in battle. They hoped, if humanly possible, to prevent a repetition of this experience. The advances made in the use of psychological testing since the end of World War I encouraged many officers to believe that techniques had been developed which would permit distinguishing the stable from the unstable, the bright from the dull, the well motivated from the unmotivated.

What should an ideal screening mechanism accomplish? It should enable the organization to accept those who will succeed in their assignments and to reject those who would fail. The assumption underlying any screening procedure is that by properly assessing an individual's strengths and weaknesses it is possible to determine whether he will be able to meet a specific performance test.

Reliance on screening presupposes that it is possible to assess the qualities of an individual at the time of the examination and also to predict how he will respond to future situations. Effective screening, then, requires first the establishing of criteria to differentiate between those who possess the necessary qualities from those who do not and, secondly, the evaluation of the group to be screened in terms of these criteria.

In some instances it is relatively easy to decide upon a criterion and to carry through the evaluation; frequently one or both present major hurdles. Enough was known about psychosis for the Armed Services to decide that they wanted to exclude all individuals with a history of psychotic behavior. Evaluation for this condition was more difficult, since many men with such a history whose disability was in remission at the time of their examination hid the fact of their prior hospitalization. And with the short time at his disposal even an experienced psychiatrist might be unable to find any signs to alert him to the man's condition.

The Armed Services encountered many more difficulties in establishing a criterion for intellectual ability which would enable them to differentiate between selectees who could absorb training and meet their duty assignments from those who were likely to fail. Not until late in the war did the Army succeed in developing a test which could discriminate fairly well between a man's educational background and his ability to learn and apply what he had been taught. And the Army never did succeed in developing psychological and psychiatric criteria that would reliably differentiate among selectees as to their future emotional stability.

Screening for military service had to result in one of two decisions: a man had to be either accepted or rejected. The draft-eligible group constituted a continuum along which men could be graded from the most to the least qualified with respect to each major characteristic. The screening of World War II was handicapped because, among other reasons, the Armed Services had to determine its several criteria on the basis of trial and error since it had no definite knowledge of the distribution of these characteristics among the eligible population.

A first test of the effectiveness of screening in World War II has already been made: if the objective of screening was to prevent the premature separation of large numbers of soldiers, sailors, and marines—as indeed it was—then the discharge of three quarters of a million men while the war was still under way is unequivocal proof of its shortcomings. Were these premature separations, however, the result of the inadequacy of the screen, or were they due to other factors? No direct answer can be given. But an indirect answer can be developed by exploring the relationship between those rejected and separated. Higher standards for selection, resulting in greater rejections, should be reflected in lower separations. If they did not, there would be little justification for assuming the heavy costs involved in screening out larger numbers.

A first means of testing this hypothesis—that higher selection standards result in lower separation rates—is to compare the manpower screening experiences of World Wars I and II, since in the latter war higher selection standards were used. Although the two world wars were in some ways comparable, we must first note the major differences between the two.

The peak strength in World War II was more than double that of World War I; World War II lasted for five years (from the onset of mobilization in 1940) in contrast to one and a half years for World War I; the educational level of the nation had been raised significantly in the interim; psychiatry and psychology had made striking advances which were reflected in improvements in diagnosis and therapy; and military equipment had become considerably more complex to use and maintain.

With these qualifications in mind, we can turn to the comparative data which are summarized in Table 35.

Table 35. RESULTS OF PHYSICAL EXAMINATIONS GIVEN MEN FOR MILITARY SERVICE, WORLD WAR I AND WORLD WAR II, SHOWING NUMBER OF MEN REJECTED, BY MAJOR REASON

Action and Reason for Rejection	*World War I* *	*World War II* [d] †
Examined	5,000,000 [a]	18,000,000
Rejected—all reasons	821,000 [a]	5,250,000
Physical defect	734,000 [b]	3,477,000
Emotional disorder	25,000 [c]	970,000
Mental or educational deficiency	43,000 [c]	716,000
Nonmedical ‡	19,000 [a]	87,000
INDICES OF CHANGE *World War I = 100*		
Examined	100	360
Rejected—all reasons	100	640
Physical defect	100	470
Emotional disorder	100	3,880
Mental or educational deficiency	100	1,670
Nonmedical ‡	100	460

* Primarily men aged 19–36 in 1918. † Men aged 18–37 as of 1 August 1945.
‡ Comprised of all men rejected on essentially moral grounds.
[a] Examined: composed of all men inducted, enlisted, rejected, or deferred as morally unfit. PMG, *Second Report*, tables 61 and 79, pp. 168 and 223; Britten and Perrott, *PHR*, LVI, No. 2.
[b] Rejected: All Reasons less Emotional Disorder, Mental or Educational Deficiency, and Non-Medical.
[c] Based on data in Love and Davenport, *Defects*, table IV, pp. 424–28.
[d] Tables 7 and 8.
Note: Figures for World War I comprise data given for men rejected by local boards (Vg.) plus men rejected at camp from among the "second million" (P2) expanded to all men rejected at camp by use of the expansion factor derived by Britten and Perrott, *PHR*, table 9, pp. 60–61.

This table indicates that during World War I a considerable number of the men examined were rejected—about 1 out of 6—primarily for reasons of physical disability. Only slightly more than

1 out of 75 was rejected because he was judged to be mentally deficient or emotionally unstable.

The difference in screening results in the two wars can be seen in the different rejection rates which are summarized in Table 36.

The first and most striking finding is the fact that the rejection rate in World War II was 80 percent above that of World War I. Differences between the two were least marked in rejections for physical defects, where the rate for World War II was only about one third higher. But this relatively modest increase must be evaluated in terms of the substantial improvement in the health of the nation during the intervening period. The higher rejection rate reflected either a raising of the criteria or more careful evaluation of selectees or, as is most likely, a combination of both.

Table 36. RATE OF REJECTIONS FOR MILITARY SERVICE, BY MAJOR REASON, WORLD WAR I AND WORLD WAR II

REASON FOR REJECTION	RATE OF REJECTIONS PER 1,000 MEN EXAMINED [a]	
	World War I *	*World War II* †
All reasons	164	292
Physical defect	146	193
Emotional disorder	5	54
Mental or educational deficiency	9	40
Nonmedical ‡	4	5

* Primarily men aged 19–36 in 1918. † Men aged 18–37 as of 1 August 1945.
‡ Men rejected on essentially moral grounds. [a] Calculated from Table 35.

Much more striking is the more than fourfold increase in the rejection rate for mental and educational deficiencies in the face of a significant rise in the educational level of the population. In World War I an estimated 29 percent of men of military age had no more than six years of schooling, while in 1941 only 14 percent had so little education. Thus, the marked increase in rejection rates must reflect a significant raising of the criteria.

There is little reason to doubt that of the 43,000 rejected in World War I virtually all were truly mentally deficient, but the majority of the 716,000 rejected during World War II were predominantly educationally deprived. If, as has been estimated, only about one fourth of the latter were truly mentally deficient—they were unable to perform even unskilled work except under close supervision in a protective environment—the rejection rates for true mental defectives were approximately equal in both wars.

The most outstanding contrast is in the proportions rejected for emotional disorders: World War II had a rate 11 times as great as World War I. Since there is no basis for believing that the emotional state of the American public has declined during a generation when its health and educational levels were improving, the only tenable explanation for this tremendous rise in the rejection rate was the establishment of a new criterion, reflecting a new philosophy of screening.

The establishment of much higher standards for selection for military service in World War II would lead us to anticipate considerably lower separation rates—for that, after all, was the purpose of the new criteria. Table 37 presents the rejection and separation rates for all mental and emotional reasons for the two wars.

During World War II the Army rejected men for mental and emotional reasons at a rate almost 7 times that which prevailed during World War I. But instead of this being reflected in a smaller proportion of separations for these causes, the rate of separations during World War II was in fact more than 5 times as high. Although World War II was longer and in many respects more intense, the finding of a separation rate which was so much higher despite a much more selective policy must be considered a distinct disappointment. Surely the expectation that higher rejections would result in lowered separations was not borne out.

The unexpected result must never be ignored. The paradoxical finding of high separation rates despite the high rejection rates may be grounded in faulty assumptions about the people examined, inadequate screening procedures, the mistaken belief that it is possible to predict the future behavior of people on the basis of what can be learned about their present qualities, or the neglect of the impact of organizational policies and situational stress on people's performance. Although our data will not permit us to weigh the relative importance of these several factors, they will help to clarify how they together led to such a paradoxical result.

We are going to try to answer several important questions suggested by these data. The first is crucial: how good must a man be to serve effectively in the Army? What cutoff points should be

Table 37. MEN REJECTED FOR MILITARY SERVICE AND ENLISTED MEN SEPARATED FROM THE ARMY FOR EMOTIONAL OR MENTAL REASONS, WORLD WAR I AND WORLD WAR II

CATEGORY	NUMBER [a]		RATE PER 1,000 [b]	
	World War I	*World War II*	*World War I*	*World War II*
Rejections	68,000 *	1,686,000 †	14 ‡	94 §
Separations	35,000 ‖	504,000 #	9 **	50 ††

* Primarily men aged 19–36 in 1918. † Men aged 18–37 as of 1 August 1945.
‡ Rejections per 1,000 men examined for enlisted military service April 1917–November 1918.
§ Rejections per 1,000 men examined during World War II for enlisted military service aged 18–37 as of 1 August 1945.
‖ 1 April 1917—31 December 1919.
\# 1942–1945.
** Separations per 1,000 enlisted male accessions to the Army, April 1917—November 1918 plus estimated enlisted male strength on active duty 1 April 1917 (3,950,000 total).
†† Separations per 1,000 enlisted male accessions, 1942–1945 plus enlisted male strength on active duty 31 December 1941 (10,087,000 total).
[a] Rejections from Table 35; Separations World War I: SG, *Med. Dept.*, either Vol. X, table 3, p. 155, or Vol. XV, table 50, pp. 166–89; Separations World War II: from Table 11.
[b] Rejections calculated from rejections data per 1,000 examined given in Table 35; Separations calculated from separations data per 1,000 initial enlisted male strength plus accessions. World War I: PMG, *Second Report*, tables 79, 79a, and 80, pp. 223, 226, and 227; World War II: *Strength of Army*, STM-30, pp. 52, 84, and 85.

established? Some may believe that the screening standards used in World War II, while higher than those of World War I, were not high enough and had they been raised further, the number of separations could have been substantially reduced. Our conclusion is quite different. We believe that screening tried to do too much and therefore was largely ineffective.

A second question concerns the relationship between the criteria used to evaluate an individual and his ability to perform. In World War II the criteria of assessment were derived from the theoretical assumptions of psychology and psychiatry rather than from military experience. The assumption was made of a closer relationship between the symptomatology of emotional disturbance and effective performance than was warranted by the evidence.

A third closely related question bears on the extent to which we can predict the future behavior of an individual on the basis of his assessed qualities. Considering our limited knowledge about the determinants of performance, there was little prospect of successful prediction except with respect to the extreme cases where the probability of ineffectiveness in the Army could reasonably be predicted, as in the case of individuals suffering from a psychosis or with severe mental deficiency.

These preliminary comments on the limitations of screening in World War II do not mean that the much lower criteria of World War I would have served the nation better. The educational and the psychiatric screen must be carefully analyzed before such a generalization can be substantiated. But before starting on these detailed evaluations it would be well to consider somewhat more carefully what is meant by the concept of performance in a military setting since screening is aimed at selecting those who will be able to perform in an acceptable manner.

To begin with, there is a wide range of performance demands in the military service and there are different arenas of performance on duty and off duty. A soldier may be assigned work closely analogous to his civilian job, or his assignment may be completely different. He may be trained as a rifleman and assigned to front line combat or be used as a clerk in a warehouse far back of the front. Moreover, from the time he is inducted until he is discharged a soldier is under constant surveillance; even on leave he must comport himself according to the Army's rules. If he fails to do so, he will be punished. Some men had no difficulty meeting their duty assignments but, because of various personality problems, such as alcoholism or homosexual tendencies, they frequently ran afoul of regulations. There were also dullards who could perform under strict supervision but who got into trouble when they were on their own.

Obviously, different performance demands call for different qualities. In combat, endurance and courage are crucial; in a desk assignment at a headquarters, verbal or arithmetic skills may determine whether or not a soldier can perform effectively. Much less is demanded of a private in a port battalion than of a sergeant in a combat unit in the line. A soldier who could perform satisfactorily in one assignment might prove ineffective in another.

The same screen was used to select men who could function adequately in the most demanding job—combat—and in the least demanding—duty in a service unit. And no examiner could be certain of the kind of performance demands that the soldier would encounter. Some had combat in mind; others, merely routine soldiering. A man accepted for service on the assumption that he could serve satisfactorily in a routine job might well prove ineffective if the assignment envisaged by the examiner failed to materialize. Thus the use of a single set of screening criteria variously interpreted by different examiners was one cause of later difficulties.

Although effective performance depends in part on the individual's qualities, it is also affected by the structure and actions of the organization in which he serves. Whether an organization takes the necessary action to facilitate a man's adjustment is important. Men required time to adjust from civilian to military life. They had much to learn and very little time in which to learn it. Whether a man eventually performed effectively quite often depended on whether he received the extra time or special support he needed, especially during basic training.

The willingness of the organization to make such adjustments depends on many things. An important one is its estimate of the manpower pool, that is, the availability of men to replace those who might be discharged. Army policy varied markedly from one time to another in its willingness to find appropriate assignments for those who required them. When the Army considered the manpower pool flush, it lowered its criteria for separation to a point where many on the margin were forced out; when it became concerned with dwindling manpower reserves, it raised its separation standards. These considerations emphasize that the assessment of a man's capabilities to perform must depend not only on his qualities but on his assignment. In late 1942 men were accepted for service if they could do a simple laboring job; by mid-1944 only men capable of serving as combat replacements were inducted.

The state of the manpower resources, the performance demands of the organization and its willingness to facilitate the adjustment of new men, the determination of valid criteria related to actual performance demands, and, finally, the application of these criteria to the individuals being assessed must all be considered in setting up a screen for service. Screening seeks to anticipate how individuals will perform in the future by assessing their personal qualities. One can usually distinguish the following qualities of the individual, all of which are relevant to performance: physical condition, motivation, acquired skills, learning ability, and emotional stability. As indicated in an earlier chapter we are concerned in this study with only the last four, with emphasis on the last two: intellectual capacity and emotional stability.

People are motivated to perform effectively in significantly different ways. Some clue to these differences can be found by studying the life histories of men of equal mental and physical ability. When one is found to do very well in whatever situation he finds himself—in school, on the job, in the Army—and the other performs at a level far below his potential although he gives no evidence of emotional disturbance, the explanation of the difference may well be found in different motivation. The type of work to which a man is assigned and the way in which he is treated can significantly affect his motivation. Delinquent boys, removed from their home environments, often did very well in the Army because, among other reasons, they were motivated to help their country and at the same time straighten themselves out. Important as motivation is, however, it cannot be illuminated directly by the mass data. In the companion volumes, where the use of case materials facilitates such observations motivation is seen to be an important factor in performance.

A man's performance in the Army, as elsewhere, was greatly dependent on both his current skills and his ability to acquire new ones. In general most selectees had acquired few occupational skills that were of direct military value; most men had to acquire on active duty the wide range of combat and combat-related competences on which victory depended. Since the Army could not expect to induct a large number of men with military skills, its central concern in educational screening was to identify men with sufficient intellectual ability to absorb training rapidly.

Intellectual ability and the level of educational achievement are not unrelated, and the Army at various times used these criteria interchangeably. At the beginning of the war, the educational requirement for selection was the completion of at least four years of school. The assumption was that this would mean that a man could read, write, and do simple sums. Later, tests were developed that sought to identify men who, regardless of their formal education, could reach this level of achievement with twelve weeks of special instruction.

The Army correctly assumed that it could ill afford to induct illiterate men unless they could acquire at least a basic literacy within a very short time. Early in the war and before formal special training units had been set up, they had accepted illiterates with the unfortunate results described in earlier chapters. The Army has to rely on written directives and communications. Moreover, soldiers must be able to use training manuals and other written materials. And even though the Army keeps strict control over its men, each individual has to assume responsibility for handling his own pay, returning to the post on time, and otherwise fitting himself into a complex and dynamic organization. A dullard or an illiterate might manage, but only with an unusual amount of supervisory assistance.

A man might be in superb physical condition, he might be well educated, have normal intelligence, and be well motivated; yet because he is emotionally disturbed he may be unable to perform effectively. It was the recognition of this fact that sent the Army to such lengths to develop and use a psychiatric screen. That the screen failed to live up to the high expectations held for it was largely due to the fact that an individual's performance is determined not only by his strengths and weaknesses; it is also determined by the kinds of supports and pressures that he later encounters.

This chapter has sought to identify some of the important relations between screening and performance. We have paid particular attention to the major problems that the Army faced in seeking to develop a screening mechanism that would reduce its manpower losses by preventing the induction of men who would sooner or later prove ineffective. Comparative data from the two world wars suggested that the screening used by the Army in World War II proved much less successful than had been anticipated. The reasons for this failure can be uncovered only by a careful critique of the educational and psychiatric screens which were used. The two following chapters are directed to this end.

Chapter Ten: THE EDUCATIONAL SCREEN

THE EDUCATIONAL screen was designed to select individuals for military service whose intellectual capacity was sufficient to enable them to adjust to the Army, absorb military training, and thereafter perform effectively. Although the tests used during the course of the war varied considerably, they were all geared to distinguish those who could read, write, and do sums at a fourth-grade level from those who could not. In examining illiterates, the Army sought to determine by special tests whether they were likely to reach this level of accomplishment with twelve weeks of special instruction.

Two questions must be answered. The first bears on the efficiency with which the screen was applied. Were men who met the criterion accepted and those who fell below rejected? Only after this question is answered can one utilize the data available to answer the next one. Did the criterion succeed in distinguishing between those who were able to perform satisfactorily and those who were not?

One way to judge the efficiency of the screen is to test it against such external data as the educational level of the population of military age as recorded in the U.S. Census of 1940.[23] The relationship between the two could not be perfect, since we know that the Army accepted men with less than a fourth-grade education. Moreover, some men who fell below the educational criterion were rejected on other grounds, such as physical or emotional disabilities; others were deferred because of their occupation, such as many farmers. But we can anticipate a reasonably close relation between the two.

Approximately 2½ percent of the white male population examined for military service was rejected for educational or

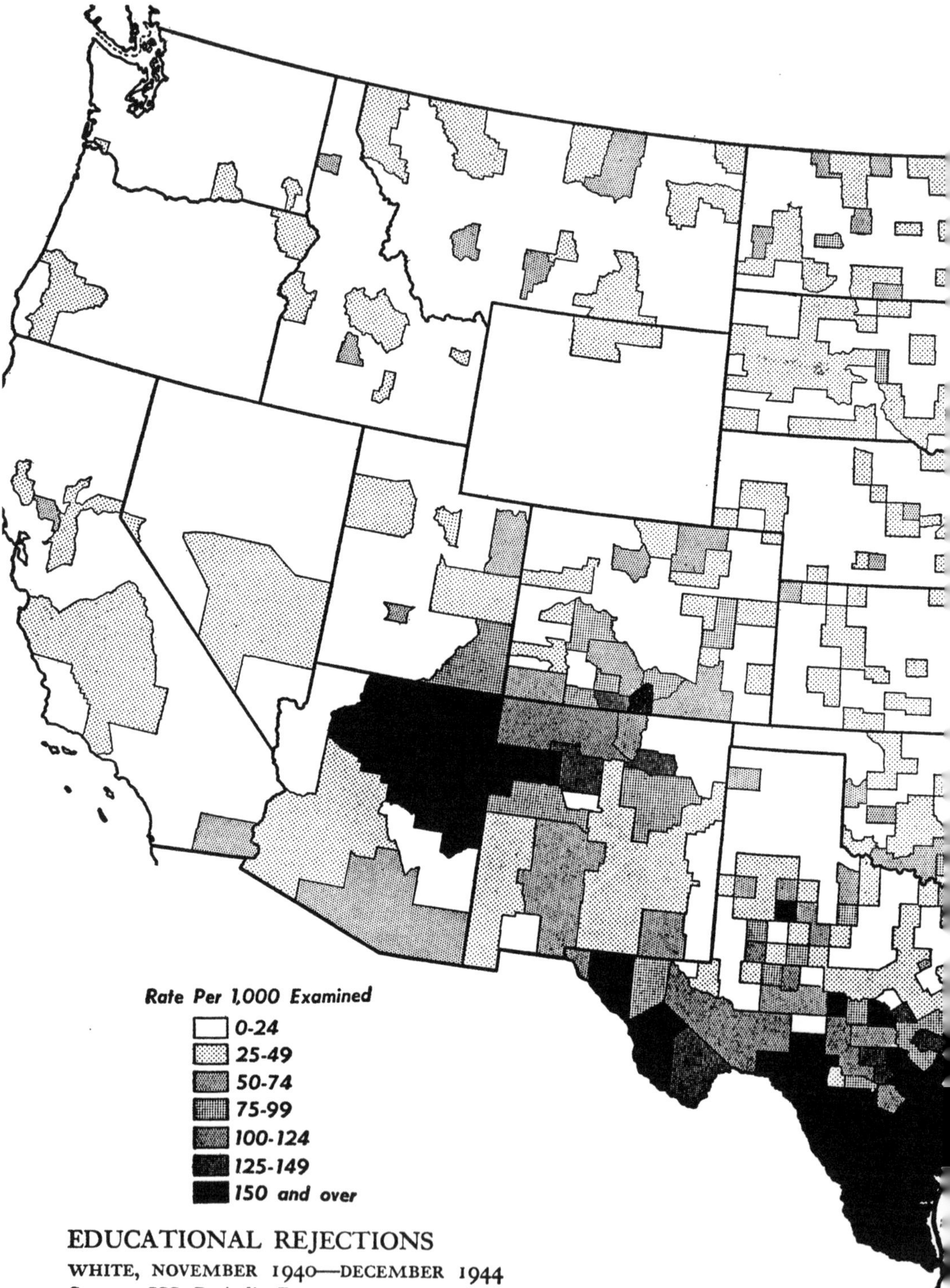

EDUCATIONAL REJECTIONS

WHITE, NOVEMBER 1940—DECEMBER 1944

Source: SSS, *Periodic Reports*

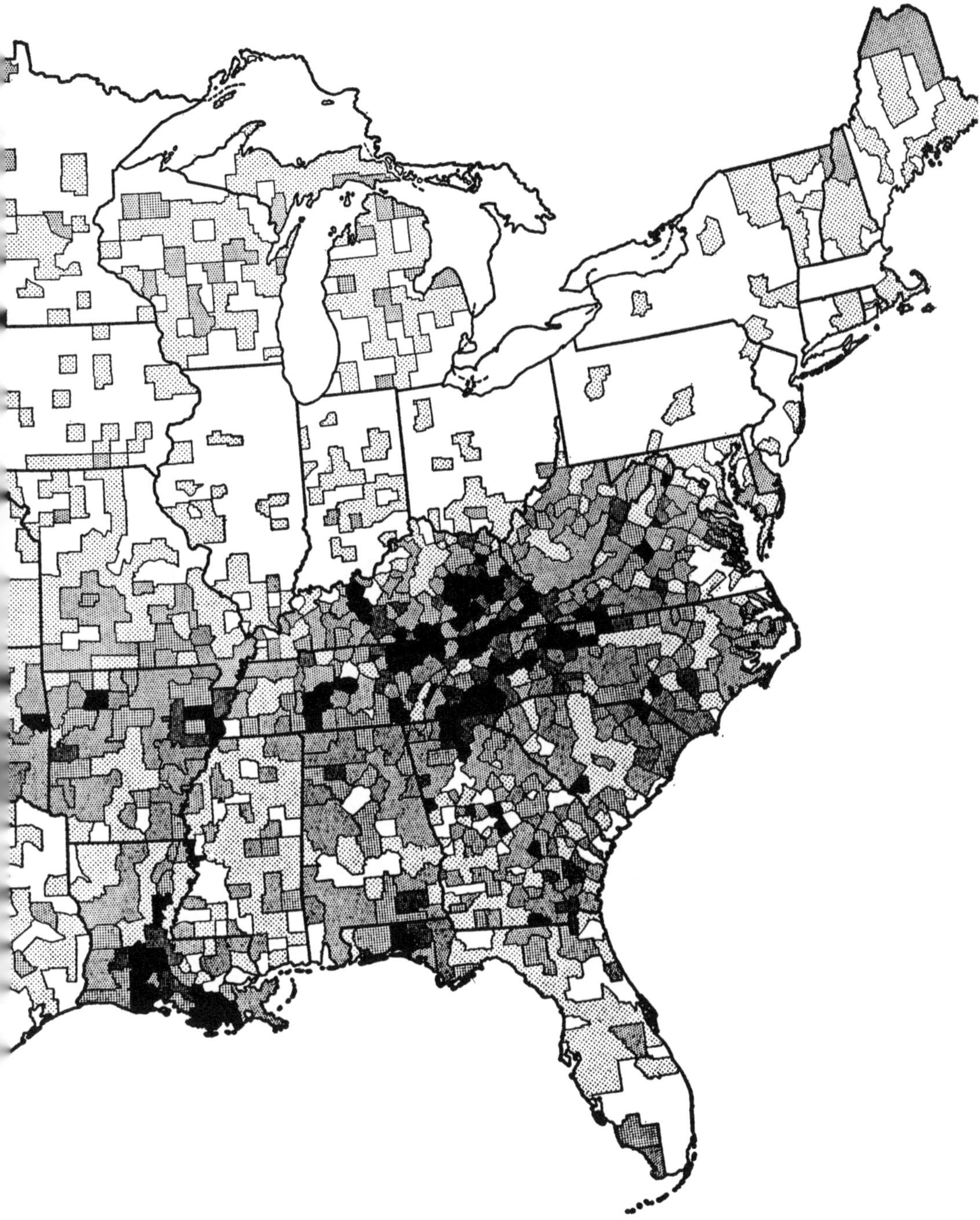

mental deficiency. This is just what we would anticipate from the 1940 Census, which shows that 2.4 percent of the comparable age group had completed less than four years of school. Although it might appear from these figures that the educational-intellectual screen was very effective, we must consider regional as well as national figures.

Since the level of educational achievement varies markedly from one region to another, the first test was to determine whether the regional rejection pattern parallels the regional educational achievement pattern. The closer the relation between the two, the more likely it is that the screen successfully identified those who did not meet the educational criterion for service.

The regional pattern of the proportion of the population rejected on educational grounds is illustrated by the map. It is based on sample data from the Selective Service System for each of the more than 3,000 counties and covers virtually the entire period of mobilization—November, 1940, through December, 1944. Only the data for white registrants are used in the current instance to avoid the distortion which would result from including the Negro data because of the very much higher rates of rejection among Negroes and their equally high concentration in particular regions. However, the Negro data have been thoroughly analyzed in *The Uneducated.*[24]

Even a cursory inspection of the map shows the marked differences from one region to another in the rate of rejections for educational or mental deficiency. With few exceptions, the pattern is one of gradual shading rather than abrupt changes, reflecting the influence of economic resources, cultural attitudes, and geography, all of which influence the ability and willingness of state and local governments to support public education.

With this map as background the relations between rejections for military service and the level of educational achievement, area by area and state by state, can be reviewed. We are handicapped by the lack of data concerning the specific educational level of those who were rejected, although it is likely that most men rejected for these reasons had not achieved the equivalent of a fourth-grade education.

If the screen were as sensitive to educational achievement as the national data imply, we would expect to find a high correlation in a state by state analysis between the percentage rejected and the proportion of the population which had not gone beyond the fourth grade in school. Such in fact was the case. A very high relationship was found to prevail (the coefficient of correlation for all races was .86; for whites alone, .94).

In spite of this high correlation, we still cannot conclude that the screen was effective in rejecting all those who should have been rejected. Actually, since for a period of months the Army accepted specified numbers of men who had not completed four years of schooling, since late in the war tests rather than school records were used to determine whether a man could eventually meet the educational criterion, and since the quality of education varies markedly among even closely adjacent communities, this very high correlation is somewhat surprising. However, it may have been affected by the fact that the quality of education tends to vary with the quantity of educational services available and that the two regions with the lowest level of educational attainment, the Southeast and the Southwest, contain virtually all of the states with high rejection rates. The relationship between rejections and educational achievement was computed for all except states of the Southeast and Southwest. A lower but still significant correlation coefficient was found (.76 for whites), which tends further to suggest that the educational screen was effective.

We can learn more about the efficiency of the screen by considering the "slippage factor" which accounted for those who should have been rejected for educational reasons but who managed to slip through the screen. A rough measure of slippage can be determined by evaluating the rates of those actually rejected for educational reasons against the rates of educational achievement in the several states and regions. Table 38 sets out the relevant data.

Table 38. RATES OF EDUCATIONAL ACHIEVEMENT, REJECTIONS FOR MILITARY SERVICE ON MENTAL OR EDUCATIONAL GROUNDS, AND SLIPPAGE FACTOR, WHITE MALES, BY REGION AND STATE, WORLD WAR II (NUMBER PER 1,000)

	EDUCATIONAL ACHIEVEMENT [a]		EDU-	"SLIPPAGE" FACTOR *	
REGION AND STATE	*3rd Grade or Less*	*4th Grade or Less*	CATIONAL REJECTION [b]	*3rd Grade or Less*	*4th Grade or Less*
New England	10	16	16	−6	0
Connecticut	9	15	14	−5	1
Maine	15	26	19	−4	7
Massachusetts	9	14	15	−6	−1
New Hampshire	9	15	20	−11	−5
Rhode Island	11	19	15	−4	4
Vermont	10	17	21	−11	−4
Middle Atlantic	13	22	11	2	11
Delaware	12	22	18	−6	4
Dist. of Columbia	4	8	4	0	4
Maryland	15	31	17	−2	14
New Jersey	10	18	10	0	8
New York	14	20	8	6	12
Pennsylvania	9	16	8	1	8
West Virginia	40	78	41	−1	37
Southeast	63	115	51	12	64
Alabama	59	110	46	13	64
Arkansas	56	109	57	−1	52
Florida	29	55	21	8	34
Georgia	70	126	38	32	88
Kentucky	78	137	61	17	76
Louisiana	86	136	54	32	82
Mississippi	39	77	28	11	49
North Carolina	56	111	61	−5	50
South Carolina	59	123	42	17	81
Tennessee	72	129	62	10	67
Virginia	63	113	57	6	56
Southwest	63	95	52	11	43
Arizona	41	68	52	−11	16
New Mexico	73	117	49	24	68
Oklahoma	28	55	28	0	27
Texas	77	110	60	17	50
Central	9	16	12	−3	4

REGION AND STATE	EDUCATIONAL ACHIEVEMENT [a] 3rd Grade or Less	EDUCATIONAL ACHIEVEMENT [a] 4th Grade or Less	EDUCATIONAL REJECTION [b]	"SLIPPAGE" FACTOR * 3rd Grade or Less	"SLIPPAGE" FACTOR * 4th Grade or Less
Illinois	8	14	9	−1	5
Indiana	8	14	14	−6	0
Iowa	5	8	11	−6	−3
Michigan	9	16	13	−4	3
Minnesota	6	10	11	−5	−1
Missouri	19	34	19	0	15
Ohio	8	14	8	0	6
Wisconsin	8	14	17	−9	−3
Northwest	8	14	13	−5	1
Colorado	15	28	19	−4	9
Idaho	5	8	9	−4	−1
Kansas	7	12	14	−7	−2
Montana	5	11	11	−6	0
Nebraska	6	10	11	−5	−1
North Dakota	12	20	16	−4	4
South Dakota	5	8	14	−9	−6
Utah	8	10	8	0	2
Wyoming	11	17	9	2	8
Far West	11	18	9	2	9
California	14	22	11	3	11
Nevada	11	18	8	3	10
Oregon	5	8	5	0	3
Washington	6	9	5	1	4
Total United States	24	41	22	2	19

* Educational achievement rate per 1,000 white (white only) males less mental and educational deficiency rejection rates per 1,000 white males.

[a] U.S. Census, 1940, Vol. IV; number of white (white only) males aged 18–34 in 1940 completing indicated grade or less per 1,000 total white (white only) males 18–34 in 1940 whose educational level was known.

[b] SSS, *Periodic Reports*, Vols. 4–14: number of white males rejected for mental or educational deficiency November 1940—December 1944 divided by thousands of white males examined plus estimated thousands of white male enlistees November 1940—December 1944 and initial white male strength 31 October 1941.

The table reaffirms what has already been noted—the close association between the high rejection rates and the heavy concentration of the poorly educated white males in the South. Moreover, the table indicates that "slippage" occurred most often in states with the lowest levels of education and the highest rejection rates. If the screen had actually kept out all who did not have the equivalent of a fourth-grade education, these states would have had "negative slippage." Many men who had formally completed the fourth grade or more would have been rejected because they did not really meet the criterion of ability to do fourth-grade work. We find, however, "negative slippage" only in a number of northern states, which indicates that they screened out not only their most poorly educated but also a considerable number of marginally educated men as well.

The tendency for slippage to increase as the level of educational achievement drops probably reflects the pressure on the draft boards exerted by a diminishing manpower pool. Since each state was assigned quotas of men to induct based on the available population of military age, those with very high rejection rates were hard pressed to meet them. Hence, they tended to adjust the criterion downward. This downward adjustment was further facilitated by the tendency of many examiners to evaluate men not in terms of a national norm, but in terms of their own local experience.

Now, on the basis of this regional analysis of the rejection rate for mental or educational deficiency compared with the rate of educational achievement, we can venture the conclusion that the screen was reasonably efficient in accomplishing its objective, which was to keep the poorly educated and the mentally deficient out of military service. But, as we have seen, it was not completely successful and was the least effective in the regions of the country where educational achievement was the lowest. This finding of the overall efficiency of the screen paves the way for a consideration of the related question of whether this criterion was a good predictor of performance; did it reject those who would not have served effectively and did it select those who could and did meet the performance standards of the Army?

The premise of selection is that the evaluation of candidates will result in accepting a group who will be able to perform better than those who are rejected. The selection process can succeed in this aim only if the criteria used are significantly related to later performance. Certainly a man's intellectual capacity will affect his ability to cope with his military training and assignments. But we cannot with equal certainty say that all men who have completed four years of school have actually mastered the required work. In some regions of the country many students are advanced from one grade to the next not on the basis of accomplishment but solely on the basis of age. Upon leaving school, some build on what they have learned in class, others forget most of what they have been taught.

In a period of manpower stringency, the standards for military service must be set as low as compatible with the desired results so that the overall manpower requirements can be met. Since intellectual ability of the population is distributed along a finely graded scale, the lower the cut-off point, the more likely it is that some will be accepted who will later prove incapable of performing effectively.

There are several considerations that bear on the determination of the cut-off point. The first desideratum is to exclude the clearly unusable group. These are the men who, even if the Army were willing and able to make a major investment in their training, would still be unable to reach a satisfactory level of performance. The true mentally deficient fall into this category.

Secondly, the cut-off point must be set with reference to the relations between manpower requirements and manpower availabilities. In the current situation when the Armed Services are moving towards a planned strength of 2.5 million, the cut-off point can obviously be considerably higher than in World War II when the peak strength was 12 million.

During the war, the appropriate educational criterion had to be very sensitive to logistical considerations. To illustrate: if the available military manpower pool comprised 20 million men and rejections for other causes would eliminate 6 million, the educational standards would have to be set at a level which would result in the educational rate not exceeding 10 percent—if an Armed Forces strength of 12 million is to be realized. But since those at or close to the margin of this educational level—those who fall between the 8th and 15th percentile in a grading of intellectual ability—might or might not be able to meet military performance standards, the Armed Forces would have to consider how much of an investment they were willing to make in terms of time, resources, and special adjustments to help this marginal group make the grade. If these costs appeared prohibitive, their options would be to cut back on their planned strength or to adjust other standards of acceptability.

The optimal cut-off point is one which would enable the Armed Forces and particularly the Army to meet their manpower requirements, keep training costs moderate, and hold the number of failures among those selected as low as possible. At the beginning of World War II there was no way to determine upon a sound cut-off point. To establish the fourth-grade level as an educational criterion was a common sense approach. And it was necessary to fall back on such an approach because of the inadequate data available about the characteristics of the population and because of inadequate personnel research. Today, more than a decade after the end of the war, these deficiencies still exist although some progress has been made both in the collection of data and in research.

More data and better research, however, could not eliminate all the difficulties. Questions remain about the extent to which intelligence, used here to mean ability to learn, can be assumed to be stable or whether it is itself subject to change; the likelihood that emotional factors, especially anxiety, affect the performance level that might be expected solely on the basis of intelligence; and finally the reduction in effectiveness likely to be introduced by poor motivation.

We are now in a position to assess how well the intellectual-educational criterion used in World War II helped to predict future performance. We are concerned solely with minimum acceptable performance, not with the entire range of performance. One clear indication of ineffective performance is the discharge of a soldier prior to demobilization for reasons of inaptitude. We have seen that some 122,000 soldiers (81,000 white and 41,000 Negro) were separated during the course of World War II for lack of adaptability—i.e., inaptitude. This amounts to a rate of slightly more than 12 per 1,000 enlisted male personnel. This appears to be a modest rate of loss.

Here, as elsewhere, a single figure is likely to be misleading. Although the rate is small, the failures were the equivalent of eight 15,000-man divisions. Clearly, it would be advantageous to improve the predictive value of the screen to avoid such sizable losses.

The test of the predictive value of the screen requires that we consider not only the national figures but also regional data to determine whether the screen was equally effective in rejecting those with the least potential in each area or whether it operated unevenly and if so, to what extent. Table 39 presents the relevant data in terms of the nine Service Commands into which the country was divided during the war.

In general the pattern of separations for inaptitude tended to parallel both the pattern of educational achievement and the amount of slippage which occurred. Regions with low educational achievement and higher slippage tended to have the higher rates for separations for inaptitude. The coefficient of correlation between separations and slippage for the nine Service Commands was very high—.96. Although this could be interpreted to mean that separations were a result of inefficiency in screening reflected in the slippage factor, the more likely explanation is that they were directly related to the limitations of men who met the fourth-grade criterion but who did not really possess the intellectual competence to perform effectively.

This is seen most sharply in the very high rates of separation which occurred among men originally accepted from the Fourth and Eighth Service Commands—the Southeast and Southwest respectively. These two regions not only had the lowest proportion of men having completed the fourth grade, as shown on Table 38, but also the lowest at the sixth-grade level. According to the

Table 39. RATE OF SEPARATIONS OF ENLISTED MALE PERSONNEL FROM THE ARMY FOR INAPTITUDE, COMPARED TO A MEASURE OF LOW EDUCATIONAL ACHIEVEMENT AND A MEASURE OF THE EFFICIENCY OF THE EDUCATIONAL SCREEN, BY SERVICE COMMAND GROUPS, WORLD WAR II

Item	*"Slippage" Factor in Educational Screen* [a]	*Number per 1,000 Who Completed 4th Grade, But No Higher* [b]	*Inapt Separations per 1,000 Accessions* [c]
Service Commands * with negative slippage and low proportion of marginally acceptable males	−5	8	5
Service Commands † with low slippage and medium proportion of marginally acceptable males	1	22	7
Service Commands ‡ with medium slippage and low proportion of marginally acceptable males	4	9	7
Service Commands § with high slippage and high proportion of marginally acceptable males	26	74	23

* *First:* Conn., Maine, Mass., N.H., R.I., Vt.; *Sixth:* Ill., Mich., Wisc.; *Seventh:* Colo., Iowa, Kansas, Minn., Mo., Neb., N.D., S.D., Wyo.

† *Third:* Md., Pa., Va., D.C.; *Fifth:* Ind., Ky., Ohio, W. Va.

‡ *Second:* Del., N.J., N.Y.; *Ninth:* Ariz., Cal., Idaho, Mon., Nev., Ore., Utah, Wash.

§ *Fourth:* Ala., Fla., Ga., Miss., N.C., S.C., Tenn.; *Eighth:* Ark., La., N.M., Okla., Texas.

[a] Weighted mean educational achievement rate for all males aged 18–34 in 1940 minus weighted mean mental and educational deficiency rejection rate for all males November 1940—December 1944. From Table 38.

[b] U.S. Census, 1940, Vol. IV: total males aged 18–34 in 1940 completing 4th grade but no higher per 1,000 total males aged 18–34 in 1940 whose educational level was known.

[c] SG, unpub. worksheets based on AG tabulations and AG unpub. worksheets: enlisted male personnel (excluding Regular Army) separated for inaptitude during fiscal years 1941–1945 divided by thousands of accessions during fiscal years 1941–1945. Accessions, and Separations for fiscal years 1941–1944 compiled by state of entry; Separations for 1945 compiled by state of residence at time of entry.

1940 Census, 6 percent of the white males of military age in these regions had completed less than four years of school and an additional 18 percent had completed over three but no more than six years. This is in sharp contrast to the rest of the country where the respective percentages are: $\frac{3}{10}$ percent and 6 percent.

The record for the South was 1 in 4 with not over six years of schooling; for the rest of the country 1 in 18! If the data are reviewed for all males, Negroes and whites combined, the position of the South was even less favorable: 11 percent of all Southern males of military age had less than four years of school and an additional 23 percent had less than a sixth-grade education. For the rest of the country the comparable figures are 1 percent and 5 percent. The contrast between the South, with 34 percent of its young men having had less than seven years of education, and the rest of the country, with 6 percent, is indeed striking.

Though slippage and inferior education undoubtedly accounted for much of the premature separations for inaptitude, they cannot alone explain the regional pattern. A sizable, if unknown, percentage of the potential slippage was rejected on physical or psychiatric grounds; and we know from our study of *The Uneducated*[25] that many of those accepted for service with less than a fourth-grade education who had the opportunity of attending a Special Training Unit were eventually able to meet performance standards. This suggests that many who were prematurely separated for inaptitude technically met the criterion but their educational background was sufficiently limited that they could not adjust without special training. Some came on active duty before the Special Training Units were established in June, 1943; others were not sent to one because they were assumed to be literate since they had completed five or six grades of school.

If the criterion had been raised, separations from military service for inaptitude would probably have been greatly reduced. Why then did the Army not move to raise the cut-off point? The answer can be found in the logistics of the manpower problem. Of the 18 million men who were examined, slightly over 700,000 were rejected for mental or educational deficiency. This is approximately the number that should have been rejected in the fourth-grade standard had been rigidly adhered to. If the cut-off point had been raised to exclude all men who had not completed the sixth grade, 2.5 million would have been rejected. If completion of the eighth grade had been used as a criterion, nearly 4 million would have been lost. These few estimates explain the excessive losses of manpower which would have resulted from a modest raising of the cut-off point—for each grade beyond the fourth, between 500,000 and 1.2 million additional men would have had to be rejected.

Since to raise the cut-off point would have been prohibitive, could the Army have followed any other policy that might have yielded a better overall result? It probably could—if the Army had set up a double screen that would have used both the school grade completed as a criterion and had also tested all who might have been educationally or intellectually deficient to determine their learning ability. If on the basis of such testing a selectee appeared to have the ability to absorb military training, he would have been accepted regardless of his educational achievement. This was actually done during the latter part of the war. With a double screen, a selectee would have been rejected if his test result showed inadequate ability to absorb military training, even if his record showed him to have completed the fourth, fifth, sixth, or seventh grade—which was not the practice during the war. Had the Army moved in this direction, it would probably also have had to readjust its training program to provide many marginal soldiers with additional support during their first weeks of military service.

The magnitude of the losses that the Army suffered because it inducted men with inadequate intellectual ability is not completely reflected in the 122,000 who were prematurely separated for inaptitude. We have seen in earlier chapters the extent to which those prematurely separated for psychoneurosis or because they had undesirable traits comprised a disproportionately large number whose education was considerably below the average. Among those separated for psychoneurosis the rate for men with less than a grammar-school education was almost 1½ times as great as for those with more education.

It is not possible to determine from the mass data how many soldiers were discharged on grounds other than inaptitude whose major disability was in fact their limited intellectual capacity. But that it probably was a substantial number can be seen in the constant warnings by various staff agencies to the field not to "abuse medical channels" in separating men prematurely—which meant to avoid separating a soldier with a certificate of disability for psychoneurosis because this was the easiest way of getting rid of him.

In the absence of an independent analysis of those who were rejected on educational grounds, only a rough approximation can be ventured about how many of them could have served effectively. Conventional estimates of true mental deficiency in the population vary between 1 and 2 percent. Of the 18 million who were screened for service, those totally unfit to serve because of mental deficiency would number between 180,000 and 360,000. The World War I rate of rejection for this reason was 1 percent. If the 2 percent rate is applied for World War II, 360,000 of the 716,000 who were rejected for mental or educational disability must be presumed to have been mentally deficient and therefore unsuitable for military service. That would leave more than 350,000 who could probably have made the grade, especially if they had been given the same or possibly a little more of the type of assistance provided by the Special Training Units. However, possibly as many as 100,000 of this group could not have passed the other screens, particularly the physical or emotional ones. Hence, a conservative estimate of the total that might have been salvaged by improved educational screening is one quarter of a million.

We do not say that the Army should have inducted these 250,000 potentially usable men during World War II. As we have seen, the Army had to be concerned with the added costs involved, and many of these men would have required even more than the twelve weeks' special training program. But the figures do underscore the cost to the nation during a major war because so many of its young men had not had even a minimum of formal education.

The nation's failure to provide adequate educational facilities during the 1920s and '30s, and the failure of many young persons to take advantage of the educational opportunities which were provided resulted in a loss to the Armed Forces of at least 372,000 men (an estimated 250,000 rejected solely for educational reasons and 122,000 prematurely separated for inaptness). This loss is equivalent to twenty-five 15,000-man divisions, or eight divisions each supported by 30,000 troops. This loss is well in excess of all battle deaths suffered by the Armed Forces during World War II.

Chapter Eleven: THE PSYCHIATRIC SCREEN

THE EVALUATION of the psychiatric screen used by the Army in World War II must begin with a description of the terms and a delineation of the objective. The psychiatric screen sought to assess a man's emotional stability, that is, his ability to cope with future stress. There are a series of related terms in common use such as emotional maturity, personality integration, and, more recently, the technical expression of "ego strength." Emotional stability is related to but distinguishable from motivation, which is more directly dependent on a man's system of values and goals than on the resilience and integration of his psyche.

Emotional stability runs a wide gamut. A very disturbed person, such as a psychotic individual in an agitated state, is at one end of the scale, while at the opposite extreme is a man who is able to withstand such severe stress and strain as exist in concentration camps. In contrast to intelligence, which is usually a relatively stable factor during the life span of a person, emotional stability is likely to undergo substantial differences from one period of an individual's life to another. Most adolescents are somewhat emotionally unstable, and this is also true of many elderly people. There is probably no man who, when confronted with a major crisis, does not show at least some signs of a temporary loss of stability.

While many individuals become emotionally unstable only under special circumstances, others are somewhat unstable throughout all or most of their lives, and still others can lose their stability if the customary supports of their lives are suddenly withdrawn. How do we measure emotional stability and what can the indices predict? Extreme emotional disturbance results in pronounced symptoms that can be identified as clinical entities such as paranoia, hysteria, or compulsion neurosis. If a man is suffering from a hallucinatory psychosis, it is extremely unlikely that he will be able to meet performance standards. But with a less extreme condition, even when a clear-cut clinical syndrome can be recognized, the prediction of a man's future behavior is much less certain. The further an individual's symptoms are removed from gross pathology, the more tenuous is the prediction of behavior.

The Army sought to reject individuals whose emotional stability was such that it raised questions about whether they could cope successfully with the stress inherent in military service. To exclude such potential casualties from the service the Army prepared a check list of clinical categories and proceeded to reject any selectee who was found to be suffering from one or more of these conditions. But while such psychiatric categories were suitable for screening the extreme cases—it made good sense for the Army to exclude all who were clearly psychotic—they were not effective in considering men with less severe emotional disturbances. In attempting to estimate a man's future performance in the military service, it is not enough to know that he is suffering from anxiety or a phobia. The important point is the nature and the severity of his condition and whether it will specifically interfere with the performance of his military duties. Impotence is a sign of serious emotional disturbance, but alone it need not bar a man from service.

Enough has been been said to suggest the complex nature of screening for emotional stability. A review of what transpired with respect to psychiatric screening in World War II should add to our understanding of manpower logistics. Unlike the appraisal of the intellectual-educational screen, there is no external criterion such as the educational achievement of the population as reported in the Census which can be used as a basis for measuring the efficiency of the psychiatric screening. In appraising the costs and returns of the psychiatric screen it will be necessary to rely on more indirect methods to reach even tentative judgments.

PATTERN OF REJECTIONS

Since there is no clear-cut evidence to the contrary, we will begin by postulating a reasonable degree of uniformity in the incidence of emotional disturbance throughout the country which we would expect to see reflected in uniform rejection rates for psychiatric causes. As a first test of this assumption, a map was prepared for each county in the country depicting the rejection rates for psychiatric reasons of the white population examined. We omitted the data for Negroes since preliminary investigation disclosed that they had been evaluated differently, particularly in the South where so many were rejected for educational reasons. Once again the basic data were derived from the 20 percent sample of the Selective Service examinations covering more than four years. This sample covered 2,794,727 examinations as a result of which 169,624 were rejected for psychiatric reasons.

An inspection of the map reveals that, contrary to expectation, the rejection rates were far from uniform. There is a surprising variability among regions, among states, and even among counties within the same state. The only patterns that can be discerned are differences in rejection rates between the North and the South and an East-West gradient moving along the upper Mississippi then cutting through Missouri, Oklahoma, and Texas. West of this line the rates decline. Except for some inexplicable differences among some neighboring counties the map shows that the change in rates in adjacent areas tends to be gradual.

Several areas warrant particular comment. In the Northeast, the rates of rejection for psychiatric disability in New Hampshire and Vermont are considerably above the regional average. Rejections in Colorado were considerably higher than in the rest of the Northwest. The coastal area of the Far West had rates considerably above the more sparsely settled hinterland. And, as we noted earlier, some states, such as Missouri, Oklahoma, and Texas, had both high and low areas.

We cannot expect such extraordinary and somewhat inconsist-

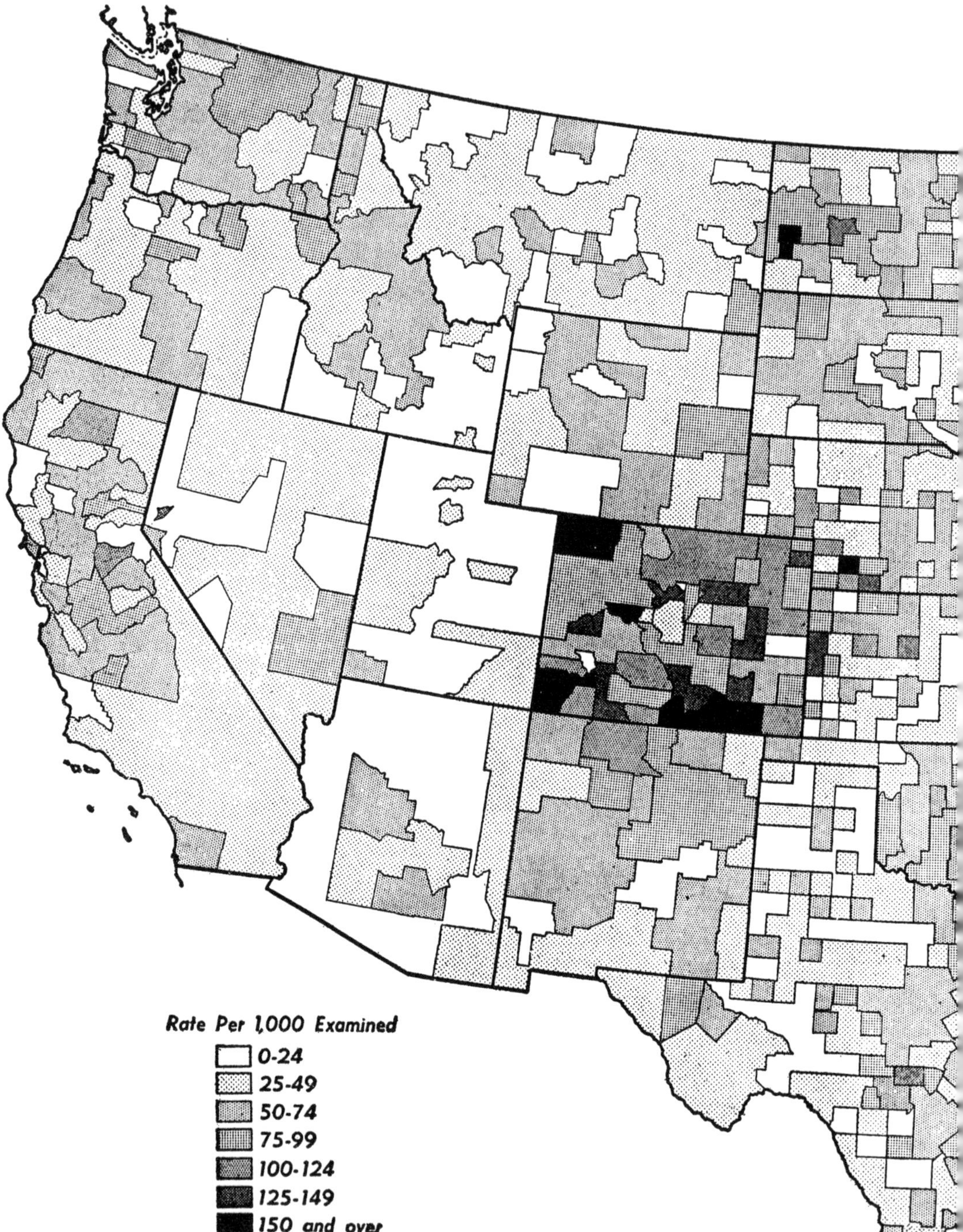

PSYCHIATRIC REJECTIONS

WHITE, NOVEMBER 1940—DECEMBER 1944

Source: SSS, *Periodic Reports*

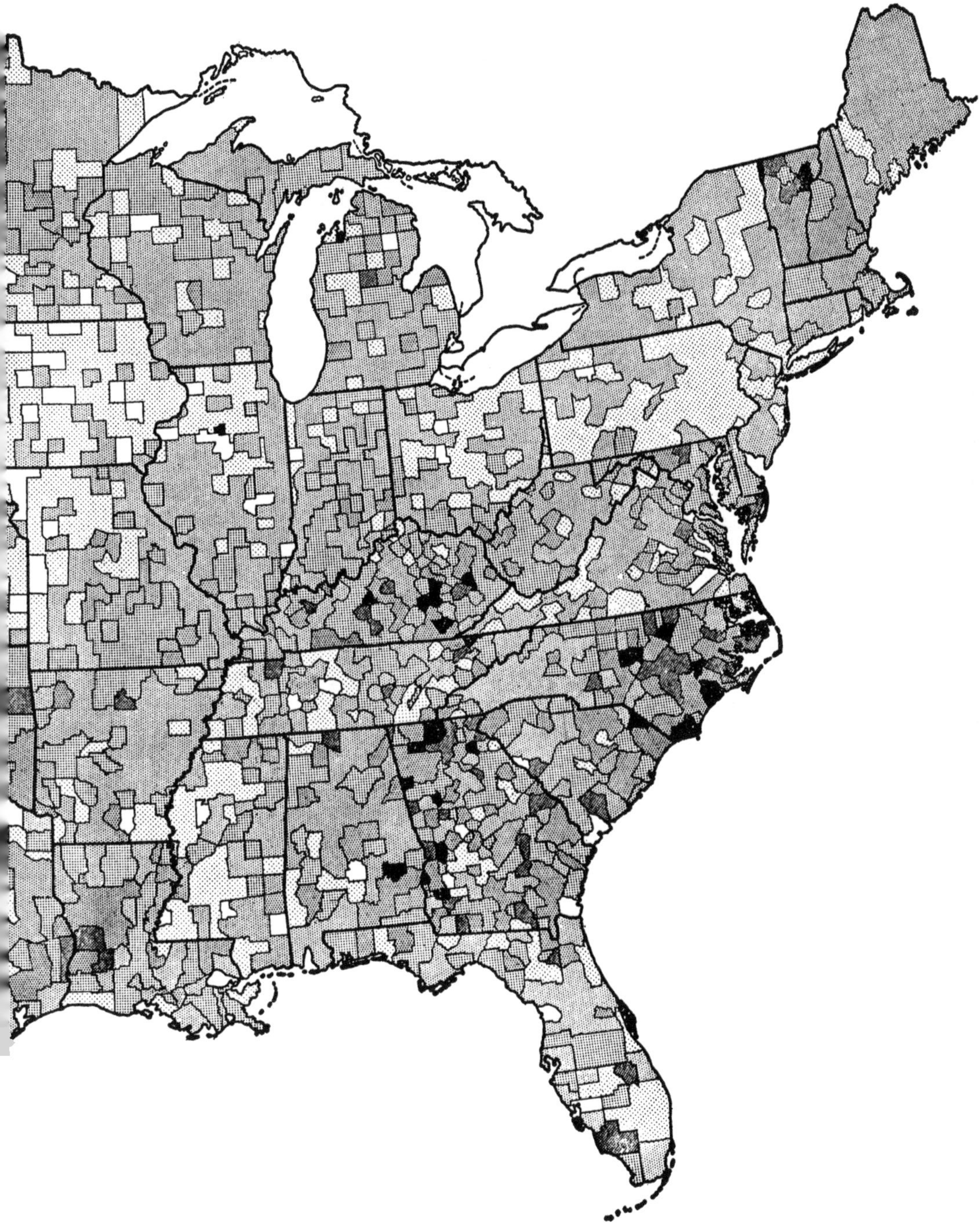

ent variations to be due to a single factor. We shall have to look for a composite of interacting variables and influences, some concrete, some rather intangible. To aid us detailed information on psychiatric rejections for white males is presented by state in Table 40.

Table 40. RATES OF EDUCATIONAL ACHIEVEMENT AND REJECTIONS FOR MILITARY SERVICE ON PSYCHIATRIC GROUNDS, WHITE MALES, BY REGION AND STATE, WORLD WAR II (PER 1,000)

Region and State	*Educational Achievement 6th Grade or Less* [a]	*Psychiatric Rejections* [b]
New England	56	54
Connecticut	48	53
Maine	80	41
Massachusetts	52	54
New Hampshire	52	73
Rhode Island	79	44
Vermont	64	85
Middle Atlantic	70	40
Delaware	77	64
District of Columbia	33	63
Maryland	125	72
New Jersey	65	39
New York	52	39
Pennsylvania	64	30
West Virginia	202	58
Southeast	257	56
Alabama	277	53
Arkansas	244	50
Florida	146	42
Georgia	281	67
Kentucky	265	69
Louisiana	273	58
Mississippi	183	41
North Carolina	277	68
South Carolina	275	63
Tennessee	271	46
Virginia	258	43
Southwest	191	42
Arizona	145	21
New Mexico	228	46

Region and State	Educational Achievement 6th Grade or Less [a]	Psychiatric Rejections [b]
Oklahoma	138	59
Texas	211	37
Central	47	45
Illinois	39	42
Indiana	44	53
Iowa	29	27
Michigan	49	57
Minnesota	36	44
Missouri	88	44
Ohio	44	42
Wisconsin	49	47
Northwest	41	36
Colorado	71	69
Idaho	25	26
Kansas	35	26
Montana	41	22
Nebraska	29	38
North Dakota	67	46
South Dakota	28	35
Utah	20	16
Wyoming	47	30
Far West	43	32
California	50	32
Nevada	43	22
Oregon	24	25
Washington	26	35

[a] U.S. Census, 1940, Vol. IV: number of white (white only) males 18–34 in 1940 completing indicated grade or less per 1,000 total white (white only) males 18–34 in 1940 whose educational level was known.

[b] From a 20% sample reported in SSS, *Periodic Reports*, Vols. 4–14: number of white males rejected for psychiatric reasons per 1,000 white males examined, November 1940—December 1944, plus initial white male strength 31 October 1941.

In each region there are marked variations: In New England, the state rates vary from 41 to 85; in the Middle Atlantic, from 30 to 72; in the Southeast, 41 to 69; in the Southwest, 21 to 59; in the Central region, 27 to 57; in the Northwest, 16 to 69; and in the Far West, from 22 to 35. The variation around the national average of 54 rejections per 1,000 examined ranges from a low of 16 to a high of 85.

If we assume that these variations cannot reflect true differences in the incidence of emotional illness in the population, we must look for alternative explanations. It may have been that different examiners applied different standards or introduced their own interpretation of established standards, either because of differences in professional orientation or as a direct result of varying pressures to meet manpower quotas. While this might illuminate some of the striking regional differences, it cannot explain why neighboring counties which made use of the same induction stations and examiners could have had such disparate rates.

Another possible explanation is a confounding of the rejection categories. Since the examiners were permitted such a short time for each examination, they might easily have mistaken educational deficiencies for psychiatric disturbances or medical defects for psychiatric disabilities. Two aspects of confounding must be distinguished. The first is a matter of statistical accounting. Individuals with multiple defects might have been put in different categories by different examiners. We do not know the exact number of men with multiple defects. Selective Service data indicate that an estimated 35 percent of the white and 40 percent of the Negro registrants who were rejected for educational or psychiatric reasons would also have been rejected on physical grounds. Slightly over 1 million registrants, then, were probably rejected solely because of an educational or psychiatric disability. An additional 600,000 had multiple defects which would have justified their being rejected on physical grounds. However, they were rejected primarily on psychiatric or educational grounds. To this total must be added a smaller, but unknown, number of men with multiple defects who were rejected on physical grounds. Since such a large number of men had multiple defects, variations in classifying rejectees could significantly affect regional rates. During one period of the war efforts were made to reduce differences in reporting by instructing the field that in classifying men with multiple defects psychiatric causes for rejection should take precedence.

The second aspect of confounding involves the differential diagnosis of men with ill-defined conditions. Those who were suffering from neurocirculatory asthenia, ulcers, and other so-called psychosomatic conditions were rejected on either physical or psychiatric grounds, depending on the inclination of the examiners. In this connection it is important to recall that for a considerable part of the war some induction stations were operated without a psychiatrist on the staff and that it was the exceptional station that had available an experienced group of psychiatrists throughout the war.

Another approach which is worth exploring in our search for explanations of the variability in rejection rates is to examine the internal consistency of the rates for rejection for various diagnostic categories. If we find that the rates vary widely, this would point to a confounding among psychiatric categories and serve as presumptive evidence of confounding among psychiatric and other causes of rejection. Table 41 presents the regional rates of rejection for psychoneurosis, psychopathy, and psychosis, and the relationship between the rejection rates for psychoneurosis and psychopathy.

All the rates vary among regions except for the rates for psychosis which, as we might expect because of the relative ease of diagnosis, are relatively constant. Some regions, such as the Central states, have high rates for psychoneurosis but low rates for psychopathy; the Southeast, in contrast, is high in both; and the Far West low in both. The table shows that there is no consistent relation between rejections for psychoneurosis and psychopathy. The latter category, the one least clearly defined, was probably used as a catch-all for doubtful cases that could not readily be placed in one of the other categories.

One additional facet of variability in psychiatric rejection rates requires mention—the possibility that these rates were in part related to differential educational achievement. We observed in an earlier chapter that there was a positive relationship between low educational achievement and the rates of separation from the Army for psychoneurosis. Since we do not have any firm data about the educational achievement level of psychiatric rejectees, we will have to use an indirect approach. The problem is complicated by the fact that most selectees were first examined for their mental ability

Table 41. RATE OF REJECTIONS (PER 1,000) FOR MILITARY SERVICE ON PSYCHIATRIC GROUNDS, TOTAL AND WHITE EXAMINEES, BY MAJOR DIAGNOSTIC CATEGORY AND BY REGION, NOVEMBER 1940—DECEMBER 1944 [a]

REGION [c]	MAJOR DIAGNOSTIC CATEGORY [b] *Psychoneurosis*	*Psychopathy*	*Psychosis*	RATIO OF PSYCHONEUROSIS TO PSYCHOPATHY
	TOTAL EXAMINEES			
New England	29	18	4	1.6:1
Middle Atlantic	21	14	4	1.5:1
Southeast	28	21	2	1.3:1
Southwest	21	18	4	1.2:1
Central	29	12	3	2.4:1
Northwest	21	10	3	2.1:1
Far West	18	9	3	2.0:1
	WHITE EXAMINEES			
New England	29	17	4	1.7:1
Middle Atlantic	21	12	4	1.8:1
Southeast	30	21	3	1.4:1
Southwest	21	16	4	1.3:1
Central	28	11	3	2.5:1
Northwest	21	10	3	2.1:1
Far West	18	9	3	2.0:1

[a] SSS, *Periodic Reports*, Vols. 4–14. See also Table 40, note b.
[b] 20% sample differentiates between psychoneurosis, psychopathy, and psychosis within psychiatric reasons.
[c] For states included in each region, see Table 38.

and those who failed were rejected. Since the numbers rejected by the educational screen varied substantially from one region of the country to another, there is no point in comparing directly the level of educational achievement of the draft eligible population and the numbers rejected by the psychiatric screen. The only way to explore whether the number is significantly related to the educational achievement of the population rejected on psychiatric grounds is to compare the psychiatric rejection rates with those marginally educated persons who had not been rejected by the educational screen. We found psychiatric rejection rates to be higher in states with relatively large numbers in this marginal group. Actually there is a small, but significant, correlation (.49). This suggests that at least part of the regional variability of psychiatric rejection rates may have been due to differential educational achievement.

Table 42. RATES OF REJECTIONS (PER 1,000) FOR MILITARY SERVICE ON MENTAL OR EDUCATIONAL AND ON PSYCHIATRIC GROUNDS, BY SERVICE COMMAND, WORLD WAR II AND KOREAN WAR

	WORLD WAR II [a]		KOREAN WAR [b] *	
SERVICE COMMAND [c]	*Educational*	*Psychiatric*	*Educational*	*Neuro-psychiatric*
First	17	54	90	30
Second	11	40	132	51
Third	30	40	192	20
Fourth	97	53	410	5
Fifth	25	52	174	8
Sixth	15	49	102	32
Seventh	16	41	90	12
Eighth	77	48	327	8
Ninth	12	30	84	21

* July 1950—December 1951. Examinees include only males given preinduction examination. As a result, Korean War rates are somewhat higher than if enlistees were included in examinees.
[a] From a 20% sample reported in SSS, *Periodic Reports*, vols. 4–14. See also Tables 38 and 40, note b: state data in sample grouped by service command.
[b] SG, Med. Stat., DA AGO Form 316.
[c] For states included in each Service Command see Table 39.

There are also corroborative data from the Korean experience which suggest that when substantially higher educational achievement is required for military service, it is likely that fewer individuals will be rejected on psychiatric grounds. The influence of raising the educational cut-off point is clear from Table 42 which points up the very low psychiatric rejection rates associated with very high rejection rates due to a failure to pass the revised screen of the Armed Forces Qualification Test. During this period the Army also changed its psychiatric screening to exclude only the severely disturbed. The lower psychiatric rejection rates, however, reflect in large part the higher educational standards.

Organizational and administrative factors governing the operation of induction stations during the war must also be considered in our search for explanations of variability in the rejection rates. In an earlier study which we undertook as a step in delineating this larger investigation, several revealing findings emerged.[26] In the opinion of the psychiatrists who cooperated in that study the following factors played a prominent role in adversely affecting the quality of the examinations and the validity of the results: the shortage of time; the constant shifting of examining and supervisory personnel; the use of physicians with limited or no psychiatric experience; the fact that the examiners were frequently unfamiliar with the population being screened; the use of different criteria of required performance because of the examiners' unfamiliarity with conditions in active military service; the desire on the part of some examiners to limit the number of potential claimants for pensions; and the need to meet fluctuating manpower requirements.

The largely erratic pattern of psychiatric rejection rates probably reflects all of the factors that we have reviewed. Although it is possible that there are significant variations in the incidence of emotional instability in the population, the rejection rates alone do not support such a conclusion if only because so many forces operated to influence them.

As to the psychiatric screen itself, our preliminary conclusion in view of these considerations must be that it was not effective. The men who were rejected for psychiatric disability were not a homogeneous group of men clearly disqualified for military service. It is probable that many of those rejected could have served as well or better than others who were accepted. But this point should be held in abeyance until we have had an opportunity to compare the patterns of psychiatric rejection rates with the rates of those who were prematurely separated for ineffective performance on psychiatric grounds.

PREDICTIVE VALUE

This brings us to the question of the predictive value of the psychiatric screen. We must remember that emotional stability is not a unitary factor but refers to the total personality of the individual, which is conceived of as a dynamic system of interacting forces. Emotional stability is the result of the interaction of innate endowment and life experiences, those of childhood being the most important. Prediction here involves an estimate of whether a particular individual is likely to break down if exposed in the future to stress, which in turn is an unknown variable.

In principle, it should be possible to grade individuals on a scale as to the degree of their emotional stability. But emotional stability is not constant for it is subject to change as the individual encounters new experiences. How such new experiences affect his emotional stability will depend on whether they constitute a stress or a support for him. For all but a few individuals combat was experienced as a major stress and some broke down even in contemplation of being sent into the line. A few found release on the battlefield: for the first time in their lives they were permitted to express their aggression with approval.

Stress has three dimensions: intensity, duration, and quality. Many found Army life tolerable but could not adjust to combat. Others could cope with combat if they had a respite from fighting every couple of weeks, but broke if they were kept in the line consecutively for many weeks. Differential intensity of stress is seen in different kinds of combat situations—from uneventful patrols to intensive shelling. Intolerable duration of stress was experienced by some men who saw service on an isolated outpost for many months. If even a mildly stressful situation lasts too long, or is repeated too frequently, it may become as upsetting to the individual as a more intensive situation experienced only once. This is the cumulative effect of prolonged stress.

The quality of stress is more individualized than either intensity or duration. A soldier who has always been afraid of water may experience near-panic when he embarks for overseas, and may lose complete control of himself if his ship is torpedoed and he is forced to jump into the water. A man's responses to stress are hard to foretell because his reactions to new situations are difficult to predict. Most men found separation from their homes and friends difficult. But to the minority who had failed to make a niche for themselves in their communities, the Army offered purpose, companionship, and leadership, all of which served as major supports.

To the extent that psychiatric screening sought to foretell whether each individual would break down in military service in the face of uncertain situations of stress and supports, the effort had to fail. But the selection process was actually geared to a less ambitious goal, to eliminate those who were most likely to break down. A psychiatric screen can surely reduce somewhat the number who would break down on active service. Even if it could do better, the question is whether it should try to do so. Assuming that the screen rejected all who showed any signs whatever of emotional instability, it could still not prevent psychiatric breakdowns in service—for the most stable man if subjected to extreme stress as can occur in war will break down. Moreover, the higher the cut-off point, the larger the number rejected. If every man who might break down emotionally were rejected, who would serve?

In assessing the predictive value of the psychiatric screen the crucial question is whether the number prematurely separated for psychiatric reasons was lower than it would have been in the absence of the screen. The paucity of reliable data makes this very difficult to determine. The national figures on rejections and separations do not provide a basis for an answer and there are no Census data available on the incidence of psychiatric disability in the entire population to serve as a statistical yardstick. The comparative figures for World War I and World War II which were presented earlier

(Table 37) indicated that in spite of a very much higher rate of rejections in the later war, there was an almost sixfold increase in premature separations. But the difference in the characteristics of the two wars and the procedures followed warns us to interpret these data with caution.

An alternative is to compare again on a regional basis the rejection and separation rates for World War II. Even if the base population was not homogenous, the screen should have resulted in equalizing the groups accepted for service at least to the extent that each man met the minimum criteria of emotional stability. If men from different regions were exposed to the same orders of stress, the regional separation rates should have been approximately the same. Since each Service Command was responsible for furnishing between 600,000 and 1,500,000 men to the Army, we can postulate that the stress factor operated without prejudice to any major region. Even if an entire division of the National Guard, composed largely of men from one state, was engaged in very heavy combat, the numbers involved were too small to alter this assumption that stress was more or less equally distributed among men from different regions. The only exception relates to Negro troops. Since they were overwhelmingly assigned to service units and thus may be presumed to have been subjected to less, or at least different orders of, stress, the regional analysis will be more accurate if it is focused on the experience of white troops only.

Table 43 sets out the separation rates for psychiatric reasons by the Service Command from which the men were inducted.

Contrary to the expectation that the separation rates would be similar, they show considerable variability, much more than can be explained by chance alone. These figures and the analysis of regional rejection data may reflect different criteria in the initial screening—that is, regions using lower cut-off points would have fewer rejections but high separation rates. Table 44 presents the relevant data.

Once again the results are surprising. The Service Commands with the highest rejection rates do not have the lowest separation rates. If anything, the two appear to vary in the same direction. The positive relationship is tenuous, but certainly there is no inverse correlation—higher rejection rates are not associated with lower separation rates.

What are the possible explanations? The assumption that higher rejection rates are necessarily the result of applying higher standards for induction may not be justified. As we have seen, the psychiatric screen was probably used to reject marginal selectees who were more educationally deprived than psychiatrically handicapped. The same blurring of categories occurred in separations, for, as we noted previously, towards the end of the war many who should have been separated for inaptitude were discharged through medical channels because it was an easier method of discharge.

Table 43. RATE OF SEPARATIONS OF ENLISTED MALE PERSONNEL FROM THE ARMY FOR PSYCHOSIS AND PSYCHONEUROSIS, TOTAL AND WHITE, BY SERVICE COMMAND, WORLD WAR II [a] *

Service Command [b]	*White*	*Total*
First	34	34
Second	41	41
Third	32	32
Fourth	37	36
Fifth	32	32
Sixth	35	36
Seventh	26	27
Eighth	29	30
Ninth	30	29

* Rate of separations (1942–1945) per 1,000 accessions (fiscal 1941–1945).

[a] Data for 1942–1944 from special tabulations, AG, Stat. & Acctg., Np. tab., CHR; data for 1945 from SG, Med. Stat., unpub. worksheets: "Disability Separations for Psychosis and Psychoneurosis," divided by thousands of accessions, fiscal years 1941–1945 from AG, Stat. & Acctg., unpub. worksheets.

Note: White accessions obtained from total accessions by subtracting Negro inductions given in SSS, *Victory*, table 153, pp. 610–11, and an estimate of enlistments derived by distributing total Negro enlistments and ERC calls from *Strength of Army*, STM-30, pp. 84–85 on basis of data in SSS, "Total Enlistments," unpub. table.

[b] For states included in each Service Command see Table 39.

Table 44. RATES OF REJECTIONS (PER 1,000) FOR MILITARY SERVICE AND SEPARATIONS OF ENLISTED MALE PERSONNEL FROM THE ARMY ON PSYCHIATRIC GROUNDS, TOTAL AND WHITE, BY MAJOR DIAGNOSTIC CATEGORY AND BY SERVICE COMMAND, WORLD WAR II

	REJECTIONS [a]		SEPARATIONS [b]	
SERVICE COMMAND [c]	*Psychoneurosis*	*Psychosis*	*Psychoneurosis*	*Psychosis*
		TOTAL		
First	29	4	28	6
Second	21	4	34	7
Third	21	4	26	6
Fourth	28	2	30	6
Fifth	28	3	27	5
Sixth	32	3	29	7
Seventh	23	4	22	5
Eighth	24	3	25	5
Ninth	17	2	24	5
		WHITE		
First	29	4	28	6
Second	21	4	34	7
Third	21	4	26	5
Fourth	31	2	32	5
Fifth	28	3	26	5
Sixth	32	3	28	6
Seventh	23	4	22	4
Eighth	24	3	24	5
Ninth	17	2	23	5

[a] SSS, *Periodic Reports,* Vols. 4–14. See also Table 40, note b: 20% sample differentiates between psychoneurosis, psychopathy, and psychosis within psychiatric reasons.

[b] Data for 1942–1944 from special tabulations, AG, Stat. & Acctg., Np. tab., CHR; data for 1945 from SG, Med. Stat., unpub. worksheets: "Disability Separations for Psychosis and Psychoneurosis," divided by thousands of accessions, fiscal years 1941–1945 from AG, Stat. & Acctg., unpub. worksheets.

[c] For states included in each Service Command see Table 39.

Such blurring is suggested by the positive correlation between psychiatric rejections and lower education on the one hand, and psychiatric separations and lower education on the other. The relationship between emotional instability and educational retardation can be illustrated by the learning troubles experienced by many upset children. A poorly educated soldier is also likely to find it difficult to absorb military training and to fulfill his duty assignments. His ineffective performance is likely to lead to his separation. The sharp differences between the Southeast and the Far West bear directly on this point. As shown in Table 40, the Southeast had a white rejection rate of 56 for all psychiatric causes; the Far West of 32. While cultural factors such as rurality, poverty, minority race problems, delayed industrialization, can help to explain the higher rates of emotional instability in the Southeast, each of these factors is also related to the differentially low educational achievement characteristic of the region. Consequently, we must consider carefully the educational factor in an effort to understand the psychiatric figures.

While it would appear that the educational factor explains much about the paradoxical relationship between psychiatric rejection and separation rates, we cannot tell whether it accounts for all, or only part, of the variability among regions. It is possible that the variations in both rejection and separation rates reflect to some extent a true differential incidence of emotional stability in different regions.

Our appraisal of psychiatric screening in World War II points to two conclusions: the screen was not very effective and it had little predictive value. Can we therefore conclude that the Army would have saved more manpower if it had operated without a psychiatric screen or, possibly, that it should have made efforts to reject much larger numbers of potential failures. The answer must be in terms of two quite different considerations: the knowledge required to establish an effective screen and the logistical cost involved in putting it into effect.

INHERENT DIFFICULTIES

But we are immediately faced with a series of difficulties. Almost nothing is known about the distribution of emotional instability in the population. Very little is known about how individuals make use of their assets to balance their liabilities when faced with new and difficult situations. Psychiatrists are much better informed about people's weaknesses than about their strengths. One thoughtful psychiatrist who participated in the screening for military service in World War II remarked that he and his colleagues knew too much about the weaknesses of their patients to be able to judge how they would perform. Dynamic psychology has never made a systematic study of the relationship between a man's emotional disabilities and his capacity to meet specific performance standards. Much more progress has been made in developing static diagnostic categories than in elaborating a dynamic approach in which various types of emotional instability are appraised in terms of their possible interference with a man's performance.

Even if more were known about the relationship between a man's emotional stability and his performance, we would have to make allowance for the influence of new situations with their varying orders of stress and support in order to predict how he will perform in the future. Since we cannot take account of such unknowns, the reliability of any screening operation geared to an estimate of future performance must be questioned. But a screen can identify men with such severe emotional disabilities that an estimate of future inadequate performance will be reasonable. This was accomplished in large measure by the screen used in World War II. To the extent that the logistical situation would permit rejecting more than these most obvious potential failures, military screening would have been more effective if it had focused on the group of men who had had relatively little education—less than eight years—and on men with physical defects which, though they did not disqualify for military service, represented a handicap. The emotional stability of a man in either group might have made the difference between success and failure. If skilled psychiatrists could truly assess such men's emotional resilience, psychiatric screening could contribute greatly to a maximum utilization of military manpower in a major war.

A second set of considerations in establishing a screen are more practical than theoretical. We have used the term logistical to describe these factors since screening is not an end in itself but has merit only as it enables an organization to discharge its mission more effectively. Among the relevant considerations are the size and quality of the manpower pool and the utilization practices of the organization.

During a war the combat mission of the Armed Services has very high priority, but since the fighting forces can win only if men have weapons to fight with and if ships are available to transport them to the combat areas, they cannot usurp all available manpower. Furthermore, the Army itself has hundreds of different tasks which must be performed in order to accomplish its mission. If it proceeds on the theory that every man accepted for service must be able to perform effectively in the most difficult assignment, it may set a standard that is unrealistic with regard to both its true needs and the condition of the manpower pool. But if the Army uses its screening procedure for selecting men with different qualities for different types of assignments, it will facilitate the accomplishment of its mission. It can further help itself by simplifying its more complex jobs and by providing additional training to qualify men for tasks within their potential competence. In this manner it can escape from having to rely exclusively on excessively high standards of selection.

During the early part of World War II the Army made its selection standards higher than would otherwise be necessary by insisting that all men had to be convertible into infantrymen even though no more than two out of five servicemen would eventually serve in ground combat units. This doctrine of maximum convertibility is largely responsible for the fact that almost 1 million men were rejected on psychiatric grounds. But even if an effort had been made to screen out still larger numbers, as some enthusiasts of psychiatric screening recommended, it is doubtful that the number of premature separations would have been materially reduced. As we have pointed out, even men with a high degree of emotional stability, if exposed to specific orders of stress, may break.

Although there are no other large-scale studies to prove our contention that many of those who were rejected because of emotional weakness could have served as well as many who had been accepted, it is supported by sample investigations that have been carried out. Egan and his colleagues [27] studied 2,000 men who were originally rejected for service but who on reexamination were later accepted. They found that four out of five served satisfactorily. Frye's follow-up study [28] of students whom he had treated at Yale for emotional disturbance and whom he considered

Table 45. EFFICIENCY OF PREDICTION BY PSYCHIATRISTS OF UNSATISFACTORY PERFORMANCE, 505 INDUCTEES, KOREAN WAR [a]

AREA OF MILITARY SERVICE	UNSATISFACTORY PERFORMERS		EFFICIENCY OF PREDICTION IN PERCENT
	Number Predicted	*Actual Number*	
Zone of Interior	27	16	59
Overseas non-combat	43	7	16
Korea, rear zone	14	2	14
Combat support	18	2	11
Front Line Combat	21	3	14
Total	123	30	24

[a] Glass, *et al., Psychiatric Prediction,* table 10, p. 20.

unfit for military service but who were accepted points in the same direction. Many of the presumed failures turned out to be not only satisfactory but superior servicemen. More recently Glass and his colleagues [29] have presented data about men already in service who were assessed as likely failures by both their own commanders and by psychiatrists, but who actually performed quite well. During the Korean conflict six examining psychiatrists made a careful evaluation of 505 inductees early in their training cycle and prognosticated their future performance. They predicted four times as many failures as subsequently occurred, as indicated by Table 45.

Aita,[30] who served during World War II as a psychiatric examiner in an induction station, divided a sample of men who were accepted into two groups—those who were likely to become successful soldiers and those who, because of various personality disorders, probably would not. On the basis of follow-up data Aita concluded that the psychiatric examiner was not able to predict future military performance with sufficient accuracy to warrant the exclusion of any except the seriously disturbed. Plesset,[31] who served as a division psychiatrist during the war, found that many soldiers whom he had labeled as poor risks for combat did quite well; this finding generally confirms the results of the other investigations reviewed above.

In addition to the manpower losses because of the unwarranted assumptions underlying the screening process which we have already outlined, a too rigid psychiatric screening procedure will cost an organization dear in professional personnel. Well-trained psychiatric personnel are likely to be in short supply and those available must be allocated to meet a large number of competing needs. A rigid screen is also hampered by the time element. Instead of the two- or three-minute examination which was the norm in World War II, a skilled examiner needs a minimum of half and in certain cases a full hour to make any reasonable assessment of a man's potential. But if this amount of time were allotted for each psychiatric examination, it would have required about 1,200 psychiatrists working full time throughout the five years to screen all the selectees. And even if so large a number of psychiatrists could have been found and induced or directed to carry out this work, they would have become a major bottleneck during periods of maximum inflow when as many as 3,000 men were processed in a single day through a single induction station.

What then can be concluded about psychiatric screening in the face of these major theoretical and logistical limitations? The disappointing results of the experience of World War II were the inevitable consequence of unrealistically high expectations. Psychiatric screening for military service that is reasonable in terms of the numbers rejected and the resources required to carry out the examining procedure cannot prevent the acceptance of many men who when exposed to the major stress of combat or even, in some cases, to noncombat situations will break down.

ADJUSTMENT POTENTIAL

We have analyzed the gross statistical data bearing on the large numbers rejected for service or prematurely separated for psychiatric reasons and have arrived at the conclusion that screening can be efficient only if it is directed toward eliminating the most likely potential failures and the marginal cases. It may now prove rewarding to review the path which we have traveled. A mountain looks different when it is viewed from the base instead of the peak. What of the basic concept of emotional stability? Has it held up well? Retrospectively, it appears that what we have called emotional stability might better be considered adjustment potential. The two are related but they can be differentiated. Emotional stability has a clinical connotation; it is grounded in the structure of the personality. In contrast adjustment potential is a broader concept: it is a composite of the psychological, cultural, educational, social, occupational, and other qualities, experiences, and skills that determine the ability of a person to cope with a new environment and new demands.

If we bear this distinction in mind, we can state that there were significant differences in the adjustment potential of different regional populations. It may well be that had our data permitted a more refined analysis, such differences could also have been ascertained for demographic groups. It is now reasonable to postulate that the smaller the differences among regions of the country in income, education, the level of industrialization, and other major factors, the less likely it is that we will find significant differences in the adjustment potential of the population. For differences in adjustment potential are largely the outgrowth of differences in developmental experiences and acquired skills. It is because of this that one group finds it easier than another to meet the standards set by a modern technological organization. The more similar the demands that an individual must meet in military life are to what he has been accustomed in civilian life, the greater is the likelihood of his adjustment to the demands of the environment.

Some confirmation of this latter conclusion can be found in the several sample analyses carried out by the Selective Service System during World War II and reported on in its monograph series.[32] These studies reveal that the rural areas had an overall higher disqualification rate—for physical, educational, and psychiatric reasons combined—than did urban areas. Further, the rejection rate for farm areas was above that for rural non-farm areas. Finally, in general the larger the urban community, the lower was the disqualification rate for each cause.

The Selective Service System also reported on the prevalence of psychiatric defects among its registrants examined during the first three years. These findings revealed a higher rate of psychiatric disability among the white farm group than among the white non-farm group. It is interesting that no significant difference was found between Negroes on and off the farm. The rate of psychiatric defects varied for both the farm and non-farm populations from one region to another and with respect to both groups the differences were found to be statistically significant. This is true irrespective of whether Negroes are included or excluded from the totals. With the single exception of the West, the white farm population was consistently found to have a higher rate of psychiatric defects than did the non-farm population. While educational achievement is probably responsible for part of these differences, there is a complex of factors associated with rurality that might help explain the higher incidence of psychiatric defects found among the agricultural population.

Our concern with the social rather than the psychological factors in the concept of an adjustment potential does not, of course, deny the more narrow, clinical factor of "emotional stability." Because of their emotional development, some people will be more stable than others, and this factor of psychological stability or instability will affect the way in which they are able to adjust to new situations or new demands. But if, as we are now suggesting, adjustment potential is not the same as emotional stability, successful adjustment may not be solely, or even largely, the result of greater emotional stability and, except for individual instances of severe disturbance, the reverse is also true: emotional instability does not necessarily preclude successful adjustment or performance.

The question that remains is whether there would still be a differential incidence of emotional instability among regions of the country after account is taken of the effects of varying adjustment potential. There is one piece of evidence which suggests that such a difference may in fact exist. Late in the war a paper and pencil self-administered, standardized psychiatric screening tool was introduced, designed to identify men who should be more carefully examined by psychiatrists. The results of the Neuropsychiatric Screening Adjunct showed less variability than the results of the clinical psychiatric examinations in the same regions at the same time. Yet even these results, which were not affected by such operational considerations as whether a man was fit for military service, did not eliminate differences between the major regions. While the variations shown by the NSA do not correspond exactly to the pattern of our data, substantial differences between North and South were found. While the test was administered to all registrants who were literate, a possible confounding between educational and emotional defect cannot be ruled out because of the significantly lower educational achievement in the Southeast and Southwest. Table 46, derived from data reported by Stouffer,[33] presents the relevant information.

The foregoing analysis was unable to settle definitively the question whether there are regional variations in the emotional stability of the population. But it did shed some new and important light on the problem of variations in the adjustment potential of the population.

The analysis demonstrated that a close connection exists between rejections and separations for psychiatric causes and educational achievement. And we know from earlier analyses of the close connection between lack of adaptability in the Army and poor educational background. We are therefore justified in concluding that there are significant variations in the adjustment potential of the population that derive in the first instance from variations in their educational achievement.

Table 46. PERCENT OF MEN REJECTED FOR MILITARY SERVICE ON PSYCHIATRIC GROUNDS AND PERCENT OF MEN RECEIVING CRITICAL NSA SCORES OR SIGNS, LITERATE PREINDUCTION EXAMINEES, BY SERVICE COMMAND, AUGUST 1945 [a]

Service Command [b]	*Psychiatric Rejections*	*Receiving Critical Scores and/or Signs*
First	21.3	28.1
Second	12.0	30.4
Third	16.3	32.7
Fourth	16.1	36.1
Fifth	13.8	26.7
Sixth	13.8	27.3
Seventh	17.0	29.7
Eighth	10.5	33.9
Ninth	8.2	32.9
Summary:		
Mean	14.3	30.9
Standard deviation	3.7	3.0
Coefficient of deviation	25.7	9.7

[a] Stouffer *et al.*, *The American Soldier*, Vol. IV, tables 2 and 4, pp. 551–52, 556–57.
[b] For states included in each Service Command see Table 39.

What are the implications for psychiatric screening growing out of our shift from the concept of emotional stability to adjustment potential and its different incidence among population groups? It is our considered conclusion that in the screening process most of the effort should be directed to assessing critically the pattern of a man's behavior prior to his call-up to determine whether he has previously encountered difficulty in meeting the ordinary demands of his home environment. Special attention should be devoted to the man who has not acquired the basic skills and competences which are almost essential in adjusting to the Army. Only if a look at a man's past behavior raises serious questions would it be worthwhile to evaluate him psychiatrically. In evaluating those on the margin, as well as those well below the standard, psychiatric screening has a constructive role to play. As for all the others, the citizen's behavior is the best clue to the soldier's performance.

Chapter Twelve: THE MORE EFFECTIVE UTILIZATION OF MANPOWER

SINCE World War II represented one of the great crises in the nation's history, the expansion of the Army from 200,000 men to over 8 million between 1940 and 1945 is an important story in its own right. The utilization of military manpower during that period has been the concern of this book. The student will want to steep himself in the details; others will be primarily interested in how the story of this major episode can contribute to improved manpower and personnel policy in a world not yet freed from the threat of war. This concluding chapter will therefore seek to delineate the guidelines for both military and civilian manpower policy that can be extracted from this study.

The generalizations that can be distilled are limited by the framework within which this particular investigation was carried out. This volume has focused on the way in which military manpower policy affected the utilization of the many millions who were screened for and inducted into the Armed Services, particularly the Army. At each stage emphasis has been placed on tracing the influence of manpower policy on effective manpower utilization. In our companion volumes the focus is broader and considers how the individual's personal strengths and weaknesses as well as the stresses and supports in his environment affect his performance.

The first, and from many points of view the most important, finding growing out of the present study is the extent to which manpower policy is determined by the past. How much time and effort must be devoted to training people to acquire new skills in a period of crisis or expansion depends in considerable measure on their previous education and experience. If the school system has done its job well, the Armed Forces or civilian industry will be able to move rapidly. If large numbers have failed to acquire a basic education, valuable time and resources will have to be devoted to teaching essential skills. The more highly specialized our society becomes and the more it must rely on highly trained personnel, the more important is the quality and preparation that young people receive for work and life.

The contemporary uneasiness about the state of our nation's scientific and professional manpower reflects a growing awareness that actions taken today—or not taken today—will materially affect our position a decade or two hence. For a man must spend almost ten years after his graduation from high school in completing his professional or scientific training. Moreover, the quality of education that young people receive in high school will significantly influence their career development.

We can see the extent to which the Armed Forces were handicapped during World War II by the failure of our society to make an adequate investment in the education of its young people by recalling the following figures: More than 700,000 poorly educated young men, many wholly illiterate, were rejected; the Armed Forces attempted to train another million men who had inadequate education and turn them into effective servicemen. It is clear, then, that inadequate educational background was a most important factor in ineffective performance.

The Armed Forces were further handicapped because in previous years the nation had not supported military training. During the 1920s and '30s Congress had made such small appropriations for the Army and the Navy that there were too few trained officers and noncommissioned officers to handle the training mission during the rapid expansion of the Army which began with the partial mobilization of 1940. The failure to invest today in training tomorrow's leaders is always costly. American business has begun to learn this lesson and it is therefore ever more concerned with executive development.

While the Congress has made provision for possible future mobilizations by erecting standby plants and stockpiling strategic materials, it has as yet not fully appreciated the importance of large-scale investments to raise the skill level of the American population. For the reasons already enumerated and for the additional reason that in any future emergency time will be extremely limited, the level of competence of our population at the outset of hostilities may well prove decisive.

Next in importance to adequate education and training for effective manpower utilization is careful manpower planning. Unless comprehensive information is gathered about the nation's human resources and unless such studies are paralleled by estimates of future requirements, manpower policy in an emergency will have to be developed largely on an ad hoc basis.

This volume should have made clear that in its use of manpower the Armed Forces had to pay a high price because they had to improvise as they went along. They had little knowledge of the characteristics of the manpower pool and they were slow to develop estimates of their future requirements. As a result, they pursued policies which resulted in a serious underutilization of manpower. For example, early in the war when the Army was sorely in need of leaders, it did not call the more experienced men who were most likely to possess leadership qualities. Again, in 1941 and early 1942 assuming that the manpower pool was flush, the Army rejected large numbers with minor defects, only to be innundated by them a little later when it found that it could meet its peak requirements only by accepting them. Its unhappy experience with the Army Specialized Training Program resulted from a failure to estimate how pressed it would be in the future for capable men for ground force units.

War cannot be adequately planned for. All contingencies can not be foreseen. Many plans will have to be modified or scrapped. But failing to plan is no answer. The more an organization knows about its resources, the more thoroughly it explores its future requirements, the more effectively it will be able to meet the unexpected.

A third finding concerned the potentialities and limitations of selection. At the beginning of the war the Army hoped that it could avoid serious manpower wastes by rejecting for service men who, because of one or another defect, were assumed to be unable to perform effectively on active duty. But these relatively high criteria had to be modified to enable the Army to meet its peak requirements.

Selection criteria must always be set with reference to the size of the manpower pool and the scale of the organization's needs. Business is constantly adjusting its selection criteria to changes in the labor market, raising them when many are seeking employment and lowering them when few are available for work. The more knowledge an organization has about the availability of the present and potential manpower supply, the better able it is to establish realistic selection criteria.

The desire to avoid personnel waste through improved selection is widespread: it is characteristic not only of the Armed Forces but of business, academic institutions, government, and the professions. Yet the military experience of World War II forces one to recognize that selection is at best a limited instrument. It can be used to reject individuals who because of gross handicaps are likely to prove ineffective. But the more refined the criteria become, the less likely that they will prove practical. Effective performance in a large organization depends on more than the individual's personal qualities and characteristics: it is greatly influenced by policies, leadership, and the actual situations in which the individual is placed.

Thorough personnel evaluations are costly to undertake, require considerable time, and cannot be carried out except by a trained staff. In an emergency, time and competent staff are always scarce. But even if refined screening could be carried out, it would still be of limited value because individuals change with time. President

Eisenhower underwent a physical examination just prior to his heart attack and was found to be in excellent health. The newspapers frequently carry reports on the suicide of a brilliant artist or scientist whose career was in full tide.

The major lesson that can be extracted from the largest screening operation in the country's history is the inherent limitations of relying too heavily on selection to insure the more effective utilization of manpower. While selection can be used to reject severely handicapped individuals who are likely to fail, it cannot do more than this. Selection is a useful and even necessary facet of a comprehensive personnel program, but training and assignment must be relied upon to fit the individual into an organization so that he can perform effectively. The Army was faced with a truly herculean task in World War II because it had to convert in the shortest possible time such large numbers of peace-loving civilians into efficient soldiers.

Industry also engages in large-scale conversion programs though it is not generally aware of this fact. Every year more than a million young people leave high school to start work; and several hundred thousand complete college or professional school to enter employment. Many problems that the Army encountered have their parallel in this school-to-work transition that characterizes our civilian society.

The first step in a successful conversion program is to assess the knowledge, aptitudes, and interests of recruits prior to placing them in a training program or in a work assignment. But the larger the numbers that have to be handled, the more difficult it is to take account of each individual's strengths and weaknesses. The Army was confronted with a daily inflow in the tens of thousands.

In determining a man's training and duty assignment the Army relied primarily on his score on the Army General Classification Test, using this as a rough measure of his ability. Yet the Army was never able to introduce much flexibility into its training system and thus to allow adequately for the differing capacities and potentials of recruits. Industry also tends to assign newcomers to the same training program. And colleges and professional schools are reluctant to grant advanced credits to students who demonstrate special competence. Every large organization is disinclined to differentiate among its newcomers before it has had an opportunity to assess them directly.

The Army did not differentiate initially among recruits except in the Air Corps but singled out those with potential leadership abilities primarily as a result of their performance in basic or advanced training. Our British allies were more venturesome and economical: in the selection of officer personnel, they were willing to give more weight to a man's civilian background and performance and to cut to the bone his trial period as an enlisted man.

Our system not only held back superior men but handicapped those who required more than the average amount of time to complete their training. We found it just as difficult to make exceptions for the slow as for the superior learner. It was not until the summer of 1943, when the Army was well on the way to achieving its peak strength, that it finally established formal special training units at reception centers to assist illiterates and slow learners get off to a good start.

But it was rarely that an individual became disturbed because his progress was slower than it might have been under a more flexible training system. More frequently, men lost confidence in themselves because they could not keep up with their unit. Even more difficulties arose when the Army assigned men to duty far beyond or far below their competence.

Most men were able to reconcile themselves to assignments that made few demands on them since they realized that an Army at war could not possibly find the right job for every man. However, when the Army failed to identify men with skills which were in short supply, such underassignment resulted in a serious waste of manpower. Moreover, the Army frequently trained men for many months in a specialty only to find when they were ready to be assigned that it has grossly overestimated its requirements. Even a man with a scarce skill was seldom assigned directly to a position where he could use his special competence. The many shortcomings in the training and assignment system inevitably resulted in a wasteful utilization of manpower. Some soldiers became so disturbed by their experiences in training or on duty that they had to be discharged as ineffective.

The Army faced a particularly difficult problem in developing an equitable policy for sharing risks. A soldier's assignment had implications far beyond whether he could make use of his aptitude and training, or even whether he had appropriate rank and pay. In large measure a soldier's assignment determined his chances of surviving. Yet it was not possible for the Army to equalize onerous duty among all who served.

As the war progressed, however, the General Staff came to recognize that it was wasteful, as well as unjust, to keep men in the line for long periods. Unfortunately, it was frequently very difficult, because of a shortage of personnel and transportation, for commanders to withdraw troops for rest, rehabilitation, or rotation. There is no way of calculating how many soldiers, resenting the fact that the Army was unable to be equitable simply refused, consciously or unconsciously, to continue in a combat assignment. A man's willingness to sacrifice depends on his faith in the integrity of the organization to which he belongs. Neither business nor the military can ignore this fact.

Since no policy ever carries itself, it must be monitored. The larger the organization, the more dispersed its units, the greater is the need for controls. Lack of adequate follow-up was another shortcoming in the Army's personnel policy in World War II. The senior staff was reluctant to invest even modest resources in evaluating the personnel policies in effect, because among other reasons it did not want to interfere with important operational missions. Since many policies were developed in response to pressing needs, time frequently found them wanting, especially as the war moved into a new stage. While evidence from the field eventually pointed up the need for revision, the staff could have avoided many problems by initially establishing tighter controls.

Another key to the effectiveness of policy is the availability of competent personnel to carry it out. The more elaborate the policy, the greater the demands on the personnel, the less likely it is that it can succeed. The Regular Army had few personnel specialists. While many recruits learned quickly, they were frequently transferred to another assignment just as they became competent. A recent Secretary of the Army once remarked that the weakest link in the Army's personnel system has always been the corporal or sergeant at the reception center. If he makes a mistake, the recruit is likely to finish his service before it is corrected.

While large civilian organizations are in a better position to test or pretest their personnel policies and train their personnel staffs so that their policies will be carried out effectively, they, like the military, are confronted by one major challenge—to meet the need for general rules and regulations while retaining as much flexibility as possible so that every individual can make his optimal contribution.

The more effective utilization of manpower has been found to be as elusive as it is important. While selection, training, and assignment procedures have much to contribute, the history of the manpower logistics in World War II emphasizes that the strength of a democracy in an emergency depends in the largest measure on its prior investment in its people, the soundness of its planning, and the effectiveness and flexibility of its policies.

THE LESSON

IF man is to progress, he must learn from experience. It is the only way. World War II was a most costly experience; the American people alone lost more than a quarter of a million young men in combat. More than twice that number of young Americans were disabled.

A major war tests the minds and souls of men and much that is hidden in ordinary times becomes revealed. World War II illuminated much that was previously obscure about the structure of our democracy and the people who are both its servants and masters.

The war demonstrated the great strength of a free people. The tried and tested institutions of a democratic society were found to be both flexible and resilient, and thus were able both to meet and surmount the emergency. And the society showed great ingenuity in improvising new institutions to meet the demands of the day. Large costs were inevitably incurred because so much had to be created without the advantage of prior planning and pilot models, but victory was gained.

As for the people, the war revealed the tremendous advantages that accrue to the side which has the better educated, the more skilled, the more flexible population. But in addition, the war provided a lesson that the nation has not yet fully assimilated. This is the lesson.

There were millions of men so poorly educated, so emotionally disturbed, or so without motivation, that they could not respond to their country's need or, if they did, they were soon found deficient. In World War II the Army mobilized 89 divisions. The nearly

2½ million men who failed, either because of their own deficiencies or because of limitations in manpower policies and procedures, represented the equivalent of some 165 divisions, or about 55 divisions if one makes allowance for direct support troops. On several occasions our generals were barely able to hold the line because of their depleted manpower reserves. World War II is far behind us but the lesson which we paid for dearly we have not yet learned.

The United States has only 6 percent of the world's population. It cannot possibly win the peace nor, if need be, repel an aggressor by numbers alone. Our one chance for security and leadership is to develop our human resources to their optimum. We have no more time to learn the lesson of World War II: we must invest in our people—men and women, young and old, white and Negro, urban and rural—so that each and every person has an opportunity to develop his full potentialities and to use them for his own benefit and the benefit of the nation. As President Eisenhower has said: "The people are the shield of the Republic."

ABBREVIATED TITLES USED IN TABLES

AG, MRBr., ETN-43	Unpublished report: "Analysis of Enlisted Men Showing Year of Birth and Marital Status Based on 'Personnel Survey' of the Army as of 31 December 1943," ETN-43. Machine Records Branch, Office of the Adjutant General, War Department, Washington, D.C., 18 April 1944.
AG, MRBr., ETN-104	Unpublished report: "Analysis of Enlisted Men Showing ACGT Groups by Enlistment/Induction Period (Negro and Others) Based on 'Personnel Survey' of the Army as of 30 June 1944," ETN-104. Machine Records Branch, Office of the Adjutant General, War Department, Washington, D.C., 1 September 1944.
AG, BRBr., STN-94	Unpublished report: "Analysis of the United States Army Personnel by Identity and Year of Birth, 30 June 1944, Based Upon 'Personnel Survey' of the Army," STN-94. Machine Records Branch, Office of the Adjutant General, War Department, Washington, D.C., November 1944.
AG, MRBr., XTQ-13	Unpublished report: "Strength of the Army as of 31 October 1940" XTQ-13. Machine Records Branch, Office of the Adjutant General, War Department, Washington, D.C.
AG, Stat. & Acctg.	Unpublished worksheets prepared in the Statistical and Accounting Branch, Office of the Adjutant General, Department of the Army, Washington, D.C.
AG, Stat. & Acctg., CHR	Special tabulations of a 5% sample made for the Conservation of Human Resources Project by the Statistical and Accounting Branch, Office of the Adjutant General, Department of the Army, Washington, D.C., 1952.
AG, Stat. & Acctg., Np. tab., CHR	Special tabulation giving separations for neuropsychiatric diseases by service command. Made for the Conservation of Human Resources Project by the Statistical and Accounting Branch, Office of the Adjutant General, Department of the Army, Washington, D.C., June 10, 1955.

AG, Stat. & Acctg., Rep. sample, CHR	Special tabulations of a representative sample. Made for the Conservation of Human Resources Project by the Statistical and Accounting Branch, Office of the Adjutant General, War Department, Washington, D.C., October 13, 1955.
Armed Forces, *Demob.*	*Demobilization of the Armed Forces: Hearings before the Committee on Military Affairs, United States Senate, Seventy-Ninth Congress, First Session, on S. 1355.* Statement of Brigadier General Gerald C. Thomas, USMC, September 19, 1945.
Army Air Forces, *Stat. Digest*	*Army Air Forces Statistical Digest World War II,* Office of Statistical Control, War Department, Washington, D.C., December 1945.
Britten and Perrott, *PHR*	R. H. Britten and G. ST. J. Perrott, "Summary of Physical Findings on Men Drafted in the World War," *Public Health Reports,* Vol. LVI, No. 2, 10 January 1941.
Glass *et al., Psychiatric Prediction*	A. J. Glass *et al., Psychiatric Prediction and Military Effectiveness.* Walter Reed Army Institute of Research, Walter Reed Army Medical Center, Washington, D.C., March 1956.
Health of Army	*Health of the Army,* vol. 1, report 2. Office of the Surgeon General, War Department, Washington, D.C., 31 August 1946.
Love and Davenport, *Defects*	A. G. Love and C. B. Davenport, *Defects Found in Drafted Men.* Prepared under the direction of the Surgeon General, M. W. Ireland, War Department, Government Printing Office, Washington, D.C., 1920.
Marine Corps, unpub. summaries	Unpublished special summaries: "U.S. Marine Corps Officer Personnel on Active Duty, Strength, Accessions, and Separations, Men and Women, Quarterly, 1940 through 1945," and "U.S. Marine Enlisted Personnel on Active Duty, Strength, Accessions, and Separations, Men and Women, Total and Negroid, Quarterly, 1940 through 1945." Office of Personnel, Headquarters, U.S. Marine Corps, Washington, D.C.
NAVPERS-15115	*Yearbook of Naval Personnel Statistics,* NAVPERS-15115. Bureau of Naval Personnel, Navy Department, Washington, D.C., May 1945.
Navy, *Annual Report of SG*	*Annual Report of the Surgeon General, U.S. Navy, Chief of the Bureau of Medicine and Surgery, to the Secretary of the Navy Concerning Statistics of Diseases and Injuries in the United States Navy,* for the calendar years 1942, 1943, 1944, and 1945. Bureau of Medicine and Surgery, Navy Department, Government Printing Office, Washington, D.C.

Navy Records	Unpublished table 172, "Accounting Gains and Losses of Navy Enlisted Personnel during Calendar year 1945" and table 179, "Accounting Gains and Losses of Navy Enlisted Women's Reserve during the Calendar Year 1945." Records Division, Bureau of Personnel, U.S. Navy, Washington, D.C.
Palmer *et al.*	R. B. Palmer, B. I. Wiley, and W. R. Keast, *The Procurement and Training of Ground Combat Troops.* Historical Section: Army Ground Forces, one of the series "The United States Army in World War II," subseries "The Army Ground Forces." Historical Division, Department of the Army, Government Printing Office, Washington, D.C., 1948.
PMG, *Second Report*	*Second Report of the Provost Marshal General to the Secretary of War on the Operations of the Selective Service System to December 20, 1918.* Government Printing Office, Washington, D.C., 1919.
Res. Br., U.S. Army	Research Branch, Information and Education Division, U.S. Army. Survey S-95 conducted in the United States during January and February 1944 to determine attitude toward the Army; sample size: 3,600. Survey S-99 conducted during January and February 1944, concerned with problems relating to psychoneurosis; sample size: 4,800.
SG, *Med. Dept.*	*The Medical Department of the United States Army in the World War.* The Surgeon General, War Department. Data available in either Vol. X, *Neuropsychiatry,* P. Bailey, *et al.*, Government Printing Office, Washington, D.C., 1929; or Vol. XV, *Statistics,* Part 2, A. G. Love, Government Printing Office, Washington, D.C., 1925.
SG, Med. Stat.	Unpublished table: "Disability Separations for Psychosis and Psychoneurosis, U.S. Army and Air Force Enlisted Men, 1945." Medical Statistics Division, Office of the Surgeon General, Department of the Army, Washington, D.C., 11 May 1955.
SG, Med. Stat., DA AGO Form 316	"Summary of Registration Examinations for Induction," DA AGO Form 316, reported in unpublished table, "Results of Preinduction Examinations under the Military Training and Service Act of 1951 and the Selective Service Extension Act of 1950 by Army Area, State, and Territory (July 1950 through December 1951)." Medical Statistics Division, Office of the Surgeon General, Department of the Army, Washington, D.C., 22 May 1952.
SG, unpub. worksheets	Unpublished worksheets prepared in the Office of the Surgeon General, War Department, Washington, D.C.

SSS, Monograph 10	*Special Groups*, Special Monograph 10, Selective Service System, Government Printing Office, Washington D.C., 1953.
SSS, Monograph 15	*Physical Examination of Selective Service Registrants*, Special Monograph 15. Selective Service System, Government Printing Office, Washington, D.C., 1948.
SSS, *Periodic Reports*	*Periodic Reports of Physical Examinations*, vols. 4–14, Summary and Detailed Reports of the results of a 20% sample taken during World War II. National Headquarters, Selective Service System, Washington, D.C.
SSS, "Total Enlistments"	"Total Enlistments by Branch of Service and State, November 1, 1946," National Headquarters, Selective Service System, Washington, D.C.
SSS, *Victory*	*Selective Service and Victory*. The Fourth Report of the Director of Selective Service, Government Printing Office, Washington, D.C., 1948.
Stat. Ab. U.S. 1957	*Statistical Abstract of the United States: 1957*. 78th ed. U.S. Bureau of the Census, Washington, D.C., 1957.
Stouffer *et al.*, *The American Soldier*	Samuel A. Stouffer *et al.*, "Studies in Social Psychology in World War II." Vol. I: *The American Soldier, Adjustment during Army Life*, 1949. Vol. IV: *Measurement and Prediction*, 1950. Princeton, N.J., Princeton University Press.
Strength of Army, STM-30	*Strength of the Army*, STM-30. Strength Accounting Branch, Office of the Adjutant General, War Department, Washington, D.C., June 1946.
U.S. Census, 1940, Vol. IV	Sixteenth Census Reports on Population, 1940: Volume IV; *Characteristics by Age*. Government Printing Office, Washington, D.C., 1943.

NOTES

1. Pearce Bailey *et al.*, *Neuropsychiatry*, Vol. X of *The Medical Department of the United States Army in the World War* (War Department, Washington, D.C., Government Printing Office, 1929).

2. Robert R. Palmer, Bell I. Wiley, and William R. Keast, *The Procurement and Training of Ground Combat Troops* from series *The United States Army in World War II* (War Department, Washington, D.C., Government Printing Office, 1948), p. 92.

3. Bailey, *Neuropsychiatry*, Chapter IV, "Detection and Elimination of Individuals with Nervous or Mental Disease."

4. Eli Ginzberg and Douglas W. Bray, *The Uneducated* (New York, Columbia University Press, 1953).

5. Eli Ginzberg, John L. Herma, and Sol W. Ginsburg, *Psychiatry and Military Manpower Policy: A Reappraisal of the Experience in World War II* (New York, King's Crown Press, 1953), p. 13.

6. *Ibid.*, p. 12.

7. *Ibid.*, p. 13.

8. Ginzberg, *The Uneducated, passim.*

9. Palmer, *The Procurement and Training of Ground Combat Troops*, pp. 482–88.

10. Norman Q. Brill and Gilbert W. Beebe, *A Follow-Up Study of War Neuroses*, "VA Medical Monograph Series" (Washington, D.C., Government Printing Office, 1955).

11. Eli Ginzberg, "Criteria for a Military Monpower Policy," *America's Manpower Crisis* (The Report of the Institute on Manpower Utilization and Government Personnel, Chicago, Public Administration Service, 1952), pp. 50–51.

12. The following is a selected listing by date of the more important Army policy directives dealing with utilization and release of men with psychiatric disabilities. It includes those specifically mentioned in this chapter.

4 Sept. 1942: "Circular Letter No. 99." Office of the Surgeon General, Services of Supply, War Department, Washington, D.C.

1 Dec. 1942: "Memorandum No. W615-61-42." The Adjutant General's Office, War Department, Washington, D.C.
5 Dec. 1942: "Circular No. 395." War Department, Washington, D.C.
7 Dec. 1942: "Circular No. 397." War Department, Washington, D.C.
4 Feb. 1943: "Circular No. 39." War Department, Washington, D.C.
25 March 1943: "Memorandum No. W600-30-43." The Adjutant General's Office, War Department, Washington, D.C.
26 April 1943: "Memorandum No. W600-39-43." The Adjutant General's Office, War Department, Washington, D.C.
29 July 1943: "Memorandum No. W600-62-43." The Adjutant General's Office, War Department, Washington, D.C.
14 July 1943: "Circular No. 161." War Department, Washington, D.C., Section III.
31 July 1943: "Circular No. 176." War Department, Washington, D.C., Section I.
21 August 1943: "Circular No. 189." War Department, Washington, D.C., Section III.
26 August 1943: "Memorandum No. W615-64-43." The Adjutant General's Office, War Department, Washington, D.C.
9 Nov. 1943: "Circular No. 290." War Department, Washington, D.C.
11 Nov. 1943: "Circular No. 293." War Department, Washington, D.C.
3 Dec. 1943: "Circular Letter No. 194." Office of the Surgeon General, Army Service Forces, Washington, D.C.
3 Feb. 1944: "Circular No. 48." War Department, Washington, D.C.
5 Feb. 1944: "Circular No. 40." Army Service Forces, War Department, Washington, D.C.
1 April 1944: "War Department Technical Bulletin TB MED 28." War Department, Washington, D.C.
26 April 1944: "Circular No. 164." War Department, Washington, D.C.
24 May 1944: "Circular No. 205." War Department, Washington, D.C.
29 May 1944: "Circular No. 212." War Department, Washington, D.C.
10 June 1944: "Circular No. 175." Army Service Forces, War Department, Washington, D.C.

6 July 1944: "Circular No. 208." Army Service Forces, War Department, Washington, D.C.
12 Sept. 1944: "Circular No. 370." War Department, Washington, D.C.
23 Sept. 1944: "Circular No. 318." Headquarters Army Service Forces, Washington, D.C.
27 Jan. 1945: "Circular No. 32." War Department, Washington, D.C.
13 March 1945: "Circular No. 81." War Department, Washington, D.C.
2 June 1945: "Circular No. 162." War Department, Washington, D.C.
30 June 1945: "Circular No. 196." War Department, Washington, D.C.
29 Dec. 1945: "Circular No. 391." War Department, Washington, D.C.

13. Ginzberg, *The Uneducated*, pp. 85–87.

14. Ginzberg, *The Uneducated.* Eli Ginzberg, *The Negro Potential* (New York, Columbia University Press, 1956).

15. Samuel A. Stouffer *et al.*, "Studies in Social Psychology in World War II." Vol. I: *The American Soldier, Adjustment During Army Life*, pp. 113 ff.; Vol. II: *The American Soldier, Combat and Its Aftermath*, pp. 420 ff (Princeton, N.J., Princeton University Press, 1949).

16. Norman Q. Brill, Gilbert W. Beebe, Regina L. Loewenstein, "Age and Resistance to Military Stress," *United States Armed Forces Medical Journal*, IV, No. 9 (September, 1953), pp. 1247–66.

17. Bureau of Medicine and Surgery, Navy Department, *The Statistics of Disease and Injuries (The History of the Medical Department of the United States Navy in World War II).* (Washington, D.C., Government Printing Office, 1950), III, 55.

18. Brill, *A Follow-Up Study of War Neuroses*, p. 31.

19. Stouffer, *The American Soldier*, I, 117 ff.

20. Elliot D. Cooke, *All But Me and Thee: Psychiatry at the Foxhole Level* (Washington, D.C., Infantry Journal Press, 1946), p. 96.

21. Ginzberg, *The Negro Potential.*

22. See for example abstracts of studies in: Nolan D. C. Lewis and Bernice Engle (ed.), *Wartime Psychiatry* (New York, Oxford University Press, 1954), Section IX.

23. *United States Census, 1940*, Vol. IV: *Characteristics by Age.*

24. Ginzberg, *The Uneducated*, pp. 49 ff.

25. *Ibid.*, Chapter VI.

26. Ginzberg, *Psychiatry and Military Manpower Policy: A Reppraisal of the Experience in World War II.*

27. J. R. Egan, Lionel Jackson, and Richard H. Eanes, "A Study of Neuropsychiatric Rejectees," *The Journal of the American Medical Association*, CXLV (February 17, 1951), pp. 466–69.

28. Clements C. Frye, "A Study of Rejection Causes, Success and Subsequent Performance of Special Groups," *The Selection of Military Manpower—A Symposium*, ed. L. Carmichael and L. C. Mead (Washington, D.C., National Academy of Science—National Research Council, Publication 209, 1951), pp. 133–48.

29. Albert J. Glass *et al.*, *Psychiatric Prediction and Military Effectiveness* (Washington, D.C., Walter Reed Army Institute of Research, March, 1956).

30. John A. Aita, "Efficacy of the Brief Clinical Interview Method in Predicting Adjustment," *Archives of Neurology and Psychiatry*, LXI (February, 1949), pp. 170–76.

31. Marvin R. Plesset, "Psychoneurotics in Combat," *The American Journal of Psychiatry*, CIII (July, 1946), pp. 87–90.

32. Selective Service System, *Physical Examinations of Selective Service Registrants*, "Special Monograph No. 15" (Washington, D.C., Government Printing Office, 1947), Vol. III, Appendix F.

33. Samuel A. Stouffer *et al.*, "Studies in Social Psychology in World War II." Vol. IV: *Measurement and Prediction* (Princeton, N.J., Princeton University Press, 1950), Chapter IV.

BIBLIOGRAPHY

Books and articles cited either in Table sources or Notes are not repeated in the Bibliography.

BOOKS

Appel, J. W. *Cause and Prevention of Psychiatric Disorders in the U.S. Army in World War II.* Unpublished manuscript.

Bartemeier, L. H., *et al. Report of Special Commission of Civilian Psychiatrists Covering Psychiatric Policy and Practice in the U.S. Army Medical Corps, European Theatre, 20 April to 8 July, 1945.* Washington, D.C., Office of Scientific Research and Development, and Office of the Surgeon General, War Department, July 1945.

Blum, Albert A. *The Army and Industrial Deferment During World War II.* Washington, D.C., Industrial College of the Armed Forces, 1955–1956.

Brosin, Henry W. *Report to the Surgeon General of the U.S. Army on Tour of Medical Installations of Far East Command, 10 September to 18 October, 1953.* Unpublished manuscript, Office of the Surgeon General, Washington, D.C., 1953.

Cline, Ray S. *Washington Command Post: The Operations Division* (The United States Army in World War II, War Department.) Washington, D.C., Government Printing Office, 1951.

Carmichael, Leonard, and Leonard C. Mead (ed.). *The Selection of Military Manpower—A Symposium.* Washington, D.C., National Academy of Sciences—National Research Council, Publication 209, 1951.

Goldberg, Samuel. *Army Training of Illiterates in World War II.* New York, Bureau of Publications, Teachers College, Columbia University, 1951.

Goldhamer, Herbert, and Andrew W. Marshal. *The Frequency of Mental Disease: Long-Term Trends and Present Status* ("Air Force

Project Rand," R-157). Santa Monica, The Rand Corporation, July 1949.

Gouldner, Alvin W. *Studies in Leadership*. New York, Harpers, 1950.

Grinker, Roy Richard, and John P. Spiegel. *Men Under Stress*. Philadelphia, Blakiston, 1945.

——. *War Neuroses*. Philadelphia, Blakiston, 1945.

Group for the Advancement of Psychiatry, Hospital Committee. *Statistics Pertinent to Psychiatry in the United States*, Report No. 7. Topeka, Kansas, March 1949.

Harris, F. Gentry, Joseph Mayer, and Herman A. Becker. *Report on Psychiatric and Psychological Data*. ("Experiences in the Study of Combat in the Korean Theatre," I.) Washington, D.C., Walter Reed Army Institute of Research, Walter Reed Army Medical Center, November 1955.

Huzar, Elias. *The Purse and the Sword: Control of the Army by Congress Through Military Appropriations*. Ithaca, N.Y., Cornell University Press, 1950.

Kardiner, Abram, and Herbert Spiegel. *War Stress and Neurotic Illness*. New York, Hoeber, 1947.

Kopetzky, Samuel J. *Report of the Medical Officer, New York City Headquarters, Selective Service System; October 15, 1940 to May 8, 1945 (V-E Day)*. New York, National Committee for Mental Hygiene, August 1950.

Kubie, Lawrence S. *Personal Report on Psychiatric Mission to the E.T.O.* Unpublished manuscript addressed to Colonel William C. Menninger, Army Service Forces, Office of the Surgeon General, Washington 25, D.C., August 9, 1945. (Note: This supplements Bartemeier, L.H., *et al.*)

Lantz, Herman R. *Social Factors in Mental Disorders: A Study of 1,000 Psychiatrically Diagnosed Cases*. Unpublished manuscript.

Marshall, Samuel Lyman Atwood. *Men Against Fire: The Problem of Battle Command in Future War*. Washington, D.C., Infantry Journal Press, 1947.

Menninger, William C. *Psychiatry in a Troubled World*. New York, Macmillan, 1948.

Millett, John D. *The Organization and Role of the Army Service Forces*. (The United States Army in World War II, War Department.) Washington, D.C., Government Printing Office, 1954.

The OSS Assessment Staff. *Assessment of Men: Selection of Personnel for the Office of Strategic Services*. New York, Rinehart and Company, Inc., 1948.

Rees, John Rawlings. *The Shaping of Psychiatry by War*. New York, Norton, 1945.

Rioch, David McK. *Problems of Preventive Psychiatry in War*. Washington, D.C., Army Medical Service Graduate School, Walter Reed Army Medical Center, October 1954.

U.S. Adjutant General's Office. *Predicting Proficiency of Enlisted Men of Limited Ability*, PRB Technical Research Report 1099. Prepared by Mary A. Morton *et al.*, Washington, D.C., February 1957.

——. Administrative Service Division, Departmental Records Branch. *Guide to the Records of the Adjutant General's Department, 1940–1945*. Washington, D.C., June 1950.

——. Administrative Service Division, Departmental Records Branch, *Guide to the Records of Headquarters Army Service Forces, 1942–1946*. Washington, D.C., December 1949.

——. Recruiting and Induction Section, Appointment and Induction Branch. "Armed Forces Induction Stations." Washington, D.C., various dates 1941–1945.

U.S. Armed Forces Information School, Carlisle Barracks, Pa. *The Army Almanac, A Book of Facts Concerning the Army of the United States*. Washington, D.C., Government Printing Office, 1950.

U.S. Army Artillery School, Department of General Subjects. *Special Leadership Problems*. Fort Sill, Oklahoma, September 1951.

U.S. Army Service Forces. *Health* ("Monthly Progress Report," Section 7). Washington, D.C., War Department, various issues, March 1943–August 1945.

U.S. Army Service Forces Headquarters, Statistics Branch, Control Division. *Statistical Review, World War II*. Washington, D.C., War Department, 1946.

U.S. Army Surgeon General's Office. *The Bulletin of the U.S. Army Medical Department*, IX, Supplemental Number—"Combat Psychiatry" (November 1949). Washington, D.C.

——. *Health of the Army*. Washington, D.C., War Department or Department of the Army, various issues August, 1946–date. (Note: This publication replaced the Army Service Forces' *Health*, "Monthly Progress Report," Section 7, as of July 1946.)

——. *Medical Statistics of the United States Army* ("Annual Report of the Surgeon General") calendar years 1941–1955. Washington, D.C., Government Printing Office, various dates 1942–1957.

——. Neuropsychiatric Consultants Division. *Annual Report of the Neuropsychiatric Consultants Division to the Surgeon General*, 1943, 1944, 1944–1945. Washington, D.C., 1943, 1944, 1945.

U.S. Army Surgeon General's Office. Neuropsychiatric Consultants Division. *Reports of the Neuropsychiatric Consultants of the Service Commands to the Surgeon General.* Washington, D.C., 1945.

U.S. Department of the Army. *History of Personnel Demobilization in the United States Army*, Pamphlet No. 20-210. Prepared by John C. Sparrow, Washington, D.C., Department of the Army, July 1952.

U.S. Department of Defense, Research and Development Board, Committee on Human Resources. *A Review of Research on Psychiatric Screening for the Armed Forces.* Washington, D.C., 1 September 1952.

——. Research and Development Board, Committee on Human Resources, Panel on Human Relations. *Symposium on Motivation*, HR-HML 201/1. Washington, D.C., 5–6 March 1953.

——. Research and Development Board and Personnel Policy Board. *Report of Working Group on Human Behavior under Conditions of Military Service.* Washington, D.C., June 1951.

U.S. Department of Labor, Bureau of Labor Statistics. *Armed Forces Rejections During the First Year of the Korean War.* Washington, D.C., November 1952.

U.S. Naval Personnel Research Field Activity, San Diego, California. *Evaluation of Screening Standards for Recruit Preparatory Training*, Technical Bulletin 55-11. Prepared for publication by the Bureau of Naval Personnel, Washington, D.C., June 1955.

——. *A Review of Current Screening Standards for Recruit Preparatory Training.* Research Report 55-3 NAVPERS-18456. Prepared for publication by the Bureau of Naval Personnel, Washington, D.C., November 1955.

U.S. Navy, Personnel Analysis Division, Billet and Qualification Research Branch. *Review of Physical Profiling Systems in the United States and Abroad*, NAVPERS-18348. Prepared for publication by the Bureau of Naval Personnel, Washington, D.C., July 1953.

U.S. Navy Department. *Annual Report of the Secretary of the Navy*, fiscal years 1941, 1942 and 1946. Washington, D.C., Government Printing Office, 1941, 1942, and 1947.

U.S. School of Aviation Medicine, Randolph Field, Texas. *Preservice Personality Problems and Subsequent Adjustments to Military Service*, Report 55-138. Prepared by Merrill Roff, Randolph Field, Texas, April 1956.

U.S. Selective Service System. *Analysis of Physical Examinations; Summary of Data from 19,923 Reports of Physical Examinations*, Medical Statistics Bulletin No. 1. Prepared by Harold O. Folk, Kenneth H.

McGill, and Leonard G. Rowntree. Washington, D.C., November 10, 1941.
——. *Causes of Rejection and Incidence of Defects: Local Board Examinations of Selective Service Registrants in Peacetime, An Analysis of Reports of Physical Examinations from 21 Selected States*, Medical Statistics Bulletin No. 2. Prepared by Thomas I. Edwards, Kenneth H. McGill, and Leonard G. Rowntree. Washington, D.C., August 1, 1943.
——. *Outline of Historical Background of Selective Service from Biblical Days to January 1, 1952.* (Revised, 1952 edition.) Prepared by Irving W. Hart, Chief Information Officer, Washington, D.C., Government Printing Office, 1952.
——. *Periodic Reports of Physical Examination.* Vols. I–III. Washington, D.C. Vol. I: Summary and Detailed Reports, April 1942–September 1943; Vol. II: Summary and Detailed Reports, April 1942–May 1946; Vol. III: Summary and Detailed Reports, November 1940–September 1945.
——. *Physical Examinations of Selective Service Registrants During Wartime; An Analysis of Reports for the Continental United States and Each State, April 1942–December 1943*, Medical Statistics Bulletin No. 3. Prepared by C. H. Greve, Kenneth H. McGill, and Leonard G. Rowntree. Washington, D.C., November 1, 1944.
——. *Physical Examinations of Selective Service Registrants in the Final Months of the War*, Medical Statistics Bulletin No. 4. Prepared by C. H. Greve, Kenneth H. McGill, and Richard H. Eanes. Washington, D.C., June 1, 1946.
——. *A Preliminary Experiment in Predicting Success and Failure in Military Service of Men Previously Rejected for Neuropsychiatric Reasons.* Washington, D.C., April 24, 1950.
——. "Reports of the Director of Selective Service," Reports Nos. 1–4. Washington, D.C., Government Printing Office, 1942–1948.
No. 1. *Selective Service in Peacetime*, 16 September 1940—8 December 1941.
No. 2. *Selective Service in Wartime*, 7 December 1941—5 December 1942.
No. 3. *Selective Service as the Tide of War Changes*, 5 December 1942—30 June 1944.
No. 4. *Selective Service and Victory*, 1 July 1944—31 December 1945.
——. "Special Monographs." Washington, D.C., Government Printing Office, Nos. 1–18, 1946–1954.
No. 1. *Background of Selective Service.*

No. 2. *The Selective Service Act.*
No. 3. *Organization and Administration of the System.*
No. 4. *Registration and Selective Service.*
No. 5. *The Classification Process.*
No. 6. *Industrial Deferment.*
No. 7. *Agricultural Deferment.*
No. 8. *Dependency Deferment.*
No. 9. *Age in the Selective Service Process.*
No. 10. *Special Groups.*
No. 11. *Conscientious Objection.*
No. 12. *Quotas, Calls, and Inductions.*
No. 13. *Reemployment and Selective Service.*
No. 14. *Enforcement of the Selective Service Law.*
No. 15. *Physical Examination of Selective Service Registrants.*
No. 16. *Problems of Selective Service.*
No. 17. *The Operation of Selective Service.*
No. 18. *Evaluation of the Selective Service Program.*

U.S. War Department. *Instruction in Special Training Units*, Pamphlet No. 20-8, April 1944. Washington, D.C., Government Printing Office, 1949.

——. *Mobilization Regulations No. 1–9*, as revised. Washington, D.C., various dates 1940–1945.

The War Reports of General of the Army George C. Marshall . . . General of the Army H. H. Arnold . . . (and) Fleet Admiral Ernest J. King. Philadelphia and New York, Lippincott, 1947.

Watson, Mark Skinner, Chief of Staff. *Prewar Plans and Preparations.* (The United States Army in World War II, War Department.) Washington, D.C., Government Printing Office, 1950.

ARTICLES

Berlien, Ivan C. "Neuropsychiatry in Armed Forces Induction Stations, Rehabilitation Centers, and Combat Divisions," *Bulletin of the Menninger Clinic*, VIII, No. 5 (September 1944), pp. 146–50.

Brill, Norman Q. and Gilbert W. Beebe. "Some Applications of a Follow-Up Study to Psychiatric Standards for Mobilization," *The American Journal of Psychiatry*, LIX (December 1952), pp. 401–10.

"Causes of Noneffectiveness," *The United States Air Force Medical Service Digest*, V (January 1954), pp. 2–7, 13–16.

Campbell, John D. "Psychiatry and Mobilization," *The Journal of the American Medical Association*, CXLVI (May 12, 1951), pp. 87–93.

Glass, Albert J. "Current Problems in Military Psychiatry," *The Jour-*

nal of the American Medical Association, CL (September 6, 1952), pp. 6–10.

——. "Psychiatric Prediction and Military Effectiveness," *U.S. Armed Forces Medical Journal*, VII (October 1956 and November 1956), pp. 1427–43 and 1575–88.

Hamburg, David A., T. Grady Baskin, and Anthony C. Tucker. "Prediction of Immediate Psychiatric Breakdown in Military Service," *U.S. Armed Forces Medical Journal*, V (May 1954), pp. 625–36.

Karpinos, Bernard D. "Evaluation of the Physical Fitness of Present-Day Inductees," *U.S. Armed Forces Medical Journal*, IV (March 1953), pp. 415–30.

Kubie, Lawrence S. "The Detection of Potential Psychosomatic Breakdowns in the Selection of Men for the Armed Services," *Annals of the New York Academy of Sciences*, XLIV (December 22, 1942), pp. 605–24.

——. "The Neurotic Potential and Human Adaptation," Presented at the Dedication of the Psychiatric Wing of the Strong Memorial Hospital, Rochester, New York, March 31, 1949.

——. "The Neurotic Potential, the Neurotic Process, and the Neurotic State," *U.S. Armed Forces Medical Journal*, II, No. 1 (January 1951), pp. 1–12.

——. "Psychiatry and Industry," *Mental Hygiene*, XXIX, No. 2 (April 1945), pp. 201–7.

——. "Technical and Organizational Problems in the Selection of Troops," *Military Affairs*. Part I (Winter 1944), pp. 243–58. Part II (Spring 1945), pp. 13–32.

Lew, Edward A. "Interpreting the Statistics of Medical Examinations of Selectees," *Journal of the American Statistical Association*, XXXIX (September 1944), pp. 345–56.

Lidz, Theodore. "Chronic Situations Evoking Psychological Stress and the Common Signs of the Resulting Strain," *Symposium on Stress*. Washington, D.C., Army Medical Service Graduate School, Walter Reed Army Medical Center, 17 March 1953.

Miner, John B. and James K. Anderson. "Intelligence and Emotional Disturbance: Evidence From Army and Veterans Administration Records," *The Journal of Abnormal and Social Psychology*, LVI (January 1958), pp. 75–81.

Rees, J. R. "Unfit on Psychiatric Grounds," *Occupational Psychology* (July 1946), London.

Reider, Norman. "The Concept of Normality," *The Psychoanalytic Quarterly*, XIX, No. 1 (January 1950), pp. 43–51.

Rowntree, Leonard G. Kenneth H. McGill, and Louis P. Hellman.

"Mental and Personality Disorders in Selective Service Registrants," *The Journal of the American Medical Association*, CXXVIII (August 11, 1945), pp. 1084–87.

Silber, Earle. "Adjustment to the Army," *U.S. Armed Forces Medical Journal*, V (September 1954), pp. 1340–48.

INDEX

www.ingramcontent.com/pod-product-compliance
Ingram Content Group UK Ltd.
Pitfield, Milton Keynes, MK11 3LW, UK
UKHW020214290926
15470UKWH00001B/171

9 780837 184678